"What makes Baer's valu███████████████████ its
breadth of information, is ████████████████

███████████████████████████████████████ ..eekly

Obsessive-compulsive disorder wreaks havoc on the lives of six
million Americans. *Getting Control* offers a clinically proven
plan to treat OCD and help put an end to distressing symptoms. In Dr. Lee Baer's completely revised and updated edition of his classic book OCD sufferers will discover how to:

*Assess symptoms

*Set realistic goals

*Create therapeutic exercises

Plus:

*Which medications really work

*Effective new treatments for violent and sexual obsessions

*The role audiotapes play in treating obsessive thoughts

. . . and much more

Lee Baer, Ph.D., is Associate Professor of Psychology in the
Department of Psychiatry at Harvard Medical School, as well
as Director of Research at the OCD Clinic at Massachusetts
General Hospital and the OCD Institute at McLean Hospital.
An internationally recognized expert in the treatment of OCD
and related disorders, Dr. Baer is the author of more than a
hundred scientific papers about OCD, and the co-editor of
Obsessive-Compulsive Disorders: Theory and Management. He lives
in Massachusetts with his family.

Judith L. Rapoport, M.D., is the author of *The Boy Who
Couldn't Stop Washing.*

LEE BAER, Ph.D.

GETTING CONTROL

REVISED EDITION

Overcoming Your Obsessions and Compulsions

WITH A FOREWORD BY JUDITH L. RAPOPORT, M.D.

A PLUME BOOK

To Carole Ann

PLUME
Published by the Penguin Group
Penguin Putnam Inc., 375 Hudson Street, New York, New York 10014, U.S.A.
Penguin Books Ltd, 27 Wrights Lane, London W8 5TZ, England
Penguin Books Australia Ltd, Ringwood, Victoria, Australia
Penguin Books Canada Ltd, 10 Alcorn Avenue, Toronto, Ontario, Canada M4V 3B2
Penguin Books (N.Z.) Ltd, 182–190 Wairau Road, Auckland 10, New Zealand

Penguin Books Ltd, Registered Offices: Harmondsworth, Middlesex, England

Published by Plume,
a member of Penguin Putnam Inc.
This is a revision of an authorized reprint of a hardcover edition published by Little, Brown
and Company. For information address Little, Brown, 3 Center Plaza, Boston, MA 02108-2084.

First Plume Printing, July, 1992
First Plume Printing (Revised Edition), July, 2000
10 9 8 7 6 5 4 3 2 1

Copyright © Lee Baer, 1991, 2000
All rights reserved

LIBRARY OF CONGRESS CATALOGING-IN-PUBLICATION DATA:

Baer, Lee.
     Getting control : overcoming your obsessions and compulsions / Lee Baer ; with a
foreword by Judith L. Rapoport.
         p. cm.
     Includes index.
     ISBN 0-452-28177-6
     1. Obsessive-compulsive disorder—Popular works. 2. Behavior therapy—Popular
works.   I. Title.
RC533.B24   2000
616.85'227—dc20   92-5032
                                                                            CIP

Printed in the United States of America

CONTENTS

● ●

FOREWORD

Dr. Baer has pulled together a most readable book for patients and their families on the diagnosis and treatment of obsessive-compulsive disorder. Unlike too many mental health practitioners, Dr. Baer does not indulge in polemics, but instead offers insights based on his unique wealth of experience in carrying out the behavioral treatment of OCD in a multidisciplinary clinic with large numbers of patients. Because of his important and unusual experience, and because interest in OCD is relatively new, this guide has a breadth and depth not to be found elsewhere. The case histories and informal style, together with the comprehensive material on both drug and behavior therapy, will allow patients and their families to make intelligent choices and initiate treatments with an ease that has not been possible before.

The section on the treatment of trichotillomania is a significant first. This disorder, whose victims are compelled to pull out their own hair (typically one strand at a time), affects millions and has been underrecognized and misunderstood. There is virtually no popular writing on this subject. Dr. Baer describes a number of cases and outlines the behavioral techniques that he has found useful in the treatment of this humiliating disorder.

Another important section of *Getting Control* is its discussion of behavioral treatment of children with OCD. Common sense tells us that children and adolescents should respond to the same techniques as do adults, and Dr. Baer provides some practical experience and advice—how to involve the parents, for example—in this relatively understudied area. And his experience indicates that behavior therapy may be just as effective for pediatric subjects as for adults.

Getting Control is a model for how-to books aimed at patients with any psychiatric disorder, but it is particularly welcome to sufferers of OCD, for whom so little is available.

Judith L. Rapoport, M.D.
Chief, Child Psychiatry Branch, National Institute
   of Mental Health
Author of *The Boy Who Couldn't Stop Washing*

PREFACE

In this book you will learn how to get control of your obsessions and compulsions with behavior therapy. We now have two proven treatments for obsessive-compulsive disorder: behavior therapy and medication. Although powerful new medications for OCD have recently received considerable publicity, information about behavior therapy remains sorely lacking.

When newspaper articles or television segments about OCD mention behavior therapy, they usually ascribe it a role secondary to medications; as a result, it is rarely described in detail. This is especially unfortunate, since many OCD sufferers could use behavior therapy to gain control of their own compulsions and obsessions. I hope that this book will rectify this situation by empowering you to get control of your OCD symptoms.

For more than two decades we have known that behavior therapy is effective for OCD. But most people with the disorder still remain unaware of its existence. Recently I treated a woman with severe OCD who provided a sad illustration of this ironical situation. Her chief problem was that she could not throw anything away. In her house worthless newspapers and food wrappers, mixed with valuable documents and stock certificates, were knee-deep. She was crippled by these hoarding rituals and other obsessive thoughts about losing something important. She could no longer work, and by the time I was asked to see her, she had voluntarily hospitalized herself on an inpatient psychiatry ward. Despite almost a decade of psychiatric treatment, her symptoms continued to get worse. She had been told that sexual issues were the root of her problem, and had to be resolved before she could improve. After years of hearing this she had come to believe it, although there was no scientific evidence that it was true. Sadly, this woman had never been told about behavior therapy, a treatment that has now given her a chance for recovery.

Perhaps as unfortunate as those OCD sufferers who are unaware of behavior therapy are those who are misinformed about it. Some patients have heard that behavior therapy forces people to do things against their will. Or they have seen a TV piece featuring a patient being physically forced to touch the inside of a filthy trash barrel. Some people choose not to try behavior therapy because of these negative, authoritarian images. This book is designed to allay these fears by presenting behavior therapy techniques as a self-help approach, in which OCD sufferers control their rate of progress at each step.

Recently I and my colleagues Dr. Michael Jenike and Dr. William Minichiello set down in a textbook for doctors and other health professionals all the current knowledge about OCD.[1] *Getting Control* is different; it is written for you, the OCD sufferer. The methods I describe in the following pages are based on my ten years of research on and clinical experience with behavior therapy as a means of controlling OCD symptoms.

This book is not intended as a substitute for behavior therapy or medication, and many readers will need professional help in dealing with their OCD symptoms. I have provided tests to help you assess the severity of your symptoms, as well as guidelines for seeking out behavior therapists and psychiatrists who specialize in treating OCD, if this seems necessary.

Most of you will find that if you work hard and follow the methods outlined in these pages, you should be rewarded with lasting decreases in your compulsions and obsessions; you also will have the feeling of accomplishment that comes from controlling your own problems.

Thanks are due to many colleagues, friends, teachers, associates, and family, without whom this book would not have been possible.

Many colleagues in the Psychiatry Department at Massachusetts General Hospital have provided a stimulating learning environment over the years, exemplified by our chief, Dr. Ned Cassem. Special thanks are due to my colleagues Drs. Michael Jenike and Bill Minichiello, who have been my teachers and friends over the last decade. Both also provided helpful suggestions on earlier drafts of this book. In addition, I am grateful to Drs. Joe Ricciardi, John Hurley, Nancy Keuthen, and Lynn Buttolph, also colleagues of mine.

1. Jenike, Baer, and Minichiello, eds., *Obsessive-Compulsive Disorders: Theory and Management,* 1st ed., 1986; 2nd ed., 1990; 3rd ed., 1998.

My editor at Little, Brown and Company, Kit Ward, gave invaluable assistance at every stage of this project, which has resulted in a book that is immeasurably better than it would otherwise have been. Kelly Aherne, Deborah Jacobs, and Beth Davey, at Little, Brown, also deserve special thanks.

My wife, Carole Ann, has been a source of constant support. Not only her emotional support, but her wisdom in suggesting changes and corrections in countless revisions of these chapters, made this book possible. Also thanks to the rest of my family: my mother, Bernice; my brother Larry; my grandmother Mary; and to P. and M., for all their loving support over the years.

Finally, thanks are due to the hundreds of patients who have shared their stories and their successes with me over the years. I have used their actual case histories liberally to illustrate important points throughout the book, in their own words, wherever possible. In all cases, the identities of actual patients have been disguised to protect their anonymity.

PREFACE TO THE
REVISED EDITION

In recent years I increasingly found myself advising my patients to ignore certain parts of *Getting Control* (for example, the section on "thought stopping") and also having to describe at length newer treatment methods that were not in the original 1991 edition. It was then that it became clear to me that it was time to revise the book in order to bring it back up to the cutting edge of OCD treatment.

When I sat down to revise *Getting Control* I was reassured to find that most of what I had written in 1991 remains as true and useful for treatment today as it did then. This further strengthened my belief that exposure and response prevention are the bedrock of treatment for overcoming contamination fears; cleaning, checking, and repeating rituals; and avoidance due to OCD. I found that the section that required the most updating was about treating obsessive thoughts. In 1991, because this was a poorly understood and understudied area, I was forced to conclude in the first edition that these symptoms usually responded poorly to behavior therapy. Happily, since that time, research has progressed independently in the areas of thought suppression and using audiotapes to improve exposure and response prevention for these obsessions. As a result, I am now able to confidently describe these new treatment methods in this revised edition. After much thought and with advice from colleagues, I was convinced to delete the whole section on "thought stopping," a technique I no longer recommended as a proven treatment for OCD. This deletion also simplified teaching about behavior therapy, since the methods of thought stopping were contradictory to the basic principle we now teach OCD sufferers: *Do not* try to fight your obsessions in any way, but *do* resist your compulsions!

Naturally, over the course of a decade, some of the information in *Getting Control* needed updating: I have included a description of all the new SRI drugs that are now on the market and being used routinely for the treatment of OCD. In addition, a new edition of the standard psychiatric manual of diagnoses is now in use, with subtle changes in diagnoses relevant to you, such as obsessive-compulsive personality disorder. I have updated the self-assessment tests in this revised edition to help you determine the severity of your OCD and depression symptoms. I have also updated the information to help you seek out behavior therapists and psychiatrists who specialize in treating OCD, which now includes Internet addresses as well.

Wherever possible, I have tried to point out future directions in the treatment of OCD. For example, I have touched upon hopeful results using cognitive therapy, and also our promising findings of successful computer-assisted behavior therapy for those who do not have access to an experienced behavior therapist. I have expanded sections on disorders that appear similar to OCD, but which require distinct treatments; my aim was to give you an idea of what treatments you should expect your doctor to prescribe for you if you suffer from one of these OCD-spectrum disorders. As a result, one positive outcome from reading this revised edition may be that you conclude that you don't have OCD, but rather have a disorder closely related to it. This would be valuable information to you, since it would direct you to treatments that can help your problem.

I again thank my colleagues at Massachusetts General Hospital and McLean Hospital, my patients, and most of all my family, for making this revised edition possible. I thank my editors at Penguin Putnam, Deborah Brody, and Amanda Patten, for agreeing that a revised edition of *Getting Control* was overdue, and for guiding me in the preparation of this revision. Once again, I have used my patients' actual case histories to illustrate important points throughout the book, in their own words wherever possible, but with identities disguised to protect their anonymity.

Finally, thanks to technological advances since the publication of the first edition, you can now e-mail me directly to tell me about your experiences using this book. I look forward to hearing from you.

Boston, Massachusetts
August 31, 1999
baer@ocd.mclean.org

CHAPTER ONE

• •

What Is OCD?

• •

"The chains of habit are too weak to be felt until they are too strong to be broken."
—Samuel Johnson (1709–1784)

You leave your house, now officially on vacation. But as you slide into the backseat of the taxi the doubts hit you: "Did I turn off the stove?" You try to ignore these thoughts, but, try as you might, you can't recall turning the gas off. Your feelings of uncertainty grow until they become unbearable. Finally, you give in and tell the taxi driver to turn around. As he waits outside, you turn the gas on and off endlessly. No matter how much you stare at the stove, you can't be certain that it is off; instead, each check adds to your nagging uncertainty. Your eyes can see that it is off, but it doesn't register in your mind.

After what feels like hours, you finally drag yourself from the stove and back to the taxi. But as you drive away you picture flames engulfing your house because of your carelessness. All through your vacation, awful thoughts of your life's treasures being incinerated torment you. Despite all your efforts, you can't drive the doubts from your mind.

Your food shopping has been uneventful and, in a way, comforting. But as you approach the checkout stand you notice that the cashier seems to have a cold. He's sniffling and blowing his nose as he prepares to ring up your groceries. Now it's too late—he's touched your food.

As you drop your grocery bags on the kitchen table at home, the doubts enter your mind. Later in the afternoon, your doubts turn to certainty; you're now sure the teenager who handled your groceries has AIDS. The virus is now everywhere, spread around your apartment by contact with your own hands, waiting to enter the myriad cracks and nicks in your skin's armor, your chair, your clothes, the pencil you hold—all contaminated. Is it already too late? Are you already infected, doomed? And what of your family, your children? Your heart pounds as terror mounts. Almost paralyzed, you scan the apartment. You spot a last hope for survival, a sink with soap and water. You scrub, beginning a sterilization that would be the envy of any surgeon in preoperative preparation. How much is enough? Wash up to your elbows, then beyond. The water must be hotter. Rinse again. Shock! How could you have missed it? The faucet handles! You touched them before you began. They must be disinfected. Now begin again on your hands. They don't yet *feel* clean. Vague feelings of uncleanliness cling to you, radiating from the pit of your stomach. As your mind races you remember reading somewhere that bleach kills germs—even viruses? Under the sink, a quart bottle. How could you have forgotten? Your clothes: they must be stripped off and bleached. The sterilization continues late into the night.

Just five years ago, you gave as little thought to taking a bus as to breathing. But things are different now. It's been a while since you've tried, so, you reason, it may be all right this time. After you drop in your fare you inch down the aisle, searching for a seat to fit your requirements: open seats to either side and directly across from you. You spot one and settle down after smoothing your skirt beneath you. But at the next stop, danger enters. This time it takes the form of a middle-aged man sitting down opposite you. Obeying unwritten laws of city etiquette, you both avert your eyes, avoiding direct eye contact. With great effort you succeed for a few minutes. But in the same way that your tongue is drawn to explore a cavity in a rear tooth, your eyes soon lock on the stranger. Again they come—grotesque sexual thoughts about the stranger dominate your mind. You're always shocked at how quickly the thoughts rise to full strength. Images of forbidden sexual acts flash in your mind's eye as your stomach heaves. You try to fight them with prayers you have memorized, but it's no use. It's no use averting your gaze now; the bizarre show, once begun, seems beyond your control. Devoutly religious, you are sickened by the depravity of the sexual acts you are committing mentally with the stranger behind his newspaper. Incredibly, even worse thoughts lie in store. The sexual obscenities become violent obscenities. In your thoughts you bury a hatchet in the groveling stranger. Closing your eyes does not dampen the carnage in your mind. Panicking now, you remind yourself that you would never do such a thing. Weakened, you ring the bell to get off at the next stop. You know it is the only hope.

Relief comes as you step heavily onto the pavement, still miles from your destination. Exhausted, you tell yourself that one day you'll try again, but for now it is easier to stay home and pray for forgiveness.

These are glimpses into the minds of three people suffering the seemingly uncontrollable thoughts and urges of obsessive-compulsive disorder. These people are not crazy; they have an anxiety disorder that dominates their lives. We are only now beginning to understand OCD and to develop proven treatments for it, including behavior therapy and drugs.

When we established the OCD Clinic at Massachusetts General Hospital in 1983, Drs. Michael Jenike and William Minichiello and I had seen fewer than fifty OCD patients among us; since then we have seen more than a thousand, and many new patients came to our clinic each week. Our colleagues tell us that similar growth has occurred at other OCD clinics around the country.

The reason for this dramatic growth is an explosion of interest in OCD among both the general public and the media. Television and radio, newspapers and magazines, all regularly run stories about OCD. This psychiatric disorder, once known only in the pages of textbooks, now is part of the popular culture.

As our knowledge of OCD grows, we now recognize that many famous figures from the past who were called eccentric actually suffered from OCD. Samuel Johnson, the prominent eighteenth-century writer quoted at the beginning of the chapter, is now thought to have had OCD symptoms. Several writers have commented on his many strange habits, which included having to enter and exit rooms in a ritualized way, always using a particular number of steps and always crossing the threshold with the same foot. In another of his many rituals, this literary giant would stretch his right, then left leg before him until he did it "correctly." While some of his contemporaries described these afflictions as a kind of epileptic convulsion, Sir Joshua Reynolds understood what is now known as the "OCD loop" that trapped his friend between uninvited obsessive thoughts and the compulsive rituals he enacted to relieve them:

> Those motions or tricks of Dr. Johnson are improperly called convulsions. He could sit motionless, when he was told so to do, as well as any other man. My opinion is, that it proceeded from a habit which he had indulged himself in, *of accompanying his thoughts with certain untoward actions, and those actions always appeared to me as if they were meant to reprobate in part some part of his past conduct* [my emphasis]. Whenever he was not engaged in conversation, such thoughts were sure to rush into his mind.[1]

Another notable victim of OCD was Howard Hughes, the millionaire playboy, pilot, and Hollywood producer. We now believe that his famed reclusiveness in his latter years was due to the obsessive thoughts and compulsive rituals of OCD.[2] As his OCD worsened, to avoid contamination Hughes drank only pure spring water. And contamination from wash water presented no problem, since he rarely washed anymore. In his hotel room, every object sat upon an ever-widening circle of tissues and newspapers to protect it from contamination by the floor or table.

To further prevent contamination, Hughes wrote volumes of painfully detailed instructions outlining steps his servants were to follow to prepare uncontaminated food for him. Among these was a three-page single-spaced memorandum titled "Special Preparation of Canned Fruit." Given the measures he required, it is no surprise to learn that Hughes generally ate but once a day, and frequently not again for several days.

1. Quoted in Boswell, *The Life of Samuel Johnson*, 1968 ed.
2. Drosnin, *Citizen Hughes*, 1985.

In his desperate crusade against contamination, Hughes once burned every thread of clothing he owned when he heard a rumor that a girlfriend from years before had a venereal disease. Suits and shirts, trousers and ties, all guilty only by some odd association, met the same fate as a seventeenth-century witch burned at the stake to expel the devil within.

Paradoxically, he could not throw away anything that came from his body. His hair and fingernails grew uncut. No urine, feces, or bodily dirt could be wasted or disposed of. All had to be saved, hoarded. He stored urine in covered jars. Anything in contact with the outside world, if only in Hughes's imagination, had to be discarded; but what came from the man himself was never to be thrown away.

Howard Hughes, at one time an American symbol of health and vigor, had become a pathetic man of mystery, progressively more debilitated by what we now recognize as OCD. His once clear mind eventually saw the outside world only through compulsive television viewing, with eyes always searching for contamination in any form.

Of course, most cases of OCD are not as severe as Howard Hughes's. But his self-imposed imprisonment illustrates how the disorder can destroy the lives of its victims and their families if left untreated. The severity of OCD can vary greatly. Some people may be very concerned with germs but still are able to carry on their work and social lives without disruption. Others, like Hughes, are crippled by their disorder; they become housebound and paralyzed.

Most magazine and newspaper stories about OCD describe only the most common kinds, such as those illustrated in the first two vignettes opening this chapter. Cleaning rituals and fears of contamination, as in the case of Howard Hughes, are symptoms of one of the most common and best-known kinds of OCD. The other most common kind involves checking rituals due to uncertainty. Indeed, I often find myself describing OCD to those unfamiliar with it as "people who can't stop washing their hands or checking locks." But there are many other forms of OCD that are less well known, yet just as devastating.

Many sufferers may never have considered themselves victims of OCD, because they don't wash their hands or check door locks. Instead, they may have fears of handling sharp objects or of shoplifting. Or, like the woman described earlier, they may have perverse sexual or violent thoughts. Some may feel compelled to repeatedly ask others for reassurance, while others cannot throw anything away.

If you have any of these less common problems, or any of a dozen other kinds of obsessions or compulsions, you will find the assessment section of this book helpful, since it describes in detail all the kinds of OCD that we know about. By the time you finish this chapter, you will have a good idea as to whether your problem may be OCD. Later chapters will then teach you how to use behavior therapy to get control of your OCD symptoms.

What Is OCD?

A frightened OCD patient once grabbed me by the arm and said he had an important question to ask me. When we were alone, he told me he had just read a newspaper article about OCD that shocked him. With a panicked look on his face he asked: "Is it true, Doc? Is OCD really a mental disorder?"

After he calmed down, I told him the answer was yes, we do consider OCD a mental disorder. "But," I told him, "so is an abnormal fear of dogs, or heights, or airplanes. In fact," I said, "OCD is grouped with these phobias in books that list psychiatric diagnoses; they all involve strong anxiety and the difficulties this causes, so they are all called anxiety disorders."

"Then it's true," he said, "I really am crazy."

Finally I convinced him that although OCD is called a mental disorder, because it affects behavior, thoughts, and emotions, this did *not* mean that he was crazy or that he would ever go crazy. Most people associate being crazy with being psychotic, or out of touch with reality. Except for their particular fears, people with OCD remain in touch with reality in all other areas of their lives. I have never seen a patient with only OCD who went on to become psychotic.

I've been amazed at the number of people with OCD who have never told even their closest family members—not even spouses—about their problems, because they feared being thought of as crazy. Obviously, people with OCD can be very secretive about their symptoms. Although their spouses may wonder why they won't wear certain clothes, or use certain washing machines, or leave the house on certain days, they may never suspect the countless rituals that are going on behind closed doors or when the house is empty.

When OCD sufferers are finally able to tell other people about their problems, they are generally pleasantly surprised by the response. Others are usually understanding and willing to help. One man told me that once he understood about his wife's problems with OCD, many of her idiosyncrasies began to make sense to him. Rather than being upset, he was amazed that she had been able to keep this suffering hidden from him over a decade of marriage, and he was anxious to help her get better. Examples like these have convinced me that the stigma of having a mental disorder is usually more in the mind of the OCD sufferer than anywhere else.

Now that we know that OCD is considered a mental disorder, specifically an anxiety disorder, let's consider its important elements. To be diagnosed as having OCD, a person must have either obsessions or compulsions that produce distress and also interfere with the person's social or role functioning.[3] A simple rule of thumb is that the term "obsessions" refers to intrusive *thoughts* that force themselves into your mind, while "compulsions" refers to *actions* you feel compelled to carry out.

In psychiatric terminology, obsessions are defined as "recurrent and persistent thoughts, impulses, or images that are experienced, at some time during the disturbance, as intrusive and inappropriate and that cause marked anxiety or distress."[4] Also "the thoughts, impulses or images are not simply excessive worries about real-life problems."[5]

Obsessions drain your energy. Since your brain expends a large proportion of your entire body's energy, it is little wonder that having these thoughts all day can leave you feeling exhausted. In every culture that has been studied, obsessive thoughts have most commonly centered on contamination, orderliness, aggression, and sexual and religious themes.

3. *Diagnostic and Statistical Manual of Mental Disorders,* 4th ed., 1994.
4. Ibid.
5. Ibid.

Compulsions, on the other hand, are defined as repetitive behaviors (e.g., hand washing, ordering, checking) or mental acts (e.g., praying, counting, repeating words silently) that the person feels driven to perform in response to an obsession, or according to rules that must be applied rigidly. The behaviors or mental acts are aimed at preventing or reducing distress or preventing some dreaded event or situation; however, these behaviors or mental acts either are not connected in a realistic way with what they are designed to neutralize or prevent or are clearly excessive.[6]

Compulsions—the most common of which are cleaning, checking to prevent a catastrophe, and repeating actions—are actions you feel compelled or forced to do. You feel as if there is a force inside you making you do or think something—wash your hands or drive back home to check that the door is securely locked. Indeed, in ancient times it was thought that the devil had entered victims of this disorder and forced them to perform their peculiar rituals. These beliefs persist to the present day: several years ago we saw a patient who sought an exorcism to cure him of OCD. This man became convinced that his actions were caused by evil demons. His searching finally led him to a religious group that agreed with these beliefs and gave him books saying that this was a common occurrence.

By definition, compulsive eating, gambling, and sexual behaviors are not considered kinds of OCD, because the individual gets some pleasure from such behaviors. People with OCD *always* hate the actions—and thoughts—that hold them in their control.

Apart from these textbook definitions of obsessions and compulsions, what does OCD *feel* like? The vignettes opening this chapter begin to give you some idea. Most people with OCD, unlike the woman in the third vignette, have both obsessions and compulsions, and they tell me that they often feel trapped in a "loop" between the two. A frightening thought enters their mind, like "I'm contaminated" or "I injured someone." As a result, they feel compelled to clean, check, or perform some other ritual to reduce such thoughts and feelings. But since these rituals don't satisfy them, they become trapped in a loop of ever-increasing obsessions and compulsions that can last for hours. Dr. Judith

6. Ibid.

Rapoport, a psychiatrist at the National Institute of Mental Health who has studied OCD extensively, describes this loop in *The Boy Who Couldn't Stop Washing* as an "obsessive-compulsive attack" that distorts the individual's view of reality.[7]

Patients have described being trapped in this loop in various ways. One stares at a light switch for an hour, and although he sees that it is off, the longer he stares at it, the less certain he is that it really is off. And so he switches it on and off repeatedly, searching for that satisfying feeling of certainty that eludes him. Another fears that she has cut herself while handling scissors. She stares at her skin and sees no wound, but after an hour she still cannot be certain that she is not injured. A trip to the emergency room and reassurance don't satisfy her, and her checking continues long into the night.

Other people, like the woman with sexual obsessions described in the third vignette, get trapped in another kind of OCD loop. Although they may have a few compulsions, like saying prayers to themselves or asking for reassurance, they get caught in a loop between their obsessions and *avoiding* situations. They therefore stay away from situations that provoke their obsessions, but the longer they stay away from them, the stronger their thoughts become. When they do venture into the situation, the thoughts are overwhelming, and they immediately return to avoiding it. And so the obsession-avoidance loop continues.

People who don't suffer from OCD can't really understand the power of these loops. For a person who has OCD it isn't easy to "just stop doing it!" as these patients are often told. The OCD sufferer usually knows that his thoughts and rituals are silly, but not when he is trapped in the middle of the OCD loop. Then it seems that his life or his sanity depends on performing these rituals. *As much as he craves the feeling of certainty that everything is alright, he cannot attain this feeling.* He feels out of control.

This book will teach you how to gain control over both of these loops by approaching them in a systematic, proven way.

7. Rapoport, *The Boy Who Couldn't Stop Washing*, 1989, p. 21.

How Common Is OCD?

Until recently, a psychiatrist or psychologist could go through an entire career without seeing a single case of classic OCD. Although OCD was once believed to be a relatively rare psychiatric disorder, recent evidence from a door-to-door federally funded survey indicates that these symptoms may occur to some extent during one's lifetime in as many as two or three of every hundred adults. Childhood and adolescent OCD are also common, indicating that this disorder does not discriminate on the basis of age. So take comfort that you are not alone in your suffering—as many as seven and a half million people in the United States may suffer from OCD at some time in their life. And, if other problems related to OCD are included, the number may be twice as large.

As a result of increased publicity, patients with OCD can now identify this disorder and are seeking treatment sooner. Whereas in the past patients often waited ten years or more before seeking help, many now undergo treatment in the first months of their disorder. Thus, milder forms of OCD presently are more common at doctors' and therapists' offices than we found in the early years of our clinic, when we saw only patients with the most severe forms of the disorder.

What Causes OCD?

Most patients want to know what caused their OCD. Many ask me if they have a chemical imbalance. Others want to know if they caused their OCD by smoking marijuana or by worrying too much. The simplest answer is that we don't yet know what causes OCD, but our research has provided some leads.[8]

We are fairly certain that OCD is partly genetically transmitted—when one identical twin has OCD, the other twin is likely to also have it, even when they have been raised apart. OCD also seems to be genetically related to some other disorders, includ-

8. For a complete review of all of the suspected causes of OCD, including recent theories about childhood strep infections (also referred to as PANDAS), consult the most recent version of the OCD textbook my colleagues and I edit (Jenike, Baer, and Minichiello, 1998).

ing agoraphobia, depression, and Tourette Disorder; relatives of OCD patients are more likely to suffer from these ailments than would be expected by chance.

Patients who ask me if they have a chemical imbalance have usually read about serotonin. This is one of many neurotransmitters, chemicals in the brain that help our nerves transmit information. We know that all the drugs that are effective in treating OCD also increase the availability of serotonin in the brain. Hence we think that this chemical is involved in OCD. But serotonin is not the complete answer.

There are almost certainly other factors that contribute to OCD. For example, by using modern scanning equipment[9] we have compared the brains of people with and without OCD, and we have found some differences, both in the way the brains work and in sizes of different parts of the brains. We are not yet sure what these differences mean, but they are providing us leads in our research.

Some patients fear that having smoked marijuana in college created their problem. There is no scientific evidence for this theory. Blaming themselves for creating the disorder only makes them feel worse.

Parents of OCD patients have sometimes been accused of causing the problem through overly strict toilet training. There is no evidence that this is true either. One study looked at this question and found absolutely no relationship between the type of toilet training and later development of OCD. Early life experiences are probably related to OCD in some way; some researchers believe that excessively harsh punishment for making mistakes may predispose people to obsessive doubts and checking rituals.[10] Growing up watching a parent or sibling carrying out OCD rituals probably leads to learning these habits, to some extent. However, most researchers agree that OCD will develop only if an individual is genetically predisposed to it.

9. PET (positron emission tomography) scans use small amounts of safe radioactive substances to tell us which areas of the brain are working hardest during different activities. MRI (magnetic resonance imaging) scans and CAT (computerized axial tomography) scans give us detailed pictures of parts of the brain. FMRI (functional magnetic resonance imaging) scans give us moment-by-moment pictures of changing blood flow patterns in the brain without any radiation exposure for the patient.
10. Rachman and Hodgson, *Obsessions and Compulsions*, 1980.

In general, for those who do develop OCD, it usually begins in late adolescence or early adulthood, commonly by age twenty-five, often during a period of stress. It is very unusual for OCD to first occur in old age, unless it is related to very severe depression (see Chapter 2 for a discussion). It is also unusual for OCD to result from an injury or illness.

Most important, no matter what causes OCD, we can now treat it with behavior therapy or medications. If OCD is left untreated, most sufferers will have the symptoms to some degree throughout their life. Although there may be times when the symptoms are less severe and permit normal functioning, they are never totally absent. Some people do have periods when their symptoms totally disappear, only to reemerge later on. And a few people will see their symptoms continually worsen.[11] But remember that this is the outlook if OCD is *untreated;* as you will learn, the outlook is much brighter if you get proper treatment.

What Are the Subtypes of OCD?

Patients with OCD exhibit a wide range of symptoms, unlike victims of many other psychiatric disorders. For example, patients with panic disorder usually experience the same kinds of symptoms: rapid heartbeat, fear of going crazy, fear of losing control, difficulty in breathing, or dizziness. And patients with depression also typically share similar symptoms: sleep and appetite changes, sadness, guilt, crying, or suicidal thoughts. But in OCD, one patient's symptoms may be totally different from another's. In fact, the kinds of OCD symptoms are distinct enough to be classified as categories, or subtypes. An individual with OCD may have several symptoms, but in general each person's symptoms fall into a particular category or subtype.

The symptoms of the most common OCD subtype are fears of contamination and cleaning rituals; these may occur alone or with other symptoms. The second most common subtype involves checking rituals, where patients fear that they have made a mistake and check their actions to reassure themselves; again, these

11. Rasmussen and Eisen, "The Epidemiology and Clinical Features of Obsessive-Compulsive Disorder," 1998.

may occur alone or with other rituals. One of several less common OCD problems, such as superstitious fears and rituals, repeating actions, obsessional slowness, and pure obsessions, may also be the major problem.

At times the differences between subtypes of patients with OCD can be so striking that it is difficult for them to believe that they have the same disorder. A patient I had referred to our OCD support group told me that the subgroups of patients found they had so little in common that at one point "the cleaners," "the checkers," and "the superstitious" had considered holding their own meetings in separate rooms. With time, however, these patients came to see the similarities of their problems. They all had seemingly uncontrollable thoughts and urges, and are now able to give support and advice to each other.

The following are descriptions and case examples of the major subtypes of OCD. The differences between the subtypes have important implications both for the way behavior therapy is implemented for each and for how well each responds to behavior therapy (these differences are described in Chapter 2). Remember that OCD is varied; you may have many of these symptoms, or you may have only one or two.

Cleaning Rituals and Contamination Fears

For some patients, fears of contamination may result in washing rituals that can continue for more than twelve hours a day for decades. Often entire areas of the house, the city, and even the country may be avoided to prevent contact with some feared contaminant. If you have contamination fears, you may also worry that you will contaminate other people. Obsessive fear of AIDS, often with resulting ferocious washing, has become more and more common. The following two cases illustrate different contamination fears and cleaning rituals.

Jane was a middle-aged woman who washed her hands a hundred times a day and used seven rolls of paper towels each week. She wouldn't touch anything that might have been touched by a person who was now dead. She was also afraid of being contaminated by "germs." As a result of these two fears, of death and germs,

Jane couldn't touch dozens of objects in her own home, including money, doorknobs, light switches, shoes, and kitchen utensils. She could not even sit on furniture that a person now deceased might have sat on in the past. Jane had persuaded members of her family to touch these objects and use them for her. As she became a prisoner in her own home because of her rituals, she became more and more depressed.

Peggy was a teacher, but she had acquired a second job: protecting herself from AIDS and cancer germs. When she came to see me, her problems had grown to the point that she had not been able to bring food into her house for six months. She spent five hours a day washing her hands and showering. If a checkout clerk looked "sickly" to her, she switched to another line. She had stopped doing her laundry because it required many rewashings due to her fears. She tried not to shake hands or brush against other people, and in her closet she segregated her "clean" clothes—those she had worn only in her apartment—from her "dirty" ones—those worn outside the apartment.

Peggy told me that she wasn't sure that touching contaminated objects would cause her to contract cancer or AIDS. But she also couldn't be sure that they wouldn't. So she kept on performing the rituals, just in case.

If you have a problem like this, you may continue scrubbing until your hands are red and raw. You may not stop at your hands but also scrub your forearms as well, up to the elbows. One patient suffered severe chemical burns on her hands from mixing bleach, ammonia, and other disinfectants as part of her hand washing.

You may wash your hands after actually touching—or just believing you've touched—a contaminated object. You may wash your hands repeatedly after shaking hands with someone you think is ill, after returning home from the outside world (and before touching anything in your house), after having sex, after touching raw meats or other uncooked foods, after touching your genitals, or even after blowing your nose. These rituals are different from normal washing. If you have OCD you can wash your hands over and over, hundreds of times a day, and still not feel clean.

If you feel that other areas of your body have also been contaminated, you may also take showers or baths lasting many hours; you may wash yourself in a ritualized way, washing each part of your body in a particular order for a particular number of times. Any interruption in your sequence or repetitions may prevent you from feeling perfectly clean, and so you may start the whole process all over again.

Checking Rituals and Safety Fears

If you perform checking rituals, you have trouble being certain that you haven't made a dangerous mistake—so you check, just to make sure. You usually fear that your mistake will hurt you or someone else. You may go back dozens of times to confirm that stove burners are off and doors are locked. But, even while staring at a locked door, you may still be unable to get the feeling that it is really locked; you can see that it is locked, but you don't believe your senses. Thus you may have to lock and unlock a single door for thirty minutes before you can finally pull yourself away, exhausted. You may frequently ask friends and family for reassurance. The following cases illustrate the power of these doubts.

Tom was a teacher tortured by fears that he had hurt one of his young students. The images were vivid: he saw himself cracking one boy's skull against the floor, strangling another with his bare hands. He would never do any of the things he feared, and these thoughts horrified him. He had fought these obsessions for twenty years, dreading each new school year and desperately waiting for the next school vacation.

Tom became an expert in inventing new and unobtrusive ways to check on the safety of the children in his class. A call to a parent when a student was out with a cold would temporarily reduce fears that he had killed the child. He would draw a chalk mark on the floor so that he could later reassure himself that he hadn't crossed over that mark to pounce on an unsuspecting student. But these measures worked only temporarily; the fears usually came back, sometimes during the school year, sometimes even for the entire summer vacation.

Bruce used to love to drive; by the time I saw him, he dreaded it. His OCD fears convinced him that, while driving, he would cause an accident without being aware of it. If he hit a bump in the road, he immediately thought he had hit a pedestrian. He would imagine a victim lying in the road while the police searched for a hit-and-run driver. In a panic he would turn his car around and circle back to check the spot. But one check never satisfied him— maybe the victim had dragged himself off the road; better turn around and check again. He became trapped in a frantic circle of checking and rechecking, like a dog chasing its tail in a losing race. When Bruce finally forced himself to break the cycle of checking, returning home afforded no peace; neither did his wife's exasperated reassurances. He then scanned television newscasts all night for the story of a hit-and-run driver. To ease his tortured conscience, he sometimes called the police to confess to a crime he never committed.

Bruce had other checking rituals. These included the common rituals of checking door locks, windows, and electrical plugs. He also feared causing a fire by being careless with electrical appliances. One day, after leaving our clinic, he frantically telephoned our secretary over and over to make sure that he had not caused a fire when he replaced the pot on the Mr. Coffee machine.

If you are subject to checking rituals, you may repeatedly ask others during a conversation whether you have insulted them. Or you may fear that you will unknowingly injure yourself. You may stay away from knives and scissors, or you may avoid a plate glass window, fearing that you might hurl yourself through it. If, nevertheless, you are unable to avoid these objects, you may check your body thoroughly to reassure yourself that you haven't been injured; but although you may search futilely for bleeding or laceration for hours, you still can't convince yourself you aren't hurt. Finally, you may find yourself making several visits or phone calls each week to your physician for reassurance.

You may, if you perform checking rituals similar to Bruce's, read the newspapers and listen to television or radio news to determine if something you feared has really happened. One patient who was afraid he had hit a pedestrian when he hit a pothole made anonymous calls to the police station asking if any hit-and-run accidents had been reported. A woman I treated who lost one of her pills while at a campground made repeated telephone calls to the ranger station to see if any children had been poisoned by taking her pill.

Or you may find it difficult to read, write, or perform simple calculations (such as balancing a checkbook) because you are continually checking that you didn't make a mistake. One woman had to quit her job as an accountant because she added columns of numbers over and over and still could not feel certain that she had not made a mistake.

Repeating Rituals and Counting Compulsions

If you perform repeating rituals, you feel compelled to repeat simple actions, like entering a room, washing a part of your body, or combing your hair, a certain number of times. And you may not feel right unless you perform the actions the "correct" number of times for you. You may be afraid that a catastrophe will befall you or a loved one if you don't complete the repetitions correctly.

To protect himself from superstitious fears, Ken developed an elaborate set of counting and repeating rituals; these had to be followed precisely if safety was to be assured. When walking down stairs he protected himself by repeating "Love God" three (and only three) times. He had to put out cigarettes in a precise pattern of movements, to be performed in the same order each time. As he showered, each part of his body had to be washed a certain number of times, in exactly the same order each time. If the order or counting was interrupted, he had to start again. Whenever he flushed his toilet, he felt compelled to flush it thirteen times, to prevent harm to himself or his family; he accepted the occasional floods in his bathroom as the lesser of two evils, although his family didn't agree.

If you perform repeating rituals like Ken's, you may spend hours reading the same page in a book to make sure that you really understood what you just read. But because you continue to be distracted by obsessive thoughts and worries, you get trapped in a cycle of having to read and reread. You may not grasp the meaning of the material you read *because* of your obsessive thoughts. One patient told me he worried about whether the letters on the page were perfectly symmetrical; once he kept returning to stare at one particular *t* in a book when he noticed that a tiny part of the top of that letter was missing.

You may have difficulty writing because you spend hours searching for the perfect word or phrase. One patient was several years late turning in a college term paper because he continually rewrote the first few lines while searching for just the right words. You may tear up and rewrite checks if you feel that your handwriting is not perfect. As a result, you may also have trouble doing simple things like addressing envelopes or writing thank-you notes.

Maybe you don't have repeating rituals but instead feel compelled to count objects like ceiling or floor tiles. One patient obsessed about the number of grains of sand on the beach and one day decided to count them one by one. You may not know *why* you count these things; you may know only that you feel uncomfortable if you resist this urge, and your eyes are drawn back to begin counting again. Almost any objects may be counted, including books in a bookcase or nails in a wall.

Compulsive Slowness

If you have *any* OCD symptoms, you are probably slowed down because you waste time performing your rituals. But for a small number of patients, slowness itself is the problem; for them it may take hours to complete simple actions like eating or getting dressed.

Because of OCD Bill was agonizingly slow to complete even routine daily activities: getting dressed took the whole morning and early afternoon; brushing his teeth took an hour. Why was he so slow? There were many reasons. Each action had to be performed in a precise, ritualistic way; if not, it had to be repeated. Many actions had to be repeated a certain number of times—for example, Bill combed his hair in a series of ten sets of ten strokes. Obsessive thoughts and worries intruded, however, breaking his concentration and ruining his carefully planned patterns. As a result, actions that were almost finished had to be started again from the beginning.

One night Bill arrived at a restaurant at 7:00 P.M., an hour before the time he had arranged to meet his date. This time he wanted to be sure that he would be well prepared and in plenty of time. Bill went to the men's room to wash his hands and comb his hair; without being aware of it, he slowly became entangled in his rituals. When he finally came out of the bathroom at 2:00 A.M., seven hours later, he was surprised to find that his date had not waited for him!

Listening to Joe speak was frustrating. Each sentence could take minutes to get out. The listener was always on the edge of his seat, tempted to suggest the next word but aware that doing so would upset Joe. For him, every . . . word . . . had . . . to . . . be . . . precisely . . . the . . . correct . . . word . . . according . . . to . . . Webster's . . . definition . . . and . . . had . . . to . . . be . . . spoken . . . only . . . when . . . the . . . time . . . was . . . perfectly . . . right. Slowness had pervaded his whole life. Eating dinner took all evening. Adding a column of numbers took half a day. Family members could often be found banging on the bathroom door after Joe had occupied it for three hours.

Superstitious Obsessions and Compulsions

For people with OCD, superstitions can grow to overshadow everything else in life. Superstitious obsessions usually boil down to a fear of death and its symbols. If you have this kind of OCD, you form connections between feared objects—that is, you associate things with bad luck and then you avoid activities and places you think cause bad luck. For example, one woman treated at our clinic could never again wear any clothes she had been wearing when she was passed by a hearse:

Nancy's fears started with concrete symbols of death: if she passed a cemetery or hearse, her day was cursed, and she returned home. Later her fears became more abstractly related to the original ones, as is common in OCD, and she began to be afraid that she had said something disrespectful about a dead person. To

Nancy, it mattered not whether she had said a bad word about Hitler or about her own grandfather; in either case the dead had been angered and would extract their punishment.

The clothes Nancy wore when she spoke ill of the dead also became omens of bad luck, and she could no longer wear them; she would even avoid stores she had visited earlier on an "unlucky" day. Coming to see me became a struggle when one day Nancy passed a display skeleton on the way to my office. Since this represented a dead person, she struggled to fight any "bad" thoughts she might have as she passed the skeleton. When she was unsuccessful in resisting these thoughts, all plans for the day had to be canceled.

If you have superstitious obsessions, you may worry that you didn't wash each part of your body the lucky number of times, or that you didn't say a prayer the lucky number of times. Or you may not be able to end an activity on an unlucky number of repetitions. For one patient, each cigarette had to be patted out four times, not three (an unlucky number), and his television set could not be left on the unlucky number thirteen.

You may have unlucky times of day and therefore may not move a muscle while the hand of the clock is passing thirteen minutes after the hour. Or you may be unwilling to buy an item if the price contains one of your unlucky numbers. One woman I helped treat couldn't eat her dinner because it contained thirteen shrimp. You may be unable to leave your house on an unlucky day, whatever personal unlucky number you may have. If you have these obsessions, you probably fear that a catastrophe will occur if you defy your numerology.

You may associate colors with superstitious fears. For example, one patient considered black the color of death, and she feared courting death if she wore black clothes. A man associated the color red with blood and death; he refused to wear clothes with red in them or to use red ink.

What distinguishes OCD superstitious fears from everyday superstitions is the strength of the belief. Besides having the fears of numbers and colors just described, you may fear passing a cemetery or being passed by a hearse or black cat. One patient avoided shopping in a department store because one day the shape of the windows reminded her of a crucifix; she then wouldn't wear clothes she had previously bought in that store. Another clinic patient even developed superstitions based on her dreams. One night she dreamed of an orange. The next day she not only avoided oranges and anything orange, but she wouldn't even say the word "orange."

Saving or Hoarding Rituals

We all keep sentimental objects or things that we may need someday. But people with hoarding rituals can't distinguish between sentimental objects and trash. They can't be certain that a scrap of paper may not have some value; to solve this problem, they just keep everything.

Sam carried more notes in his wallet and trouser pockets than many people keep in their file cabinets. His wallet was more than two inches thick and bulged from his trouser pocket. He was afraid to throw anything away for fear it might turn out to be important. His room was an archaeologist's delight, filled with newspapers from years past, food wrappers, memos announcing long-forgotten meetings, torn tickets from old movies. Sam had to periodically clear a path in this rubble to get to his bed.

Like Sam, you may worry about throwing away newspapers or scraps of notepaper. Or you may worry if you don't collect huge quantities of things like towels. One man had compulsive urges to pick up useless pieces of trash from garbage cans and one day came to our clinic carrying a hubcap he had found. It is important to distinguish obsessions about hoarding from the normal saving of valuable or sentimental objects; for people with OCD, the objects have no real value.

Because of these fears and compulsions, you may have rooms filled with old newspapers, notes, cans, paper towels, wrappers, and empty bottles. You don't throw these things away because you fear you'll be disposing of something you may one day need. Some patients even save their own feces and urine, as did Howard Hughes. One woman at our clinic photographed anything she was going to throw away or flush down the toilet; she would then save the photographs rather than the items.

Obsessions Without Compulsions

You may suffer from aggressive sexual or religious obsessive thoughts that seem forced into your mind. Although you may not perform any rituals, these obsessive thoughts can be so severe that work or social activities are impossible for you. And even simple actions, such as patting a child on the head, can become intolerable, as the following case illustrates.

Paul was an elderly gentleman who believed he was a child molester. In fact, however, the molestation occurred only in his mind. Paul had OCD and was unable to rid himself of the thought that he had sexually abused a neighbor's boy. He talked to the child's parents, his wife, his rabbi, even the child himself, and all told him the same thing: nothing had happened. But because he could not be convinced, he had been tortured by the thought for more than five years.

As with many OCD sufferers with violent or sexual obsessions, Paul was a devoutly religious man. He was appalled by his thoughts but was unable to force them from his mind. He spent hours each day re-creating the events surrounding the supposed abuse. But despite this exhausting mental and emotional effort, he was never able to feel certain that he hadn't abused the child.

Like Paul, you may have sexual obsessions that horrify you, and you may spend hours reassuring yourself that this kind of sexual contact did not take place. But if you have OCD, *you never act on these urges.*

Your obsessive thoughts may involve either specific thoughts, images, or urges toward someone of the opposite sex or may take the form of worries such as "Am I a homosexual?" when in fact you do not engage in homosexual activities. One of our patients was a contented husband and father who said he was sexually satisfied. However, he kept having the obsessive thought that he would "suddenly become gay" and make a pass at a man. He said he had never felt any sexual attraction toward men and had never acted on this urge.

Instead of having sexual thoughts, you may worry that if you have a blasphemous or sacrilegious thought you will be punished. One woman had repetitive thoughts about sexual intercourse with Jesus and, being devoutly religious, found these thoughts disgusting and "evil." Others spend hours searching their memories to determine whether they in fact did do something blasphemous. These patients tend to be very religious.

One man worried constantly about whether he was doing the right or moral thing. He couldn't use the words "devil" or "Satan" or even words that began with the letters *d* or *s*. Other patients obsess about having told a lie or having inadvertently cheated someone.

You may be plagued by thoughts that you need to know or remember insignificant information, such as license plate numbers of cars parked in front of your house, the names of contestants on television game shows, or the telephone number of a doctor you saw years ago. You may spend hours trying to remember such unimportant bits of information, and you cannot rest until you do so. You may either fear that something terrible will happen to you or to a loved one if the information is not retrieved or simply feel very uncomfortable unless you search for the information.

One man carried around a notebook in which he recorded bumper sticker and sweatshirt slogans, so that if he needed to remember them, he could easily satisfy the urge. Otherwise he would search his memory for hours.

What Problems Are Confused with OCD?

The following section describes the differences between OCD and problems that are often confused with OCD. It is important for you to be clear about what OCD is, since the treatments you will learn in this book have been proven to work, but *only* for OCD. They may not be helpful for these other problems.

Everyday Worries and Rituals

We all worry or feel compelled to do things at times. We check to make sure we left the house with our wallet. We wash our hands if they feel dirty. But these normal doubts and habits aren't bothersome; they don't interfere with everyday life. It is only when these problems are so excessive that they cause severe discomfort or disrupt daily life that OCD is diagnosed. As shown in the following examples, although the boundary between OCD and ordinary urges and thoughts can be narrow, it can determine whether a person is able to function in society.

One man uses a particularly filthy public toilet, feels dirty, and eagerly pumps wet soap onto his hands and scrubs them clean. After rinsing, he feels relief as he leaves the bathroom. For another man, no matter how long he scrubs, the feeling of dirtiness remains. He can wash and rinse until his hands are raw and bleeding, but he still feels the germs and pictures the coming disease ravaging his body. This man has OCD.

One man has recently broken up with his girlfriend; despite his attempts to distract himself, thoughts of her force entry into his mind. Wherever he goes he still thinks of her, of the good times and the painful breakup. Mercifully, with time the thoughts fade. Another man has unwanted thoughts also, but these are unbearable thoughts of perverse sex with his infant daughter. For this man, suffering from OCD, time does not heal, and the irrational thoughts intensify, invading his mind while he is with his family and at work and causing tortured guilt and intense self-doubt.

In large office buildings in a major city, no thirteenth floor is to be found among the elevator buttons. Few tenants would want to rent space on that floor; few visitors would choose that floor. Silly, they think, but why take a chance when simply numbering the thirteenth floor "14" neatly solves the problem? Compare this "normal" fear of the unlucky number thirteen with the case of a teenage girl with OCD who cannot leave her home on the thirteenth of any month. Even leaving her home or performing an important errand on any date with a three in it is tempting the fates, so she remains at home. She is also compelled to freeze in her steps when the hands of a clock pass over the number three, and she cannot watch television channels containing this unlucky number.

She believes that if she violates these superstitious rules, the fates may strike one of her loved ones to show their displeasure.

Despite surface dissimilarities, these three individuals with OCD have important points in common: they have thoughts, compulsions, or urges they cannot control, all of which are felt as controlling them in a way they don't want to be controlled. These are the hallmarks of OCD.

Several years ago, a writer from a woman's magazine called me for information about OCD. She had heard that lovers who couldn't get thoughts of their former boyfriend or girlfriend out of their mind had OCD. These people would sometimes drive by the house of their ex-lovers or harass them with phone calls. This writer was surprised to hear that such behavior was probably not OCD. I told her that these problems can run the gamut from normal feelings of missing a loved one all the way to severe personality problems causing inappropriate behavior.

Obsessive-Compulsive Personality Disorder

Another problem commonly confused with OCD is the disorder known as obsessive-compulsive personality. The adjective "obsessive" is often used to describe a punctual, orderly person; in many cases being punctual and orderly are helpful traits. Most people who are called obsessive do not have OCD. But if they have personality traits like perfectionism, stinginess, or aloofness that interfere with their life or relationships, then they may have what is called obsessive-compulsive personality disorder.

A professional's work and marriage may suffer because of endless procrastination and indecisiveness. Important deadlines pass for bills and reports as he puts off preparing the necessary material rather than face the agonizing quest for perfection in each and every word and calculation. Because of his attention to detail and perfectionism, he cannot see the forest for the trees, and although he stays late at work to finish a report, the time is wasted, with the end result an empty sheet of paper.

There is a marked difference between such people, whom we call obsessive, and those with OCD. The following table contains a list of obsessional qualities and a brief description of each.

TRAITS OF OBSESSIVE-COMPULSIVE PERSONALITY DISORDER[12]

Preoccupation with details or rules	Person spends so much time paying attention to unimportant details or rules that he or she misses the big picture
Perfectionism interferes with completing tasks	Person may put off or not finish important work because he or she is paralyzed by thoughts that everything must be perfect
Excessive devotion to work and productivity	Person may be considered a workaholic
Overconscientiousness and inflexibility about morality and ethics	Person sees moral and ethical issues as either "right or wrong" or "black or white"
Inability to discard worn-out or worthless objects	Person saves things that have no monetary or sentimental value
Insistence that others submit to his or her way of doing things	Person tolerates no deviation from his or her way of doing things among family, friends, or co-workers
Lack of generosity	Person is stingy with money
Shows rigidity and stubbornness	Person is inflexible when dealing with other people

When I show this list to audiences at my talks, most people nod their head to at least some of these symptoms. But only if you have at least four of these traits, and they cause problems in your

12. Modified from *Diagnostic and Statistical Manual of Mental Disorders,* 4th ed., 1994.

life, do we give the diagnosis of obsessive-compulsive personality disorder.

Although some of these traits *may* occur in people with OCD, notice that they have little to do with the classic violent or sexual obsessions or with the cleaning or checking compulsions described previously. The distinction between these two disorders is important, because obsessive-compulsive personality disorder may not respond to the same treatments as OCD.

Promiscuous Sex, Drug Abuse, Compulsive Overeating, and Pathological Gambling

Problems such as promiscuous sex,[13] drug abuse, overeating, and gambling are often confused with OCD. People with each of these problems appear to act compulsively: they experience a growing urge compelling them to perform some self-damaging action that they tell us they don't want to perform. Traditionally, however, the distinction between such a compulsion and OCD has been straightforward. In all these problems the person *derives pleasure* from engaging in the compulsive activity. Sex, eating, drug use, and gambling usually produce a pleasant high while they are being engaged in, even though individuals may later regret the fact that they overindulged. In contrast, OCD compulsions *never* produce pleasant feelings. Although giving in to these urges may reduce unpleasant feelings, people with OCD always hate experiencing them. Thus, the traditional criterion has been that any compulsive activity that produces pleasure is not part of OCD.

Another distinction is that people with such problems as drug abuse and gambling act on their destructive urges; people with OCD *fear* doing something wrong, but *they never do it*.

We don't know yet whether the same medication and behavioral treatments effective for OCD will also help sufferers of these

13. It is in vogue to refer to this problem as a sexual addiction. This is not a psychiatric diagnosis; instead, it describes the experience sufferers feel. (The technical diagnosis in the *Diagnostic and Statistical Manual of Mental Disorders,* 4th ed., 1994 would be "Sexual Disorder Not Otherwise Specified," since one example given for this diagnosis is "distress about a pattern of repeated sexual relationships involving a succession of lovers who are experienced by the individual only as things to be used.") Support groups for this problem now exist, as well as therapists who specialize in treating it.

disorders. Although it is conceivable that with further research we may find that they are part of the OCD spectrum and that the distinction between them and OCD has been artificial, we will not refer to these problems in our discussion of OCD.

Delusional Thoughts

A delusion is an irrational thought that a person believes strongly is true. Delusions, such as the belief that you are being followed by the FBI or that your phone is tapped by communists, are common in paranoid disorders and schizophrenia. People with these thoughts usually will need medication treatment from a psychiatrist. These problems are easy to distinguish from the classic obsessions of OCD sufferers, who are not totally convinced that their obsessions are true.

But there are other delusions that are not so easy to tell from OCD. One man told me that he felt sure that a woman in his town was in love with him. He had believed this for more than five years. Every time she told him she wasn't interested, he became more convinced that she was. When his parents told him to forget her, he took this as proof that they were in on her plan to play hard to get. And when the police arrested him for bothering her, this "proved" that she had involved the entire city in her plan to keep her love for him secret.

The delusion that someone is in love with you, despite convincing evidence to the contrary, is called erotomania. This condition is considered different from OCD. It doesn't respond to the same treatments as OCD, and it requires medication treatment by a psychiatrist.

Sometimes jealousy can become a delusion. A woman was convinced that her boyfriend was having an affair. Although there was no evidence of this, she was certain it was true. Despite reassurances from her boyfriend, her family, and friends, her beliefs became stronger. She became positive that they were involved in a conspiracy against her. Her problem was different from normal feelings of jealousy. She thought about the imagined affair day and night. She was completely sure that she was right, despite all evidence. These delusions were ruining her relationship and her life, but she could not be convinced that they *were* delusions. Thoughts like these are called jealous delusions.

Such delusional problems may be very hard to distinguish from OCD. But the distinction is important, because they usually do not respond to treatments that help OCD.

Other Illnesses with Obsessions and Compulsions

Obsessive thoughts and compulsive urges can occur in a variety of psychiatric disorders, such as schizophrenia, severe depression, and organic brain dysfunction. If obsessions and urges are due to these disorders, then the patient is not diagnosed as having OCD.

In schizophrenia major symptoms are hallucinations (either seeing things or hearing voices) and poor social relations. Other symptoms often include paranoia.

Organic brain dysfunction may be caused by a head injury, by disorders such as Alzheimer's disease, or by use of alcohol or other drugs. People with these disorders may feel compelled to perform meaningless actions over and over again but cannot explain why they are doing them. These actions are usually different from the classic OCD symptoms already described, in that OCD sufferers enact their repetitive rituals with the goal of protecting themselves or their family from harm or discomfort.

In severe depression, the patient's main symptoms are sadness, sleep and appetite changes, guilt, crying, and suicidal thoughts. Often depressed individuals have intrusive, or obsessive, thoughts about mistakes they have made in their past, or about their worthlessness, or about suicide; but these thoughts are related to the depressive disorder and differ from the obsessions and compulsions of OCD that were mentioned earlier.

What Disorders May Be Related to OCD?

As OCD research has blossomed in recent years, studies of drug treatment response and genetics have indicated that there may be a spectrum of behavior problems related to OCD. In trichotillomania patients will pull hair from their head until they produce bald spots. This temporarily reduces their tension and urges. Patients often pluck their eyelids and eyebrows smooth as well. One man had such a constant compulsion to pull, tweeze, or burn the hairs of his sideburns that he avoided not only mirrors but also plate glass windows and polished metal because he was afraid he would give in to his urge once he caught sight of his own reflection, even in public; he had previously done so after passing a shiny toaster and a glass storefront. Shaving his head smooth provided only temporary relief, and he told me that he would consider chopping his hands off if he thought this would solve his problem.

Trichotillomania is many times more common than once thought, since victims are only now beginning to come forward for treatment as a result of increased publicity. Originally patients with the disorder were seen by dermatologists, but recently many have come to psychiatrists and psychologists. Trichotillomania appears to respond to some of the same medications as OCD does, and behavior therapy treatment is also effective in many cases, as described in Chapter 7.

Tourette Disorder is a neurological problem characterized by obscene utterances, barking sounds, and jerking body movements, or tics. One patient with the disorder shocked an unsuspecting secretary at our clinic by interrupting a casual conversation with a string of obscenities and animal noises; the secretary was left wide-eyed and speechless as the patient then lapsed back into normal conversation without missing a beat. Most patients have OCD symptoms in addition to their Tourette symptoms. And, conversely, many patients with OCD as their major problem also have some tics similar to those found in Tourette Disorder. The distinction between these two disorders is often difficult to make, and it is discussed fully in Chapter 7. This distinction is very important because different medications are effective for these two disorders. Preliminary research indicates that the behavior therapy treatment called "habit reversal" (described in Chapter 7) may be helpful in Tourette Disorder.

Some patients are convinced that they have a terrible disease. No matter how many normal heart tests they have, they are sure they have heart disease. Others, no matter how much reassurance they get, are certain that their insides are rotting away with cancer. The difference is somewhat blurred between this kind of patient and an OCD patient who fears getting a disease. But while the latter *worries* that he may get a disease, the former is *convinced* that he already has it. His thoughts are called somatic delusions, or hypochondriasis, and are discussed in Chapter 7. Other patients have obsessive thoughts that some aspect of their appearance is horribly ugly, despite reassurances to the contrary. (Many of these patients initially see plastic surgeons to help improve their imagined repulsive appearance.) This problem, called body dysmorphic disorder, is also discussed in Chapter 7.

Other habits now thought to be related to OCD include skin picking, in which patients become trapped in a loop of damaging their skin and the resulting scabs; these patients often will avoid wearing clothes that reveal the affected parts of their bodies, and skin infections can ensue. Individuals with this disorder appear to respond to medication and behavioral treatments effective for trichotillomania.

Although all of these problems are distinct from classic OCD, they are thought to make up a spectrum of OCD disorders.

After reading this chapter, you should now know if you could possibly have OCD. If you think you may have one of the non-OCD disorders described here and you are not currently being treated, you should consult a clinical psychologist or psychiatrist as soon as possible for an evaluation. If, however, you suspect you have OCD symptoms, the following chapters will help you to assess those symptoms and get control of them.

CHAPTER TWO

• •

Treatment of OCD

• •

"There are no such things as incurables; there are only things for which man has not yet found a cure."
—Bernard Baruch (1870–1965)

Can we treat OCD successfully? If you had asked this question thirty years ago, the answer would have been "Probably not." Despite some reports of successful treatments, none of the methods gave consistent results. But, proving Baruch's observation true, the outlook for OCD sufferers has improved dramatically in recent years with the development of proven behavior therapy and medication treatments for OCD. As a result, we now can successfully treat the vast majority of our patients with OCD.

To assess the effectiveness of any OCD treatment, we must keep in mind that OCD symptoms can fluctuate on their own, even without treatment. Although OCD patients rarely lose all their symptoms during natural periods of remission, many may see temporary improvement over any given span of months or years.[1] Thus, we consider effective only those treatments that are proven to help more than 50 percent of patients, to accomplish this in a short time, and to result in lasting improvement.

The research studies I describe later in this chapter apply mainly to the treatment of adults with OCD. But similar behavior

1. Rasmussen and Tsuang, "Epidemiology and Clinical Features of Obsessive-Compulsive Disorder," 1986.

therapy and medication treatments appear to be effective with children and adolescents also, as described in Chapter 5.

Behavior Therapy for OCD

Behavior therapy is a form of psychotherapy that uses principles of learning to help patients change specific problems. Whereas traditional psychotherapy views problem behaviors as symptoms of an underlying unconscious conflict, in behavior therapy we teach patients how to correct their problems directly.

As an example, we know from our theories of how humans learn and unlearn habits that if you are very afraid of heights you can overcome this fear by first learning how to relax and to control your irrational thoughts about heights. Then you would use these techniques to control your anxiety while attempting an easy goal like standing on a kitchen chair. After several successes like this, you would gradually put yourself into more difficult situations, until finally you were able to comfortably look out the window of the top floor of a skyscraper or to fly in an airplane.

Following this principle, powerful behavior therapy methods were developed in the late 1950s to treat patients with phobias, or fears. Behavior therapy proved so effective that it revolutionized the treatment of these problems—for which no successful treatment had previously existed—and, as a result, is now the preferred treatment for them.

When the same methods were first applied to OCD, however, the results were not impressive. But a breakthrough came in 1966, when a British psychiatrist, Dr. Victor Meyer, instructed nurses in his hospital psychiatric ward to actively prevent patients with OCD from carrying out their rituals around the clock. When given this treatment, fourteen of his fifteen patients for the first time showed rapid improvement, which for most of them proved to be lasting.

Methods such as these have come to be the standard type of behavior therapy for OCD. The active ingredients in this treatment are *exposure* (confronting a situation you fear) and *response prevention* (keeping yourself from acting on compulsions afterward). You'll be seeing these phrases over and over in the pages that follow. And since much of this book teaches you how to apply these simple principles to your particular problems, it is essential to understand them fully.

What Are Exposure and Response Prevention?

The procedures of exposure and response prevention would be straightforward if you came to see me for behavior therapy for compulsive hand washing and showering due to fears of being contaminated by cancer "germs." Exposure would consist of gradually bringing you into contact with objects you believed to be contaminated, such as a magazine or chair in the waiting area of a cancer clinic. I would then encourage you to stay in contact with the "contaminated" object for as long as possible (*exposure*) and then to keep from washing your hands or showering for one to two hours afterward (*response prevention*).

Although less obvious, the same principles of exposure and response prevention would apply if you had other kinds of compulsive rituals. For example, if you felt compelled to retrace your route while driving to check that you had not struck a pedestrian, I would accompany you while you drove your car and encourage you to do the things that normally make you fear you've hit someone, like driving on a bumpy road or passing pedestrians in the road (*exposure*). While you did this, I would encourage you to resist the urge to stare in your rearview mirror or turn the car around to check for victims (*response prevention*).

We can state the principles of exposure and response prevention for OCD simply:

1. *Confront* the things you fear as often as possible.
2. If you feel like you have to avoid something, *don't.*
3. If you feel like you have to perform a ritual to feel better, *don't.*
4. Continue steps 1, 2, and 3 for as long as possible.

Steps 1 and 2 describe exposure (confronting the situation). Step 3 describes response prevention (not giving in to compulsions during or after exposure).

*   *   *

Most "new" ideas are really reworkings of very old ones. The great French neurologist Pierre Janet alluded to forms of treatment similar to modern behavior therapy as early as the turn of this century. Janet not only was treating his patients with what we now call exposure therapy, but he also called it by that name, which remains in use to this day.

> The guide, the therapist, will specify to the patient the action as precisely as possible. He will analyse it into its elements if it should be necessary to give the patient's mind an immediate and proximate aim. By continually repeating the order to perform the action, that is, exposure, he will help the patient greatly by words of encouragement at every sign of success, however insignificant, for encouragement will make the patient realize these little successes and will stimulate him with the hopes aroused by glimpses of greater successes in the future. Other patients need strictures and even threats and one patient told [Janet], "Unless I am continually being forced to do things that need a great deal of effort I shall never get better. You must keep a strict hand over me!"[2]

This description of behavioral treatment for OCD is still accurate today, and exposure therapy as described by Janet is still the major behavioral treatment of OCD almost a hundred years later. Sadly, this effective treatment fell out of favor soon after Janet proposed it, as Europe was swept up in the new psychoanalytic theory of Freud. While therapists became more interested in discovering the hidden meanings of obsessions and compulsions, Janet's powerful methods lay idle for decades until they were resurrected by Dr. Meyer.

Habituation: The Key to Exposure and Response Prevention

Have you ever visited friends who live near an airport or train station? You've probably wondered how in the world they can

2. Isaac Marks, "Review of Behavioral Psychotherapy, I: Obsessive-Compulsive Disorders," 1981.

stand the noise. But your friends seem hardly to notice it. Or have you ever squeezed into a painfully tight pair of shoes in the morning, only to find that by evening you've forgotten you have them on? If you've had either of these experiences, you've witnessed your body's process of habituation firsthand. "Habituation," which comes from the Latin word *habitus,* for "habit," means "to accustom; to make familiar by frequent use or practice." In other words, after long familiarity with a situation that at first produces a strong emotional reaction, our bodies learn to get used to or ignore that situation.

Habituation is a key process to understand if you want to control your compulsions and obsessions. Our research and experience with hundreds of patients show that if you continue to practice exposure and response prevention, your fears and compulsions will almost always decrease. But people's compulsions change at different rates. One person's fears may diminish in the first hour of practice, while a second person may feel better only after weeks of hard practice. There is nothing you can do about these differences, except to accept them as we accept individual differences in hair color and height. All that really matters is that with practice your fears will eventually subside.

Habituation works in many areas of life apart from OCD. For example, most of us were afraid of the dark as children. We may have felt afraid, had urges to scream or cry, and suffered with thoughts of the bogeyman and other monsters hiding under our bed. As a result, we may have begged our parents to turn the lights on or to let us crawl into bed with them.

Over the months, if we—and our parents—persisted, and we continued to sleep in the dark, our fears and thoughts of bogeymen lessened. Thus, just by changing our *behavior* (staying in the dark room), we also indirectly changed our *thoughts* (monsters) and *feelings* (fear). Read the last sentence again; this is exactly what happens in all successful behavior therapy for OCD.

Research in Behavior Therapy for OCD

Studies around the world over the past three decades have tested exposure and response prevention and confirmed that they are indeed effective in helping about three quarters of OCD patients get control of their symptoms. These studies also found that 80 percent of patients were able to complete the behavioral treatment and that the remainder could not, because of extreme fears.

While most early studies were done with hospitalized patients, we have since learned how to employ these techniques with patients outside the hospital ward. More recent studies have been done with outpatients, with excellent results. And studies conducted in Europe over the last decade have found that patients can carry out these techniques *on their own* and achieve results equal to those attained by practicing exposure and response prevention with a therapist. This book draws upon this research to show you how to use these same methods with the assistance of a helper, a family member or friend who helps you with your practice.

There are no known side effects of behavior therapy. Compulsions that are treated tend to remain better. Studies have found that almost all patients have either maintained their improvements or continued to improve as long as seven years after treatment.[3] Some patients in these studies needed booster sessions of behavior therapy along the way to hold on to their gains. No new symptoms have been discovered to arise to replace the ones that are successfully treated.

Research in the effectiveness of behavior therapy has also identified two problems that can interfere with your progress. These factors—strong belief in obsessions, and severe depression—both interfere with improvement in behavior therapy for the same reasons: they decrease the chances that you will actually complete the exposure and response prevention that are necessary for you to get control, and they interfere with the process of habituation, which, as you know, is the aim of these procedures.

Strong Belief in Obsessions

If you *always* honestly believe that your obsessions are true or that your compulsions are necessary to prevent a catastrophe, you are unlikely to respond well to behavior therapy. Should your assessment in Chapter 3 indicate that you have this problem, then

3. Baer and Minichiello, "Behavior Therapy for Obsessive-Compulsive Disorder," 1998.

you should consult a psychiatrist to see if a medication can help you to change these thoughts before trying behavior therapy.

In discussing strong belief in obsessions I do not mean hearing voices in your head; this is *not* OCD. People with OCD always know that their thoughts are a product of their own mind. If you believe that other people's voices are speaking to you or controlling you, then you should see a qualified psychiatrist or psychologist as soon as possible to get help for your problem.

Happily, the vast majority of people with OCD do not truly believe in their obsessions, *except* when they are trapped in an OCD loop of obsessions and compulsions and are feeling anxious; this is common. Only when you *always* believe in your obsessions do you have what are called overvalued beliefs. The following description demonstrates that most people with OCD don't really believe in their obsessions.

Alexis was afraid of germs. She avoided touching objects or eating food that might have touched someone who possibly had cancer or AIDS "germs." When she was not in the throes of anxiety related to her OCD symptoms, she was able to speak rationally and calmly about her fears; at these times she told me that she knew she couldn't contract cancer or AIDS just from touching something that had touched someone with either of these diseases. She had read extensively on the subject and was convinced that all the current scientific evidence pointed in this direction.

But when she tried to take home food sold to her by an "ill-looking" checkout boy, the paradox of her obsessions became clear: Alexis didn't believe that she could get ill from "disease germs," but neither was she completely certain that she wouldn't. Faced with the feared situation, she felt compelled to avoid the objects and, failing this, to scrub and disinfect the parts of her body and clothing that had come into contact with them.

Most patients with OCD fit this pattern—they do not truly believe that they will definitely get ill or have bad luck, but neither are they completely certain that they are safe. On the other hand, no amount of convincing could change the mind of the woman in the next description. She was certain she would get cancer from touching certain things.

*   *   *

Millie saw cancer germs everywhere: on the doorknob touched by someone with cancer, on a seat recently occupied by a cancer patient. As is common in OCD, her fears began slowly—causing her to avoid only things her mother, who had recently died of cancer, had touched—but spread insidiously. When I met Millie she had been unable to live in her apartment for months for fear that it was contaminated by cancer germs. She was not able to work; instead she cleaned house and baby-sat in return for board. Although she was miserable because of the changes in her life, when I questioned her it was clear that she truly believed she would contract cancer by touching "contaminated" objects. She was not sure how long the cancer would take to develop: she believed that she would get cancer but that it might not show up for one, ten, or thirty years. Thus, even if she agreed to touch "contaminated" objects and didn't become ill after days or weeks had passed, her fears remained undiminished, since she believed that the disease would still develop sooner or later.

Severe Depression

In Chapter 3 you will rate yourself by answering some questions about depressed mood. It is natural for you to feel somewhat sad or depressed if OCD has affected your social and work life. But if you find that you are *severely* depressed, then you should consult a qualified psychiatrist or psychologist as soon as possible (or ask your own doctor to refer you to one), before trying behavior therapy to treat your OCD. Getting professional help for depression is critical for two reasons.

First is the obvious fact that people who are severely depressed usually are living in difficult, substandard conditions and sometimes become suicidal. Second, their OCD is less likely to respond to behavior therapy while they are severely depressed—they are unlikely to have the energy needed for exposure and response prevention and may find this treatment ineffective even if they do try it, since the process of habituation seems to work differently when the patient is very depressed.

The next case history illustrates how an OCD patient can be treated successfully once he or she has received help for severe depression.

* * *

Like millions of senior citizens, she sat in front of her television and watched a daily parade of soap operas and game shows. But Martha was different—she was compelled to write down and remember the name of every actor or contestant on these shows. Should she be unable to remember one of these, she believed, something terrible would happen to her or her family.

Martha's problem began suddenly the year before. She had been severely depressed after her mother's death, which climaxed the deaths of several family members and close friends in a short span of time. First came the classic signs of depression: inability to eat or sleep, sad mood, and thoughts of death. Within a few weeks, however, Martha's children noticed odd new habits, or rituals, appearing. Everywhere she went, their mother would now carry a shopping bag filled with slips of paper. These bore the names, birthdays, and anniversaries of family and friends, and even license plate numbers of cars parked on her street.

When Martha came to our clinic for help with these rituals she had been put on a low dose of an antidepressant medication, desipramine, by her family doctor. As this dose was increased, she became less depressed and told me she no longer feared that anything terrible would happen if she did not remember the names and numbers she had recorded. She now agreed to work with me on behavior therapy to help rid her of these rituals. She worked at home with her son on throwing away the slips of paper she had accumulated and began watching television shows without taking any notes. And after just three sessions, Martha and her son told me that she had made remarkable improvement.

How Long Does Behavior Therapy Take?

Most patients rightfully want to know how long behavior therapy will take. Whether you try to control your symptoms on your own or while seeing a behavior therapist, the answer depends on two factors: how much exposure and response prevention practice you do, and how severe your OCD symptoms are.

Dr. John Hurley, a behavior therapist in our clinic, told me, "Patients often ask me this, so I went back over my records to find out the answer. I found that on the average I see patients for six months: at first I see them every week, then every two weeks, and finally every month. But I tell my patients that this is only if they are very determined and motivated to work hard. Other patients who are less motivated may stay in treatment much longer and make less progress. The most important thing is how willing they are to work on exposure and response prevention."

Obviously, whether you are working with a behavior therapist, with a family member, or by yourself, persistence is a vital ingredient for your success with behavior therapy.

Will Behavior Therapy Eliminate All My OCD Symptoms?

Probably not. Although your obsessive and compulsive symptoms probably will be greatly reduced with behavioral treatment, and interference with your occupational and social functioning also will be greatly reduced, the chances are that a few rituals or obsessions will remain.

To put this in perspective, I should note that even though our patients rarely get completely better with behavior therapy, they're usually thrilled with the improvements they make, since their OCD symptoms no longer interfere with their social lives or work. They may still worry about contamination more than the average person, or they may still ask themselves if the door is really locked, or they may prefer not to get married on Friday the thirteenth, but these problems no longer dominate their life.

Can Behavior Therapy Help My Child?

Parents often ask me about behavior therapy for their children with OCD. Although most of our clinic patients are adults, I have treated many children and adolescents over the years. And while not much research has been done in the area of behavior therapy for children, I have seen many children and adolescents in our clinic who got control of their OCD symptoms with behavior therapy.

In our clinic we've found three important conditions for success: first, the parents have to participate in a constructive and enthusiastic way. In some cases the parents seem to have more anxiety than the child they brought to me for treatment. The parents have to be willing to help their child carry out exposure and response prevention in a firm but calm and loving way. Second, the child must really want to get better. Since the child will be involved in the treatment, he or she must understand the plan and be willing and positive about it. Finally, the child should have a good relationship with his or her parents. When these conditions have been met, I have had good success with behavior therapy for children and adolescents with OCD.

Overall, our clinic has had success in about half of the children with OCD we've treated. Many improve by 70 percent or more. Most of the children are already on medication by the time they are referred to us, and the combination of behavior therapy and medication seems to work well for many children.

Fortunately, over the past decade Dr. John March, a leading child psychiatrist, and his colleagues at Duke University have developed a remarkably effective treatment program for children and adolescents suffering from OCD. Although their approach emphasizes the same exposure and response prevention methods that I describe here, they have found a wonderful way of communicating these ideas to children and adolescents that is both understandable and motivating. If your child suffers from OCD, go out and buy *OCD in Children and Adolescents: A Cognitive-Behavioral Treatment Manual* tomorrow; while you're at it, you should probably buy two copies and give one to any therapist who is treating your child!

Prognosis for Different Types of OCD Symptoms

Because of the variety of OCD symptoms, the way you will use behavior therapy will depend on the kind of problem you have. Behavior therapy is most straightforward for cleaning rituals. Most research has focused on these rituals, finding that they respond very well to behavior therapy. If you perform cleaning rituals, the techniques of exposure and response prevention in Chapter 5 should enable you and your helper to get control of them.

Checking rituals may be somewhat more difficult to treat with behavior therapy, largely because you probably perform your rituals mainly when you are alone and in your home; in other words, when you are responsible for your own decisions. This can make it more difficult for a therapist or helper to assist in your treatment, since you will have to do most of your exposure and response prevention on your own. If you can do this, you'll probably be able to greatly reduce your checking rituals with behavior therapy so that you are able to function more normally again, but your feelings of uncertainty, although greatly reduced, may still be present at times.

Other types of rituals, like superstitious fears and hoarding, have not been studied as extensively as cleaning and checking rituals. But if you work with a helper and use the techniques in Chapter 5, you should be able to reduce your problems. As with checking rituals, your urges, while diminished, may persist. Behavior therapy for these problems usually requires a helper to work with you.

The treatment of compulsive slowness is very difficult and complicated. If you have very mild problems with compulsive slowness, you may be able to control them by working with a helper and using the techniques given in Chapter 5. But if you have a more serious problem with slowness, you should work with a behavior therapist and a psychiatrist who will prescribe medication.

The problem of obsessive thoughts with no compulsions used to be considered the most difficult OCD disorder to treat with behavior therapy, because it results in no observable behavior on which to use exposure and response prevention. Fortunately, over the past decade we have developed effective non-medication treatments for this problem. If you find that you are avoiding situations that trigger these obsessions, then setting goals to expose yourself to these situations without performing compulsions (as I describe in Chapter 4) will probably help control this problem.

On the other hand, if you do *not* avoid situations that trigger these thoughts, you may still get relief by using audiotaped exposure or new cognitive therapy techniques (both of which are described in Chapter 5).

Medication Treatment for OCD

Until the early 1970s the psychiatric medications available for anxiety and depression, despite their success in treating these conditions, did little to reduce obsessions or compulsions. But since then several new antidepressant medications have been developed that are effective for OCD symptoms within three months of treatment. These new medications all affect the brain neurotransmitter serotonin, which was briefly discussed in Chapter 1 and will be discussed in detail in Chapter 8.

The first such "anticompulsive" drug was clomipramine, (Anafranil)[4] which has been available in most countries for several years and was approved in 1990 by the U.S. Food and Drug Administration as the first anticompulsive drug in the United States. Research at our OCD clinic, and at other centers, has proven clomipramine to be very effective in reducing OCD symptoms in most patients.

Over the past decade we have also found several other medications to be effective for OCD. These drugs include fluoxetine (Prozac), fluroxamine (Luvox), sertraline (Zoloft), paroxetine (Paxil), and citalopram (Celexa).

If these new medications are so effective, then why has behavior therapy remained so important in treating OCD? There are three major reasons. First, 20 to 30 percent of patients either refuse or are unable to take these medications, because of such conditions as pregnancy or a predisposition to severe side effects. These patients need behavior therapy. Second, about 25 percent of those who take the medications notice only small changes and do not experience pronounced improvements. Third, although medications produce significant improvements in most patients with OCD, usually these patients still retain between 30 and 50 percent of their symptoms. In most cases these individuals are very happy with the progress they have made with medication alone, but we find that the addition of behavior therapy will result in even more improvement in their symptoms. Still, some symptoms almost always persist after any kind of treatment for OCD.

4. Names in parentheses refer to the American brand name of each drug.

For most of our clinic patients, we find, a combined approach including both behavior therapy (provided by a psychologist) and medication (prescribed by a psychiatrist) works well. We also treat many patients with behavior therapy alone, with excellent results. The decision to use medication or behavior therapy, therefore, is not an either-or question in our OCD clinic. The use of medications to treat OCD is so common, and so important, that Chapter 8 is devoted to it.

The following is an example of a patient who improved markedly with behavior therapy after already having made some progress with medication.

James had severe fears of being contaminated by fiberglass and gasoline. When I met him, he had been taking fluvoxamine for two years, and though he had improved somewhat and had fewer obsessive thoughts, he still avoided most situations in which he might come in contact with these substances: entering his attic, filling up his car with gasoline, wearing clothes that might be contaminated, or touching his children when he felt contaminated. James was very motivated to work hard in behavior therapy, and because he lived three hours from our clinic, I saw him only once a month, while he practiced exposure and response prevention at home with his wife helping him. After only five sessions, James had made remarkable progress, avoiding few or no situations. These improvements have continued a year after treatment.

Most behavior therapists and psychiatrists now believe that combining behavior therapy and medication is an efficient approach to treating many patients—adults, children, and adolescents—with moderate or severe OCD. I tell my patients that taking antidepressant or antianxiety medications will not interfere with their progress in behavior therapy. If anything, it will only help them more.

In our clinic we find that patients with less severe cleaning and checking rituals do very well with behavior therapy alone. Some patients with other types of OCD problems also do well with behavior therapy alone. One man, for example, had obsessive fears about AIDS and avoided many situations. He was able to overcome his fears with behavior therapy alone and has maintained his progress now for more than a year since treatment ended. But in general, if you spend more than four hours a day performing rituals, or you are severely depressed or severely anxious, or you have only obsessions, then you should probably take a medication in addition to practicing behavior therapy.

Other Treatments for OCD

Traditional Psychotherapy

Most people who hear the word "psychotherapy" immediately think of traditional kinds of psychotherapy (also known as talking therapies). These include traditional Freudian psychoanalysis, in which patients talk about their early life and dreams. Although traditional psychotherapy can help us to understand many emotional problems, there are no scientific studies indicating that this treatment is helpful for classic OCD. It will cause no harm but does little to alleviate OCD symptoms.[5]

Because the habits of OCD are so strong, most therapists now agree, treatment must be more active to change the obsessions or compulsions of OCD. Just talking about the symptoms or their history does not seem to change them. In our clinic, we do not consider traditional psychotherapy an effective treatment for OCD symptoms. *After* our patients get their obsessions and compulsions under control, we sometimes refer them for traditional psychotherapy to help them deal with other problems.

Freud's theories taught us that people can perform rituals for reasons of which they are unaware, but his methods did not lead to effective treatments for OCD. In fact, almost every week we see at least one patient in our clinic whose OCD symptoms either did not improve or worsened, despite many years of daily psychoanalysis.

In the absence of other effective treatments for OCD, psychoanalytic psychotherapy was still the most common treatment as

5. On the other hand, this approach can be helpful in the treatment of obsessive-compulsive personality disorder, which is described in Chapter 1. (See Jenike, "Psychotherapy of Obsessive-Compulsive Disorder," in Jenike et al., *Obsessive-Compulsive Disorders: Practical Management,* 3rd ed., 1998, for more information.)

recently as the late 1960s. Up until this time, OCD was called obsessional neurosis and was thought to have one of the poorest prognoses of any of the neurotic disorders; in other words, it was untreatable. Fortunately, over the past two decades this prognosis has changed drastically, thanks to the advent of powerful behavior therapy and medication treatments.

Electroconvulsive Therapy

Electroconvulsive therapy (ECT) has long been used to treat severe depression. Patients who are unable to function in daily life or are suicidal, and whose depression has not responded to proven antidepressant medications or any other treatment, are often given painless electric shocks to their temples. These treatments are repeated several times on different days until the depression lessens.

Although this treatment sounds frightening, it is safe, and its only side effect can be a memory loss of events right before the ECT; even this memory usually comes back gradually. Most important, this treatment has helped many severely depressed patients who might otherwise have committed suicide begin to function normally again.

Because of ECT's proven effectiveness in severe depression, many psychiatrists have tried it in treating severe OCD symptoms. While there are some case reports of ECT's helping OCD, the vast majority of research has found that it is not an effective treatment for OCD.[6] We have seen dozens of patients in our clinic whose OCD symptoms were no better despite having had between five and a hundred ECT sessions. On the other hand, we have seen several patients who were only able to respond to behavior therapy for their OCD symptoms *after* their severe depression lifted following ECT. Thus, the success of ECT in some OCD cases can probably be explained by ECT's ability to relieve the depression that often accompanies severe OCD.

6. Jenike, "Somatic Treatments," in Jenike et al., *Obsessive-Compulsive Disorders,* 1st ed., 1986.

Cingulotomy

The cingulum is a part of the brain made up of nerve fibers that connect those sections of the brain controlling feelings and actions. Brain surgeons have known since the early 1950s that by making small cuts in the cingulum—performing a cingulotomy[7]—obsessive and compulsive symptoms can be reduced.[8]

To test the value of this approach, our OCD clinic recently collaborated with our colleagues Drs. Thomas Ballantine and Robert Martuza, two neurosurgeons at Massachusetts General Hospital, to study the small number of patients with very severe OCD who had had cingulotomy operations at the hospital since the 1960s. We concluded that the operations were effective for many patients with severe OCD who had not been helped by other methods.[9] As a result we began working with the late Dr. Ballantine, with Dr. Martuza, and most recently with Dr. Rees Cosgrove to carefully assess all patients referred for cingulotomy for severe OCD which had not responded to any other treatment. We saw these patients before they underwent surgery: first, to make sure that they were in fact sufferers from OCD; second, to make sure they had undergone adequate trials of both behavior therapy and medication for OCD; and third, to carefully assess the type and severity of their OCD symptoms before surgery. After surgery, we continued to follow up on these 18 patients about twice a year, either by phone or in person, to carefully assess any changes in their symptoms or quality of life. Once again, we found that the cingulotomies done at Massachusetts General Hospital gave dramatic relief to from one quarter to one half of these patients without any serious side effects.[10]

7. Cingulotomy is only one kind of brain surgery that has been used for OCD. Other small areas of the brain have been operated on to help OCD. This discussion also applies to these other operations, which include capsulotomies and limbic leucotomies. Another term for these operations is "limbic system surgery."
8. Jenike et al., "Neurosurgical Treatment of Obsessive-Compulsive Disorder," in *Obsessive-Compulsive Disorders,* 3rd ed., 1998.
9. Jenike et al., "Cingulotomy for Refractory Obsessive-Compulsive Disorder: A Long-Term Follow-up of 33 Patients," *Archives of General Psychiatry,* in press.
10. Baer, L., Rauch, S. L., Ballantine, H. T., Martuza, R., Cosgrove, R., Cassem, E., Manzo, P.A., Dimino, C., Jenike, M.A., "Cingulotomy for Intractable Obsessive-Compulsive Disorder: Prospective Long-term Follow-up of 18 Patients." *Archives of General Psychiatry,* 1995; 52(5):384-392.

Naturally, most people fear any kind of brain surgery. Pictures of patients who underwent lobotomies in the 1950s may come to mind. Such patients often became unemotional and docile after the surgery; these changes were popularized in the life story of Frances Farmer.

But the modern cingulotomy operation uses computer techniques to cut only a tiny bunch of nerve fibers. As a result, careful studies of many patients at our hospital have found, no personality changes are caused by this surgery. Some patients do suffer treatable epileptic seizures or, rarely, more serious complications after the surgery.

Of course, all surgery involves some risks, and so cingulotomy will remain a treatment of last resort. All patients should try behavior therapy and all available medications before even considering cingulotomy. However, if all the other treatments have been tried adequately and have failed, and the sufferer is crippled by OCD problems, he or she should not be afraid to discuss with a doctor the possibility of a cingulotomy.

The following case illustrates a successful cingulotomy.

John had been bothered by obsessive thoughts of all kinds every waking hour for the previous five years. Violent thoughts, sexual thoughts, counting, trying to remember names and telephone numbers—all seemed to be going on loudly and at once. He was unable to work, and often couldn't hold a conversation because of these relentless thoughts. He told me that he had reached the point of seriously considering suicide. We call his condition one of pure obsessions, because he had only obsessive thoughts and did not perform compulsive rituals.

John had come to Massachusetts General Hospital from his home in another part of the country to be evaluated for a cingulotomy. Any patient who is referred for a cingulotomy at our hospital must be approved for this surgery by a committee of doctors to ensure that the operation is appropriate and has a good chance of helping the problem.

I had two purposes in interviewing John. First, I had to confirm that he indeed had OCD. This was easy; John had the most severe case of pure obsessions I had ever seen, and the content of his obsessions was classic in OCD. Second, I had to make sure that he had already tried all other reasonable treatments for OCD. John's doctor had tried all medications thought to be effective for OCD, but none had helped the obsessions at all. When I reviewed his medical records I confirmed that he had been on the correct doses of each medication for a long enough time to expect some improvement. Similarly, several sessions of ECT had had no effect on his obsessive thoughts. Although John never had seen a therapist for behavior therapy for his OCD, he had tried this treatment on his own but could not control his thoughts or distract himself at all. I knew that behavior therapy was least likely to help pure obsessions, especially obsessions as frequent and strong as John's.

I wrote the cingulotomy committee, telling them that John had OCD and that he had failed to respond to all standard treatments besides cingulotomy. The next day, the review committee gave John the go-ahead for a cingulotomy in two days' time. The surgery went well, and two days afterward he was up and around with no ill effects.

When I telephoned John recently to see how things had gone in the six months since his surgery, it was like talking to a different person. He told me that "about two months after the surgery the thoughts began to fade away." He said he had had *no* obsessive thoughts at all over the past three months, and he was no longer depressed: "It's like a miracle. I can work again, and enjoy life. I'm just keeping my fingers crossed that they don't come back." John, his friends, and his family noticed no negative changes in his personality after the surgery, only that he was his old self again.

Most patients do not respond as quickly as John did. And some require a second operation before they see results. However, John's case shows what a dramatic impact neurosurgery performed at a hospital with OCD specialists can have *when all other treatments have failed.*

Principles of Behavior Therapy

You now know that behavior therapy is the only proven treatment for OCD that you can undertake yourself. It is also the only treatment that you can undertake yourself. Most of this book explains how behavior therapy works. Chapter 8 explains the use of medication in combination with behavior therapy.

Now let's examine each of the principles of behavior therapy in detail. The way you apply these principles to control different OCD symptoms varies quite a bit; these differences are discussed in Chapter 5. For now, however, we are concerned only with those principles of behavior therapy that are common to treating *all* OCD symptoms.

You Can Control Your Behavior—Not Your Urges or Thoughts

Let's be clear on our definitions. A behavior is an action that another person can see you perform. Turning a knob on a stove is a behavior. Touching a water faucet is a behavior. Urges and thoughts, on the other hand, are experienced only by the person who is having them. Feeling that you need to wash your hands is an urge. Worrying about whether your hands are contaminated is a thought. Although our thoughts and feelings are often compelling and fascinating to discuss, we simply cannot control them directly. We try to—and with practice we can gain somewhat better control over them—but no one can control feelings or thoughts all the time.

Just knowing this simple fact comes as a relief to many of my patients. They finally realize that they've been struggling, often for years, to control something that can't be controlled. As soon as they learn that they are responsible only for controlling their behaviors, a weight is lifted from their shoulders. They no longer have to feel like a failure for not being able to control their obsessive thoughts and urges. All they must take responsibility for is whether they actually perform a compulsion or avoid a situation they fear.

I explain to my patients that if I give them the homework assignment of turning off the stove just once, without returning to check it, their assignment is just that; they have succeeded if they turn the stove off once, without checking it, regardless of the feelings or thoughts they have while doing this. I do not hold patients responsible for controlling their feelings, thoughts, or urges during this action. How can I? They are going to have some obsessive thoughts and uncomfortable feelings whether they try to or not. But if they can control their behavior, then they have achieved their goal. And if they can repeat this process and get their behavior under control, eventually their urges and thoughts will diminish too.

The following statements illustrate this principle. You may want to copy them onto an index card, to refer to during practice assignments. If you keep them in mind, they will save you a lot of discouragement:

1. You cannot always control your thoughts.
2. You cannot always control your feelings.
3. But you *can* always control your behavior.
4. As you change your behavior, your thoughts and feelings will also change.

You Can Resist Compulsions— You Just Feel You Can't

Although the urge to perform a compulsion can be very intense, I have never seen a patient who couldn't resist a compulsion—if he or she was motivated and given enough support and encouragement.[11] We can always control our behaviors. In the most extreme example, if we were to tie our hands together or sit on our hands, we would be able to keep from checking a lock or washing our hands. What patients usually mean when they say they can't resist a compulsion is: "I am not willing to put up with the discomfort I will feel if I don't" and "I don't want to feel the anxiety that will come if I don't."

Just learning this principle is sometimes a revelation for my patients. At first they say things like "I have to check the lock" or "I have to wash my hands." I immediately correct them and have them be more precise: "I *feel* like I have to check the lock" and "I *feel* like I have to wash my hands." Once patients recognize this dis-

11. If you find that no matter how hard you try, you simply cannot resist your urges, it may be that your symptoms are more like tics than compulsions. If this is the case, the section later in this book that describes the treatment called "habit reversal" may be helpful to you (see Chapter 7).

tinction, they realize that they can always control their behaviors, provided they put in the effort and, if they need it, get assistance.

Try this for yourself. See how many times today you can catch yourself saying "I can't do that." Then see how often this is really what you meant to say. It usually isn't. Since we come to believe what we say to ourselves and others, it is important to be precise in our speech. Try to change your next "I can't do that" to something more accurate, like "I would feel uncomfortable if I were to do that now."

Compulsions, Urges, and Obsessions
Decrease Separately

All we can control directly is our behavior, and our feelings and thoughts will change as a result of this control; this we already know. But will our feelings and thoughts change simultaneously with the behavior we have changed? Probably not. As the graph shows, our behaviors usually change first, followed initially by our feelings and then by our thoughts.

SAMPLE RATES OF CHANGE WITH BEHAVIOR THERAPY OF AN OCD RITUAL

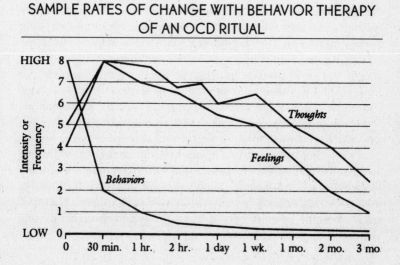

You may want to photocopy this graph and carry it with you as a reminder in your practice. I believe that it illustrates why so few people have been able to get control of their OCD on their own. At first, your urges and obsessions will probably increase, because you are confronting situations you avoided before—and you're no longer performing compulsive rituals to reduce them. Even after days of struggling to resist your compulsions, therefore, your thoughts and feelings may not have lessened at all. As a result, you may give up, just before you would have seen improvement in your feelings and thoughts.

We can only speculate that the reason for these differences in rates of change has to do with our evolution. It has always been important for humans to be flexible in response to changes in their environment and to respond with new behaviors that can be learned quickly. Our feelings, on the other hand, are more resistant to change, probably as a safety precaution for the survival of the species. Negative feelings that signal danger change more slowly, and only when we are certain that the situation is really safe. For example, if you eat something that makes you ill, feelings of nausea and distaste for that food may last for weeks or even years. They will begin to decrease gradually only if you eat the food repeatedly and find that you don't get ill. Our thoughts change at an unpredictable rate, and we don't yet know the laws controlling them. They are often influenced by negative feelings, so that if our feelings signal a danger, our thoughts immediately start to devise a plan to help us escape the danger. If, for instance, we feel we have been contaminated, our thoughts focus on ways to remove the contamination and to avoid future contamination.

Although these evolutionary explanations make sense, they are impossible to prove; instead, we can only accept that our behaviors, our feelings, and our thoughts will change at different speeds. Try not to get discouraged if, after several days of hard work reducing your compulsions, you still have strong feelings and thoughts. This is exactly what usually happens. Hang in there, keep on practicing, and the feelings and thoughts should subside too.

You Can Deal with Anxiety

As you've already learned from the preceding graph, the bad news is that your anxiety will probably increase when you first try response prevention. If you are able to accept the fact that you are going to experience some anxiety as a normal part of behavior therapy and to deal with the anxiety until it subsides, you will succeed in getting control of your problems.

The good news is that the anxiety you will feel during a practice session is likely to be much less than you expect. Remember, the anxiety will not harm you in any way. Most patients tell me that the anxiety they feel while worrying about or anticipating a practice session is much worse than the actual anxiety during exposure and response prevention.

In Chapter 5 you will learn special techniques for dealing with this anxiety. For now, make sure you understand the graph. Study it and you'll probably find it reassuring. It tells you that yes, your anxiety will rise at first, but this is only temporary. If you keep resisting your compulsions, your anxiety will begin to diminish. This is a natural process that will happen on its own.

I've found that the amount of anxiety you feel during your early exposure sessions normally indicates how much anxiety you will experience during *all* your practice sessions. One patient began with low levels of anxiety in the very first practice sessions. A man I treated told me that in all his practice sessions, "at the beginning the anxiety mounted and climbed to a fairly high level, but it very quickly decreased to a manageable amount after one minute. Then it slowly decreased the rest of the way over the next fifteen minutes." Everyone seems to have a different pattern of anxiety decrease during exposure practice; when you begin your practice, try to identify *your* own unique pattern.

Similarly, your success in your first few practice sessions will probably predict your overall improvement. I find that if you make a lot of progress in your first few sessions of exposure and response prevention, you'll tend to make large changes overall—another reason to work extra hard in the beginning.

A Helper May Be Vital to Your Success

My patients rarely have a problem *understanding* the principles of exposure and response prevention, but at first they may have trouble *applying* them. People who do not suffer from OCD cannot fully appreciate the agonizing urges, thoughts, and uncertainty that the patient experiences. But for OCD sufferers, these experiences are precisely what can make following these simple rules so difficult at times.

The assistance of a family member or friend can sometimes make the difference between success and failure in behavior therapy. I have become so convinced of the importance of a helper that I tell all my patients in their first session that their chances of success will be much better if they have a helper to work with outside the clinic. I explain that although I am sure they would try hard on their own, I know that their promises to me and themselves may turn to disappointment and frustration once they are alone with their urges.

The woman in the following description was able to get control of her obsessions and compulsions with the aid of her parents and husband, who acted as helpers for her. At the very first session, I met with her and these family members and explained the principles and techniques of behavior therapy.

As her baby grew inside her, so did Audrey's fear of contamination. She could still hear her obstetrician warning her to always keep her hands clean during and after her pregnancy; because of her OCD, she carried this common warning to extremes. Her fear spread rapidly until it encompassed her entire house. She was no longer able to eat or touch many objects in the house for fear of becoming contaminated and harming her unborn baby. Although she knew that her fear was excessive, she still scrubbed her hands immediately after she touched something she believed to be contaminated. As a result of her OCD symptoms, Audrey worried in her eighth month of pregnancy that once her baby was born she would not be able to care for it.

I treated Audrey with behavior therapy alone, since she could take no medications during her pregnancy. She worked hard in my office during our six sessions and also between sessions, in her home, with the assistance of her helpers. With them, she gradually confronted the objects she feared (such as clothes, shoes, cabinets, and dresser drawers) without scrubbing her hands. Her fears began to recede over the first two weeks of treatment. Soon she was again able to eat at home, do laundry, and touch objects around the house. Her fears of contaminating her unborn child continued to subside until they were only slightly greater than normal concerns of pregnancy.

Audrey's example shows that even severe OCD symptoms can be controlled quickly with hard work and assistance from helpers. Audrey did most of the practice on her own, with the help of family members. My role was to provide information and encouragement, as it is in writing this book for you.

Home practice is vital to most behavioral treatment of OCD, since most rituals occur in the OCD sufferer's own home. Therefore, for anyone attempting to change OCD rituals with behavior therapy, the assistance at home of family members and friends is often critical for success.[12]

As they did in Audrey's case, helpers assist by setting goals, carrying out practice assignments, and giving the patient encouragement when the going gets tough. These functions are similar to those I would perform if I were your behavior therapist; in fact, you may think of your helper as a sort of surrogate behavior therapist. Thus, you should rely on your helper, ask for advice, and, most important, accept his or her encouragement; behavior therapy is simple, but it's not always easy! Working with your helper will help ensure that you succeed in getting control of your obsessions and compulsions.

Because your obsessions and compulsions are often of a very personal or embarrassing nature, your helper should be someone

---

12. Some patients tell me that they work better on their own and would prefer to try exposure and response prevention without a helper. I tell them that if they feel strongly about this, they should try the exposure and response prevention practices (described in chapters 4 and 5) for one week. If at the end of this time they tell me that they are succeeding in doing this practice without avoiding situations or doing compulsions, then I tell them to continue working alone. On the other hand, if they are having trouble doing the practice correctly while alone, they need to have a helper work with them immediately.

you trust and respect. You should have your helper read Chapter 10, in which I describe the role of the helper fully.

Exposure and Response Prevention Should Last at Least One Hour

As we've seen, anxiety and discomfort decrease at different speeds for different people who are exposed to the situations that trigger their compulsions. However, exposure and response prevention periods of one to two hours seem to result in the best improvement for most OCD patients.

You've probably tried to resist your rituals at some time. But when you found that your urges and anxiety increased, you gave in and performed your rituals. You also were likely to find that your compulsions felt stronger after this experience. If this has happened to you, then you've learned firsthand that if your exposure time is too short, you can actually increase your fears and the frequency of your rituals. It works this way: each time you are in a situation that produces unpleasant feelings, you get a strong urge to complete a ritual to make yourself feel better. Usually you will feel better soon after performing the ritual, either once or many times. But by doing this you are teaching your body that the *only* way to feel better is to complete the ritual.

If, instead, you resist the urge and *stay in the situation long enough for the feelings to begin to subside*—and one to two hours is usually long enough—then you are teaching your body that you can feel better *without* the ritual. That is what getting control of your urges and actions is all about.

Behavior Therapy Requires Patience

Finally, always keep in mind that persistence and knowledge are ingredients for your success. What should you consider a fair trial of behavior therapy? You should put in a total of at least twenty hours of exposure and response prevention. You can do this either daily, or two or three times a week. If you will commit yourself to this amount of practice of the techniques you'll learn in Chapter 5, you will probably get control of your symptoms. You can do your twenty hours of exposure in a week, a month, or a year, and, surprisingly, you will probably improve to the same extent in each case.

But be prepared to experience good days as well as difficult days. Your progress may not always be smooth. You may wake up one morning and feel wonderful, and wake up the next and know that it is going to be a difficult day. Or you may see large improvements on some days, and seem to be stuck on others. Be sure to practice the same way every day and to take advantage of your helper. He or she will remind you of your improvements—and will keep you from giving up. Also, remind yourself that success often means simply hanging on after others have let go.

In the following chapters you'll learn not only more about behavior therapy techniques, but also how to tailor these techniques to fit your own particular problems.

CHAPTER THREE

• •

Test Yourself

• •

"Know thyself."

—*Admonition of the oracle of Apollo
at Delphi (c.650–550 B.C.)*

The tests in this chapter will help you to assess which OCD symptoms you have, and the severity of these symptoms before treatment. This information will enable you to plan your behavior therapy effectively. You will then be able to return to this chapter and retake these tests later on to evaluate your progress.

As you learned from the case examples in Chapter 2, it is important for you to assess the strength of your belief in your obsessions or compulsions, and your level of depression. This chapter provides tests for rating these significant factors. Since people with OCD often avoid the situations that produce their obsessions and compulsions, it is sometimes possible for them to score fairly low on a measure of OCD severity because they are staying in their house most of the day. You will therefore also find tests for determining how many situations you are avoiding.

When you finish taking these tests, you will interpret the results. At this point you will be well on your way to setting your particular goals for behavior therapy.

Since you will be taking these tests frequently to assess your progress, don't write your answers directly in the book. Either use a separate sheet of paper or make a photocopy of each test (copies of all the tests in this chapter also appear in the Appendix).

Assessing the Type of Your OCD Symptoms

First, you need to clearly specify the symptoms of OCD that you have. To do this you will use the symptom checklist section of the Yale Brown Obsessive-Compulsive Scale, which is known as the YBOCS and was developed by Dr. Wayne Goodman, Dr. Steven Rasmussen, and their associates. Although the YBOCS was designed to be administered by a doctor, with Drs. Goodman and Rasmussen's permission I have modified parts of it so that you can respond on your own. Doing so will give you meaningful information for planning your treatment and assessing your progress.

As you review the checklist, which includes all known symptoms of OCD, check off those symptoms that you have. Because this is a long, exhaustive list, you will check some of the symptoms but not all of them. Don't worry too much about whether or not to check a particular symptom—if a symptom is a major problem for you, then it will be obvious to you without thinking too much. If you are not sure what a particular symptom means, look at its corresponding description or examples in the column to the right. You may also review Chapter 1 for further descriptions of particular symptoms.

YALE BROWN OBSESSIVE-COMPULSIVE SCALE SYMPTOM CHECKLIST (GOODMAN, RASMUSSEN, ET AL.)[1]

Check only those symptoms that are bothering you right now. Items marked with an asterisk (*) may or may not be OCD symptoms. To decide whether you have a particular symptom, refer to the description or examples of each item in the right-hand column.

---

1. Used by permission of the authors.

OBSESSIONS

Aggressive Obsessions

___ 1. I fear I might harm myself.

Fear of eating with a knife or fork, fear of handling sharp objects, fear of walking near glass windows.

___ 2. I fear I might harm other people.

Fear of poisoning other people's food, fear of harming babies, fear of pushing someone in front of a train, fear of hurting someone's feelings, fear of being responsible by not providing assistance for some imagined catastrophe, fear of causing harm by giving bad advice.

___ 3. I have violent or horrific images in my mind.

Images of murders, dismembered bodies, or other disgusting scenes.

___ 4. I fear I will blurt out obscenities or insults.

Fear of shouting obscenities in public situations like church, fear of writing obscenities.

___ 5. I fear doing something else embarrassing.

Fear of appearing foolish in social situations.

___ 6. I fear I will act on an unwanted impulse.

Fear of driving a car into a tree, fear of running someone over, fear of stabbing a friend.

___ 7. I fear I will steal things.

Fear of "cheating" a cashier, fear of shoplifting inexpensive items.

___ 8. I fear that I'll harm others because I'm not careful enough.

Fear of causing an accident without being aware of it (such as a hit-and-run automobile accident).

___ 9. I fear I'll be responsible for something else terrible happening.

Fear of causing a fire or burglary because of not being careful enough in checking the house before leaving.

Contamination Obsessions

___ 10. I am concerned or disgusted with bodily waste or secretions.

Fear of contracting AIDS, cancer, or other diseases from public rest rooms; fears of your own saliva, urine, feces, semen, or vaginal secretions.

___ 11. I am concerned with dirt or germs.

Fear of picking up germs from sitting in certain chairs, shaking hands, or touching door handles.

___ 12. I am excessively concerned with environmental contaminants.

Fear of being contaminated by asbestos or radon, fear of radioactive substances, fear of things associated with towns containing toxic waste sites.

___ 13. I am excessively concerned with certain household cleansers.

Fear of poisonous kitchen or bathroom cleansers, solvents, insect spray, or turpentine.

___ 14. I am excessively concerned with animals.

Fear of being contaminated by touching an insect, dog, cat, or other animal.

___ 15. I am bothered by sticky substances or residues.

Fear of adhesive tape and other sticky substances that may trap contaminants.

___ 16. I am concerned that I will get ill because of contamination.

Fear of getting ill as a direct result of being contaminated (beliefs vary about how long the disease will take to appear).

___ 17. I am concerned that I will contaminate others.

Fear of touching other people or preparing their food after you touch poisonous substances (like gasoline) or after you touch your own body.

Sexual Obsessions

___ 18. I have forbidden or perverse sexual thoughts, images, or impulses.

Unwanted sexual thoughts about strangers, family, or friends.

___ 19. I have sexual obsessions that involve children or incest.

Unwanted thoughts about sexually molesting either your own children or other children.

___ 20. I have obsessions about homosexuality.

Worries like "Am I a homosexual?" or "What if I suddenly become gay?" when there is no basis for these thoughts.

___ 21. I have obsessions about aggressive sexual behavior toward other people.

Unwanted images of violent sexual behavior toward adult strangers, friends, or family members.

Hoarding/Saving Obsessions

___ 22. I have obsessions about hoarding or saving things.

Worries about throwing away seemingly unimportant things that you might need in the future, urges to pick up and collect useless things.

Religious Obsessions

___ 23. I am concerned with sacrilege and blasphemy.

Worries about having blasphemous thoughts, saying blasphemous things, or being punished for such things.

___ 24. I am excessively concerned with morality.

Worries about always doing "the right thing," having told a lie, or having cheated someone.

Obsession with the Need for Symmetry or Exactness

___ 25. I have obsessions about symmetry or exactness.

Worries about papers and books being properly aligned, worries about calculations or handwriting being perfect.

Miscellaneous Obsessions

___ 26. I feel that I need to know or remember certain things.

Belief that you need to remember insignificant things like license plate numbers, the names of actors on television shows, old telephone numbers, bumper sticker or T-shirt slogans.

___ 27. I fear saying certain things.

Fear of saying certain words (such as "thirteen") because of superstitions, fear of saying something that might be disrespectful to a dead person, fear of using words with an apostrophe (because this denotes possession).

___ 28. I fear not saying just the right thing.

Fear of having said the wrong thing, fear of not using the "perfect" word.

___ 29. I fear losing things.

Worries about losing a wallet or unimportant objects, like a scrap of notepaper.

____ 30. I am bothered by intrusive (neutral) mental images.

Random, unwanted images in your mind.

____ 31. I am bothered by intrusive mental nonsense sounds, words, or music.

Words, songs, or music in your mind that you can't stop.

____ *32. I am bothered by certain sounds or noises.

Worries about the sounds of clocks ticking loudly or of voices in another room that may interfere with sleeping.

____ 33. I have lucky and unlucky numbers.

Worries about common numbers (like thirteen) that may cause you to perform activities a certain lucky number of times or to postpone an action until a certain lucky hour of the day.

____ 34. Certain colors have special significance to me.

Fear of using objects of certain colors (e.g., black may be associated with death, red with blood and injury).

____ 35. I have superstitious fears.

Fear of passing a cemetery, hearse, or black cat; fear of omens associated with death.

Somatic Obsessions

____ 36. I am concerned with illness or disease.

Worries that you have an illness like cancer, heart disease, or AIDS, despite reassurance from doctors that you do not.

____ *37. I am excessively concerned with a part of my body or an aspect of my appearance (dysmorphophobia).

Worries that your face, ears, nose, eyes, or another part of your body is hideously ugly, despite reassurance to the contrary.

COMPULSIONS

Cleaning/Washing Compulsions

____ 38. I wash my hands excessively or in a ritualized way.

Washing your hands many times a day or for long periods of time after touching, or thinking you have touched, a contaminated object. This may include washing the entire length of your arms.

____ 39. I have excessive or ritualized showering, bathing, toothbrushing, grooming, or toilet routines.

Taking showers or baths or performing other bathroom routines that may last for several hours. If the sequence is interrupted, the entire process may have to be restarted.

____ 40. I have compulsions that involve cleaning household items or other inanimate objects.

Excessive cleaning of faucets, toilets, floors, kitchen counters, or kitchen utensils.

____ 41. I do other things to prevent or remove contact with contaminants.

Asking family members to handle or remove insecticides, garbage, gasoline cans, raw meat, paints, varnish, drugs in the medicine cabinet, or kitty litter. If you can't avoid these things, you may wear gloves to handle them, such as when using a self-service gasoline pump.

Checking Compulsions

____ 42. I check that I did not harm others.

Checking that you haven't hurt someone without knowing it. You may ask others for reassurance or telephone to make sure that everything is all right.

___ 43. I check that I did not harm myself.

Looking for injuries or bleeding after handling sharp or breakable objects. You may frequently go to doctors to ask for reassurance that you haven't hurt yourself.

___ 44. I check that nothing terrible happened.

Searching the newspaper or listening to the radio or television for news about some catastrophe you believe you caused. You may also ask people for reassurance that you didn't cause an accident.

___ 45. I check that I did not make a mistake.

Repeated checking of door locks, stoves, electrical outlets, before leaving home; repeated checking while reading, writing, or doing simple calculations to make sure you didn't make a mistake (you can't be certain that you didn't).

___ *46. I check some aspect of my physical condition tied to my obsessions about my body.

Seeking reassurance from friends or doctors that you aren't having a heart attack or getting cancer; repeatedly taking your pulse, blood pressure, or temperature; checking yourself for body odors; checking your appearance in a mirror, looking for ugly features.

Repeating Rituals

___ 47. I reread or rewrite things.

Taking hours to read a few pages in a book or to write a short letter because you get caught in a cycle of reading and rereading; worrying that you didn't understand something you just read; searching for a "perfect" word or phrase; having obsessive thoughts about the shape of certain printed letters in a book.

___ 48. I need to repeat routine activities.

Repeating activities like turning appliances on and off, combing your hair, going in and out of a doorway, or looking in a particular direction; not feeling comfortable unless you do these things the "right" number of times.

Counting Compulsions

___ 49. I have counting compulsions.

Counting objects like ceiling or floor tiles, books in a bookcase, nails in a wall, or even grains of sand on a beach; counting when you repeat certain activities, like washing.

Ordering/Arranging Compulsions

___ 50. I have ordering or arranging compulsions.

Straightening paper and pens on a desktop or books in a bookcase, wasting hours arranging things in your house in "order" and then becoming very upset if this order is disturbed.

Hoarding/Collecting Compulsions

___ 51. I have compulsions to hoard or collect things.

Saving old newspapers, notes, cans, paper towels, wrappers, and empty bottles for fear that if you throw them away you may one day need them; picking up useless objects from the street or from garbage cans.

Miscellaneous Compulsions

___ 52. I have mental rituals (other than checking/counting).

Performing rituals in your head, like saying prayers or thinking a "good" thought to undo a "bad" thought. These are different from obsessions, because you perform them intentionally to reduce anxiety or feel better.

___ 53. I need to tell, ask, or confess things.

Asking other people to reassure you, confessing to wrong behaviors you never even did, believing that you have to tell other people certain words to feel better.

___ *54. I need to touch, tap, or rub things.

Giving in to the urge to touch rough surfaces, like wood, or hot surfaces, like a stovetop; giving in to the urge to lightly touch other people; believing you need to touch an object like a telephone to prevent an illness in your family.

___ 55. I take measures (other than checking) to prevent harm or terrible consequences to myself or others.

Staying away from sharp or breakable objects, such as knives, scissors, and fragile glass.

___ *56. I have ritualized eating behaviors.

Arranging your food, knife, and fork in a particular order before being able to eat, eating according to a strict ritual, not being able to eat until the hands of a clock point exactly at a certain time.

___ 57. I have superstitious behaviors.

Not taking a bus or train if its number contains an "unlucky" number (like thirteen), staying in your house on the thirteenth of the month, throwing away clothes you wore while passing a funeral home or cemetery.

___ *58. I pull my hair out (trichotillomania).

Pulling hair from your scalp, eyelids, eyelashes, or pubic areas, using your fingers or tweezers. You may produce bald spots that require you to wear a wig, or you may pluck your eyelids or eyebrows smooth.

Make sure you've read all the checklist items and checked those that are bothering you now.

Now go back over the items you checked and put a *P* (to signify a *principal* problem) next to those symptoms that are interfering most with your life right now. To help you do this, ask yourself, "Which symptoms are causing me the most problems? Which are interfering most with my family life, home life, and work?"

If you don't do this, later on when you set goals for behavior therapy you may find yourself tempted to select symptoms that seem easy to change but really aren't bothering you enough to motivate you to change. Without the prospect of significant improvement in your life, you may not stick to the behavior therapy practice, thus becoming frustrated and giving up. You'll guard against this by identifying your principal problems now.

Measuring the Severity of Your OCD

Now that you've identified your major symptoms, you'll use the YBOC Scale to assess how much these problems are interfering with your life right now. Be sure to answer all the questions. You'll be using this questionnaire again later to assess your progress. Just to remind you, here again is the definition of obsessions: unwelcome and distressing ideas, thoughts, images, or impulses that repeatedly enter your mind. They may seem to occur against your will. They may be repugnant to you, and you may recognize them as senseless, and they may not fit your personality.

YALE BROWN OBSESSIVE-COMPULSIVE SCALE (GOODMAN, RASMUSSEN, ET AL.)[2]

OBSESSIVE THOUGHTS

Review the obsessions you checked on the YBOCS Symptom Checklist to help you answer the first five questions. Please think about the *last seven days* (including today), and check one answer for each question.

1. How much of your time is occupied by obsessive thoughts? How frequently do the obsessive thoughts occur?

__0 = None*
__1 = Less than 1 hour per day, or occasional intrusions (occur no more than 8 times a day)
__2 = 1 to 3 hours per day, or frequent intrusions (occur more than 8 times a day, but most hours of the day are free of obsessions)
__3 = More than 3 hours and up to 8 hours per day, or very frequent intrusions (occur more than 8 times a day and during most hours of the day)
__4 = More than 8 hours per day, or near-constant intrusions (too numerous to count, and an hour rarely passes without several obsessions occurring)

2. How much do your obsessive thoughts interfere with your social or work functioning? (If you are currently not working, please think about how much the obsessions interfere with your everyday activities.) (In answering this question, please consider whether

*If you checked this answer, also check 0 for questions 2, 3, 4, and 5, and proceed to question 6.

2. This self-report version of YBOCS, used by permission of the authors, has been modified for computer administration by Dr. John Greist, a leading researcher in OCD at the University of Wisconsin. I have modified the wording of questions 4 and 5 to clarify their meaning and to emphasize the goal of successful behavior therapy treatment for OCD: obsessions are *not* to be resisted; compulsions are *always* to be resisted.

there is anything that you don't do, or that you do less, because of the obsessions.)

__0 = No interference
__1 = Mild, slight interference with social or occupational activities, but overall performance not impaired
__2 = Moderate, definite interference with social or occupational performance, but still manageable
__3 = Severe interference, causes substantial impairment in social or occupational performance
__4 = Extreme, incapacitating interference

3. How much distress do your obsessive thoughts cause you?

__0 = None
__1 = Mild, infrequent, and not too disturbing distress
__2 = Moderate, frequent, and disturbing distress, but still manageable
__3 = Severe, very frequent, and very disturbing distress
__4 = Extreme, near-constant, and disabling distress

4. How often do you *try* to disregard these thoughts and let them pass naturally through your mind? (Here we are *not* interested in knowing how successful you are in disregarding your thoughts but only in how much or how often you *try* to do so.)

__0 = I always let the obsessions pass naturally through my mind.
__1 = I disregard them most of the time (i.e., more than half the time).
__2 = I make some effort to disregard them.
__3 = I rarely try to disregard the obsessions.
__4 = I never try to disregard the obsessions.

5. How *successful* are you in disregarding your obsessive thinking? (*Note:* Do not include here obsessions stopped by doing *compulsions.*)

__0 = Always successful.
__1 = Usually successful in disregarding obsessions.
__2 = Sometimes successful in disregarding obsessions.
__3 = Rarely successful in disregarding obsessions.
__4 = I am rarely able to even momentarily disregard the obsessions.

COMPULSIONS

Just to remind you, here again is the definition of compulsions: behaviors or acts that you feel driven to perform although you may recognize them as senseless or excessive. At times, you may try to resist doing them, but this may prove difficult. You may experience anxiety that does not diminish until the behavior is completed.

Review the compulsions you checked on the YBOCS Symptom Checklist to help you answer these five questions. Please think about the *last seven days* (including today), and check one answer for each question.

6. How much time do you spend performing compulsive behavior? How frequently do you perform compulsions? (If your rituals involve daily living activities, please consider how much longer it takes you to complete routine activities because of your rituals.)

__0 = None*
__1 = Less than 1 hour per day is spent performing compulsions, or occasional performance of compulsive behaviors (no more than 8 times a day)
__2 = 1 to 3 hours per day are spent performing compulsions, or frequent performance of compulsive behaviors (more than 8 times a day, but most hours are free of compulsions)
__3 = More than 3 hours and up to 8 hours per day are spent performing compulsions, or very frequent performance of compulsive behaviors (more than 8 times a day and during most hours of the day)
__4 = More than 8 hours per day are spent performing compulsions, or near-constant performance of compulsive behaviors (too numerous to count, and an hour rarely passes without several compulsions being performed)

7. How much do your compulsive behaviors interfere with your social or work functioning? (If you are not currently working, please think about your everyday activities.)

*If you checked this answer, then also check 0 for questions 7, 8, 9, and 10.

__0 = No interference
__1 = Mild, slight interference with social or occupational activities, but overall performance not impaired
__2 = Moderate, definite interference with social or occupational performance, but still manageable
__3 = Severe interference, substantial impairment in social or occupational performance
__4 = Extreme, incapacitating interference

8. How would you feel if prevented from performing your compulsion(s)? How anxious would you become?

__0 = Not at all anxious
__1 = Only slightly anxious if compulsions prevented
__2 = Anxiety would mount but remain manageable if compulsions prevented
__3 = Prominent and very disturbing increase in anxiety if compulsions interrupted
__4 = Extreme, incapacitating anxiety from any intervention aimed at reducing the compulsions

9. How much of an effort do you make to resist the compulsions? Or how often do you try to stop the compulsions? (Rate only how often or how much you try to resist your compulsions, not how successful you actually are in stopping them.)

__0 = I make an effort to always resist (or the symptoms are so minimal that there is no need to actively resist them)
__1 = I try to resist most of the time (i.e., more than half the time)
__2 = I make some effort to resist
__3 = I yield to almost all compulsions without attempting to control them, but I do so with some reluctance
__4 = I completely and willingly yield to all compulsions

10. How much control do you have over the compulsive behavior? How successful are you in stopping the ritual(s)? (If you rarely try to resist, please think about those rare occasions in which you *did try* to stop the compulsions, in order to answer this question.)

__0 = I have complete control
__1 = Usually I can stop compulsions or rituals with some effort and
    willpower
__2 = Sometimes I can stop compulsive behavior but only with
    difficulty
__3 = I can only delay the compulsive behavior, but eventually it must
    be carried to completion
__4 = I am rarely able to even momentarily delay performing the
    compulsive behavior

Add up your scores for questions 1 to 10, using the numbers next to
the answer you checked for each question.

Assessing the Strength of Your Belief in Your Obsessions or Compulsions

As you learned in Chapter 2, it is important to determine how
strongly you believe in your obsessions or compulsions. You will
use this information in planning your particular treatment.

The following question is adapted from YBOCS experimental
questions, by Goodman, Rasmussen, et al.

Check the one statement that best describes what you believe right
now. Do you think your obsessions or compulsions are reasonable
or rational? Would there be anything besides anxiety to worry
about if you resisted them? Do you think something would really
happen?

__0 = I think my obsessions or compulsions are unreasonable or
    excessive
__1 = I think my obsessions or compulsions are unreasonable or
    excessive, but I'm not completely convinced that they aren't
    necessary
__2 = I think my obsessions or compulsions may be unreasonable or
    excessive
__3 = I don't think my obsessions or compulsions are unreasonable or
    excessive

__4 = I am sure my obsessions or compulsions are reasonable, no
matter what anyone says

Assessing Avoidance Due to OCD

Next you will assess how many activities you are avoiding because of your obsessive-compulsive symptoms. You will use this
measure along with your score on the YBOC Scale to give you an
overall assessment of how much OCD is affecting the quality of
your life. For the question below, think about all the things in
your life that you are not doing because of obsessions and
compulsions.

The following question is adapted from YBOCS experimental
questions by Goodman, Rasmussen, et al.

Check the one statement that best describes how many things you
have avoided in the past week.

Have you been avoiding doing anything, going anyplace, or being
with anyone because of your obsessional thoughts or because you
were afraid you would perform compulsions?

__0 = I haven't been avoiding anything because of OCD
__1 = I have been avoiding a few unimportant things because of
OCD
__2 = I have been avoiding some important things because of
OCD
__3 = I have been avoiding many important things because of
OCD
__4 = I have been avoiding doing almost everything because of
OCD

Assessing Depression

Severe depression causes problems in behavior therapy for
OCD, as discussed in Chapter 2. To assess depression, you'll answer two questions I've modified from a 10 item depression

screening scale called the "Harvard Department of Psychiatry/National Depression Screening Day Scale"[3] (HANDS, for short).

For each question, carefully read each of the four choices. Check the number next to the statement that best describes the way you've been feeling over the past week.

1. How often have you been feeling blue over the past week?

__0 = None or a little of the time
__1 = Some of the time
__2 = Most of the time
__3 = All of the time

2. How often have you thought about suicide over the past week?

__0 = None or a little of the time
__1 = Some of the time
__2 = Most of the time
__3 = All of the time

Interpreting the Results

YBOCS Symptom Checklist

Look at the grouping of the items you checked to find out the subtypes your principal symptoms fall into. These will be the basis for establishing your goals for behavior therapy.

Yale Brown Obsessive-Compulsive Scale

If you answered 0 to question 6 and answered 1 or higher to question 1, then you have pure obsessions. (Confirm this by reviewing your answers to the YBOCS Symptom Checklist; if you checked

3. Baer, L., Jacobs, D. G., Meszler-Reizes, J., Blais, M., Fava, M., Kessler, R., Magruder, K., Murphy, J., Kopans, B., Cukor, P., Leahy, L., O'Laughlen, J., "Development of a Brief Screening Instrument: The HANDS." *Psychotherapy and Psychosomatics* 69:35–41 (2000).

any compulsions, then redo questions 6 through 10 on the YBOC Scale.) If you have pure obsessions, and your total YBOCS score is 10 or more, then you have moderate OCD symptoms and you should see a psychiatrist or psychologist for help. The methods in this book may also help you gain some control over your thoughts.

If you do not have pure obsessions, then compare your score to the following table (if you have obsessions only, or compulsions only, a score of 10 to 14 would correspond to the "Moderate" category below, and 15 or greater would correspond to the "Severe" category).

YBOCS Score	Severity Range	Recommendation
Less than 10	Very mild OCD symptoms	You can probably get control of most symptoms on your own, with the help of this book
10 to 15	Mild OCD symptoms*	You can probably get control of most symptoms on your own, with the help of this book
16 to 25	Moderate OCD symptoms	You may be able to get control of symptoms on your own, with the help of this book, but you would probably benefit from seeing a behavior therapist
More than 25	Severe OCD symptoms	You should see a therapist to help you get control of your symptoms

*YBOCS score of 16 or above is usually required to participate in either a behavior therapy or medication treatment study for OCD. (If obsessions only or compulsions only are present, a score of 10 or more is required.)

Strength of Belief in Obsessions or Compulsions

If you answered this question with statement 3 or 4, then you should see a psychiatrist or psychologist to help you before you deal with your OCD symptoms with behavior therapy. You may do best with a medication or cognitive therapy that can enable you to alter these strong beliefs. Behavior therapy may help you eventually, but you will probably first need help from a mental health professional. If you answered with statement 0, 1, or 2, then you do not strongly believe in your obsessions or compulsions and should benefit from behavior therapy alone.

Avoidance Due to OCD

If you selected statement 3 or 4 on the question about avoidance, your life has been severely affected by OCD. It is important that you begin treatment soon and enlist the help of a family member or a friend to help you get control of your obsessive and compulsive symptoms. If you selected statement 0, 1, or 2, then you haven't permitted your OCD symptoms to interfere with your functioning to a great extent. Your ultimate goal with behavior therapy is to have a low score on the YBOCS *and* a score of 0 or 1 on the avoidance question.

Depression Questions

If you checked any statement but 0 in question 1, ask yourself if you are feeling this way *only* because of the problems your OCD symptoms are causing you. If your answer is no and you have felt this way for several weeks or months, then you should see a mental health professional to assess if you are severely depressed and may require treatment. Other signs of depression are increased or decreased appetite, sleep problems, crying, loss of interest or energy, and decreased interest in sex.

You should always take suicidal thoughts seriously. So, if at any time you check any statement but 0 in question 2 you should see a psychiatrist or psychologist for your own protection. A score of 1 on either of these questions is not unusual in people who have become discouraged because of their OCD symptoms. With a score of 0 on the first question and 0 or 1 on the second question, you can proceed with behavior therapy as outlined in this book.

You now have a good idea of where you are starting from with your OCD symptoms. You will return to these tests many times to keep track of your progress as you get control of your symptoms.

CHAPTER FOUR

●●●●●●●●●●●●●●●●●●●●●●●●●●●●●●●●●●●●●

Setting Your Goals

●●●●●●●●●●●●●●●●●●●●●●●●●●●●●●●●●●●●●

"Goals are as essential to success as air is to life."
—*David Schwartz*

Having a clear written goal is like having a detailed road map when you start on a trip: you know exactly where you are headed and how to get there most efficiently. But without written goals, you wander around, never sure if you are getting where you want to go. Have you ever asked for directions, only to find you've forgotten them by the time you drive down the street? If so, you know what can happen if you don't write down your goals.

Setting goals to work on is one of the first and most important steps in behavior therapy. When you go to a doctor to get a medication, you've learned to simply expect that after a certain amount of time taking the medication, you'll almost magically begin to feel better. But behavior therapy is different; it's more like unlearning a bad habit. First you clearly identify exactly what the bad habit is, and then you work out a plan to change it. Thus, the goals you set must be ones you can achieve if they are to be useful to you.

When patients first come to see me, they usually have vague goals. For example, if you came to me to reduce your fears of contamination, you might say, "I just want to feel better." But I'd tell you that this goal is not specific enough to help you with behavior therapy. A more useful goal would be "I want to reduce my shower time from four hours a day to fifteen minutes a day." This is a specific and attainable goal, one toward which you can judge your progress. Perhaps you have problems with checking door locks. Rather than telling me your goal is "Just to stop doing this," you should set a more specific goal, such as "I want to leave my house and check the door lock no more than one time." In this book I will refer to this kind of goal as a long-term goal, because it is something you want to achieve by the end of treatment.

But, of course, you cannot achieve your long-term goals right away. First you must go through a series of practice exercises with exposure and response prevention to steadily approach your long-term goals. I will call these practice exercises "practice goals," because you will aim to achieve them during your exposure and response prevention practice sessions. For instance, if your long-term goal is to reduce your shower time from four hours to fifteen minutes a day, your first practice goal might be to reduce your showering to three hours a day, while working with your helper. Then, after you've accomplished this, you might decrease your time by another half hour, while still supervised by your helper. With your helper, you would continue to slowly decrease your shower time, practicing at each step until you felt comfortable. Finally, you would reach your long-term goal of showering only fifteen minutes a day, and you would time yourself, with no assistance from your helper.

As you can see, successful behavior therapy results from setting and achieving progressively more difficult practice goals; these in turn move you closer to your long-term goals. As you achieve each practice goal, keep in mind that you are one step closer to your biggest goal: getting control of your obsessions and compulsions rather than having them control you.

The rest of this chapter will teach you how to set both your long-term and practice goals. Although some of these goals will require hard work, they will be achievable. Remember, change can be hard, but it is possible—thousands of others have gotten control of their OCD problems with behavior therapy, and so can you.

Basic Principles of Setting Long-term Goals

The following six principles are your guidelines for establishing your long-term goals for behavior therapy for OCD. They explain how to concentrate on one goal at a time, how to select the first symptom for treatment, how to create attainable goals, and how to rank those goals, among other things. (You will also be using these guidelines if you want to set additional long-term goals after you've successfully met your first set of goals.) A series of charts on which you can put these principles into practice follows the explanations.

1. Work on One Major Symptom at a Time

Thoreau reminds us to "simplify, simplify." Take his advice and simplify your practice: resist the urge to work on many symptoms at once and instead concentrate on only one major symptom. Since you'll be using both exposure and response prevention, and many of your symptoms overlap anyway, you'll find that as you work on and improve one major symptom, others will improve automatically.

For example, as you work on reducing your avoidance of things that may be contaminated, your hand washing and showering will also subside. So too will your contamination obsessions. If you work on reducing your checking rituals, your avoidance of things that trigger your urge to check will recede, as will your aggressive obsessions and worries. This overlap will occur no matter what kind of OCD problem you have.

Be patient; you *will* reach your goals. Remember that it's much better to get there slowly but surely than to become discouraged and not get there at all.

2. Carefully Choose the First Symptom to Work On

Look back over the symptoms you marked with a *P* (for *principal*) on the YBOCS Symptom Checklist in Chapter 3. If you find that *all* of your major symptoms fall under one main category, such as "Cleaning/Washing Compulsions" or "Religious Obsessions," then you have no alternative—you will make your choice from this category, focusing all your energy and time on that choice during your practice sessions. In this case, to choose which major symptom you should target first, ask yourself, "Which one is interfering most with my life right now?" This approach will ensure that you will always be working on high-payoff goals that will make a significant difference in your life. Working on important goals will keep your motivation high.

If, instead, you find that you marked with a *P* symptoms of both obsessions and compulsions, then you have a different kind of decision to make. This decision is important, since you should start with a symptom that you have the best chance of controlling.

As you learned in Chapter 2, behavior therapy works directly on your problem behaviors, or compulsions. Once the compulsions are changed, your obsessive thoughts that accompany these compulsions change too. Because you cannot directly control your thoughts, you could be setting yourself up to fail if you select your first long-term goal from among your principal obsessions on the checklist. Therefore, *if possible,* choose your first long-term goal from the compulsion section of the checklist. If you marked no compulsions with a *P* but only obsessions, then you have pure obsessional disorder, and you'll have to select your long-term goals from among your obsessive thoughts.

You also learned in Chapter 2 that behavior therapy works most efficiently for cleaning compulsions. If you marked any major cleaning compulsions with a *P,* then one of these should be the target of the first long-term goal you set.

If you have no cleaning compulsions, then look for checking compulsions marked with a *P.* If you find none, look for compulsions that cause you to avoid things you fear, and make one of these your first long-term goal.

Where possible, leave such compulsions as counting or compulsive slowness and such obsessions as superstitious, violent, or sexual thoughts for later, after you've gained confidence in achieving other long-term goals.

3. Convert Symptoms to Specific Goals

On the YBOCS Symptom Checklist, you identified general symptoms like excessive hand washing and rereading or rewriting.

But as I mentioned earlier, your goals must be much more specific before you can use them to guide you in behavior therapy.

For example, if a principal symptom for you is rereading or rewriting, you should first ask yourself, "What important things do I do too much and what things do I avoid because of this problem?" You might decide that things you do too much include tearing up checks and rewriting them, going back over a page in a book dozens of times, and asking your spouse if your handwriting is adequate or needs to be rewritten. In the category of things you avoid, you might list writing a check in public, reading novels, or handwriting notes or letters to friends.

Once you have identified these specific behaviors, you will then change them from problems to statements of goals you would like to achieve. Thus, "Tearing up checks and rewriting them" might become "I will write each check only once and will not tear it up." "Avoiding handwriting notes or letters to friends" might become "I will handwrite a letter to a friend each week, without asking for reassurance or rewriting it."

Of course, your specific problems may be very different from these, but the principle is the same: you convert general symptoms into specific problem behaviors and then convert problem behaviors into specific long-term goals you want to achieve by the end of treatment.

4. Set Realistic Goals

I have found that patients with OCD often have difficulty converting their problems into long-term goals for a simple reason: they have lost touch with what normal behaviors are. They ask me, "How many times *does* the average person wash his hands in a day?" "After *which* activities does the average person wash his hands?" "How *many* times does the average person check the door and stove at night?" "Doesn't *everyone* call his doctor every week or two for reassurance about some worrisome symptom?" "How long *does* it take the average person to get washed in the morning?" "How long *should* a shower take?" "Will most people *really* walk by a cemetery and then wear the same clothes without washing them?" These are but a few of the questions I've been asked by my patients. You may have questions like these too. If you do, you have lost track of what is normal and what is extreme.

Of course, there is no single correct answer to any of these questions. To get a sense of what is normal, make a point of asking two or three friends or family members these questions. Once you have answers from two or three people, you can average these answers together and use this information to set a reasonable long-term goal for yourself. Even though you may feel as if these questions are embarrassing or foolish, you must be able to answer them before you can set your long-term goals. Ask people whom you trust and whose opinions you value. As you get control of your symptoms, you will gradually get back in touch with normal behavior, and you'll no longer have to ask other people what it is.

5. Rank Your Goals

When you set your long-term goals, keep in mind the image of a dartboard. At first, when your OCD began, there was probably a central object or situation that you feared greatly. This represents the bull's-eye of the dartboard. But with time, your fears, compulsions, and obsessions probably began to spread to other objects, which became associated with the main one; these correspond to the inner rings of the dartboard. As more time passed, other objects became associated that had even less obvious connections with the original object; these objects fall on the outermost rings of the dartboard.

When we treat OCD, we set goals that reverse this process. We start with problems at the outer rings of the dartboard, because these produce the least anxiety and are usually the easiest for you to modify. Meeting with success early on as you are changing problems that interfere with your life will give you confidence and encourage you to continue with behavior therapy. After controlling the problems at the outer rings of the dartboard, you then move to the next inner ring to set the next goal. At each ring, you will set several practice goals; you may think of these like the divisions of the dartboard that correspond to the different numbers. Once you reach the bull's-eye, and this long-term goal is successfully accomplished, treatment is over.

After you've identified your long-term goals for a major symptom, you will rank them from least difficult to achieve to most difficult, based on the amount of anxiety or discomfort the thought of performing the different actions causes you. To do this, you'll use the 100-point SUD (Subjective Units of Distress) Scale, developed by pioneering behavior therapist Dr. Joseph Wolpe. In general, you can picture the goals that produce the highest SUDS ratings, or most anxiety, near the bull's-eye of your dartboard, with the SUDS ratings dropping gradually as you move toward the outer rings.

Learning to use this scale is very easy. Begin by remembering a time in your life when you were as relaxed and calm as you've ever been. It might have been yesterday or in your childhood; it doesn't matter. All that matters is that you think of a specific situation on a specific day. Let's say it was a day on the beach during a summer vacation last year. For you, a 0 would be the way you felt that day on the beach.

Now for the other end of the SUD Scale. First, think of those times when you were the most afraid or anxious you've ever been. They might have been during an extremely dangerous situation, like a fire, or when you were dreading doing something, like getting up to read your poem to the sixth-grade class. The specific situation you think of will be a 100. Let's say it was when you were terrified of reading your poem.

Thus, a 50 would be the feeling halfway between these two situations, a 75 three quarters of the way toward the feeling in the sixth grade, and so on. When you rate yourself, don't worry about being precise; just use round numbers, like 50 or 65.

Using the scale reproduced here, you'll rate each long-term goal based on the amount of anxiety it produces for you.

0	25	50	75	100
No Anxiety	Mild Anxiety	Moderate Anxiety	Severe Anxiety	Extreme Anxiety

After you rank your long-term goals from lowest to highest SUDS ratings, you will then begin exposure and response prevention, starting with the lower-rated goals.

6. Avoid the Flat Earth Syndrome

Don't worry if you can't picture yourself achieving your long-term goals yet; this is perfectly normal. It is so common, in fact, that I've dubbed it the Flat Earth Syndrome. Think of a sailor in Columbus's time, who couldn't even conceive of sailing around the world, because he was convinced that the earth was flat and that he would fall off the edge. In the same way, many of my patients, when they begin treatment, cannot even *imagine* themselves accomplishing some of their long-term goals. One patient with contamination fears could not imagine herself one day sitting in a hospital wheelchair that many ill persons had previously sat in. A patient with checking compulsions couldn't imagine leaving her house without checking that her stove was off and her iron unplugged. A patient with superstitious fears couldn't imagine himself saying the word "thirteen" or leaving his house on the thirteenth of the month. Yet they all accomplished their goal within a matter of weeks.

Why this failure of imagination? One patient told me his theory: he believed he couldn't picture achieving his long-term goals because, although he was virtually paralyzed in his house by his fears of contamination, he had accommodated himself to these problems and had built a system around them. He wasn't happy, but he was safe. He was unable to picture attaining long-term goals because he feared that achieving them would cause his entire system to crumble, leaving him incapable of functioning. (Apparently, he subscribed to the old saying that the devil you know is better than the devil you don't know.) However, as he made progress, he realized that the imagined catastrophe wouldn't happen, and he began to picture the long-term goal.

This is a common occurrence. Don't let it bother you or prevent you from setting a long-term goal that you can't imagine achieving now. Write down the goal anyway, even if you can't imagine it. As you move toward the goal, your anxiety will decrease, and your picture of meeting it will slowly come into focus.

Setting Long-term Goals

Now that you know the basic principles, it's time to get down to the job of setting your long-term goals. I have provided a number of charts for you to use in writing down your goals. Since you will be using these charts several times, you may want to make a number of copies of all charts and forms provided in the Appendix. (Date each of your forms and keep them together in a file folder so you can keep track of your progress.)

Before you try to establish your own goals, you can learn by considering the example of Peggy, the teacher with cleaning compulsions described in Chapter 1. She was afraid of contracting cancer and AIDS from a variety of sources. Although your symptoms may be very different from Peggy's, the process you follow for setting goals will be the same. Later in this chapter, I will give you examples of setting long-term goals for other OCD problems.

Here is how Peggy set her long-term goals. First, she used a form to list as many as four obsessions and four compulsions that she had marked with a *P* on the checklist in Chapter 3.

PRINCIPAL SYMPTOMS

Include only items marked with a *P* on the YBOCS Symptom Checklist.

Date: _____

OBSESSIONS

Symptom	General Area
#11. concern with dirt or germs	contamination obsessions
#16. concerned will get ill	contamination obsessions
#10. concern or disgust with bodily waste	contamination obsessions

COMPULSIONS

Symptom	General Area
#38. excessive or ritualized hand washing	cleaning/washing compulsions
#39. excessive or ritualized bathing	cleaning/washing compulsions
#41. prevent or remove contact	cleaning/washing compulsions

Following principle 1 of setting long-term goals, Peggy knew that she had to first identify a single principal symptom to work on, so she had to choose from among the six she listed on this form. Applying principle 2, she decided that the first symptom to work on should come from among the three compulsion symptoms she listed on this form. Since all her three principal compulsions came from the same category, "Cleaning/Washing Compulsions," she checked principle 2 and found that she next had to identify which of these was most interfering with her life at the time. She asked herself this question and decided that it was number 41, "I do other things to prevent or remove contact with contaminants," since this affected almost every aspect of her life.

Therefore she selected this as the first principal symptom to work on, and she wrote in on the "Long-term Goals" form:

LONG-TERM GOALS

Date: _____

PRINCIPAL SYMPTOM: I do other things to prevent or remove contact with contaminants.

Most important things you do too much or avoid because of this problem:

1. I avoid washing machines used by strangers.
2. I avoid rooms where sick people may have been.
3. I have to wash after brushing up against strangers.
4. I eat out because I can't bring food into my house.
5. I have to separate "clean" and "dirty" clothes in the closet.

Change to *long-term goals* you want to accomplish by the end of treatment:

		SUDS Rating
1.	Use public washing machines.	80
2.	Go into rooms, use furniture, even if sick people were there.	90
3.	Brush up against strangers or shake hands without washing afterward.	70
4.	Bring food into my house and eat it there.	50
5.	Mix "clean" and "dirty" clothes together in the closet.	60

As you can see, Peggy also followed principle 3 and converted this general symptom to five specific problem behaviors that she could get control of. Next, she rephrased each problem in terms of a long-term goal that she wanted to accomplish by the end of treatment, following principle 4 and asking others for help in setting realistic goals. Finally, following principle 5, Peggy ranked each of these five long-term goals using the SUD Scale. To do this she estimated how much anxiety or discomfort attaining each of these goals would cause her now, even if she couldn't yet imagine herself doing it.

These were the long-term goals Peggy decided to concentrate on first. Next she had to determine the order in which she would work on them. Following principle 5, she arranged her long-term goals by their SUDS ratings on the next form:

RANKING OF LONG-TERM GOALS

Date: _____

Arrange your long-term goals based on their difficulty, from easiest to most difficult:

		SUDS Rating
1.	Bring food into my house and eat it there.	50
2.	Mix "clean" and "dirty" clothes together in the closet.	60
3.	Brush up against strangers or shake hands without washing afterward.	70

4. Use public washing machines.	80
5. Go into rooms, use furniture, even if sick people were there.	90

Now Peggy had her final order: she would start with her easiest long-term goal. She would then set practice goals to achieve this long-term goal.

Examples of completed forms showing long-term goals for other OCD problems follow.

Checking Compulsions

LONG-TERM GOALS

Date: _____

PRINCIPAL SYMPTOM: check that I did not make a mistake.

Most important things you do too much or avoid because of this problem:

1. I check the door for fifteen minutes whenever I go out.
2. I check the stove for ten minutes whenever I go out.
3. I check all the electric plugs in the house when I go out.
4. I don't use a calculator because I have to keep re-adding.
5. _____

Change to *long-term goals* you want to accomplish by the end of treatment:

	SUDS Rating
1. I will check the door only once when I go out.	70
2. I will check the stove only once when I go out.	80
3. I will not check electric plugs before I leave the house.	85
4. I will use a calculator to balance my checkbook and will not re-add.	65
5.	

Counting or Repeating Compulsions

LONG-TERM GOALS

Date: _____

PRINCIPAL SYMPTOM: I need to repeat routine activities.

Most important things you do too much or avoid because of this problem:

1. I get up and down seven times before settling in a chair.
2. I pick up and put down a glass seven times.
3. I have to comb my hair seven sets of seven times.
4. I avoid taking showers because it takes so long.
5. _____

Change to *long-term goals* you want to accomplish by the end of treatment:

		SUDS Rating
1. I will sit in a chair and settle down without getting up again.		65
2. I will put my glass on the table once only.		70
3. I will comb my hair once each time.		50
4. I will take a shower each day, and wash only once.		80
5. _____		_____

Sexual Obsessions

LONG-TERM GOALS

Date: _____

PRINCIPAL SYMPTOM: I have obsessions about homosexuality.

Most important things you do too much or avoid because of this problem:

1. I ask my wife/husband "Am I a homosexual?" several times a day.
2. I avoid being around men/women.
3. I read about homosexuality all the time to reassure myself.
4. I won't watch any movie, because it may upset me.
5. _____

Change to *long-term goals* you want to accomplish by the end of treatment:

	SUDS Rating
1. I will not ask my wife/husband "Am I a homosexual?" at all.	80
2. I will not avoid any situation where men/women are around.	90
3. I will stop reading books about homosexuality for reassurance.	75
4. I will watch any movie regardless of what it's about.	70
5. _____	

Setting Your Long-term Goals

Now it's your turn. Go back to the Chapter 3 checklist you completed and write on the following form up to four obsessions and four compulsions that you marked with a *P* on that list, indicating that they are the problems interfering most with your life right now. If you checked fewer than four obsessions or compulsions, just write down all those that you checked. Don't worry about the order at this point.

PRINCIPAL SYMPTOMS

Include only items marked with a *P* on the YBOCS Symptom Checklist.

Date: _____

OBSESSIONS

Symptom   *General Area*
_____   _____
_____   _____
_____   _____
_____   _____

COMPULSIONS

Symptom   *General Area*
_____   _____
_____   _____
_____   _____
_____   _____

Next, use principles 1 and 2 for setting long-term goals to decide on the principal symptom you will work on first. Then transfer this symptom onto the form below, list the things you either do too much or too little due to this symptom, and employ principles 3 and 4 to convert the problems into statements of long-term goals. Use the SUD Scale to rate each long-term goal, according to principle 5. Consult with your helper in completing this form. Use copies of the form and write in pencil, since you may want to change your initial answers.

LONG-TERM GOALS

Date: _____

PRINCIPAL SYMPTOM: _____

Most important things you do too much or avoid because of this problem:

1. _____
2. _____
3. _____
4. _____
5. _____

Change to *long-term goals* you want to accomplish by the end of treatment:

SUDS
Rating

1. _____ _____
2. _____ _____
3. _____ _____
4. _____ _____
5 _____ _____

Now use the next form to rank your long-term goals.

RANKING OF LONG-TERM GOALS

Date: _____

Arrange your long-term goals based on their difficulty, from easiest to most difficult:

SUDS
Rating

1. _____ _____
2. _____ _____
3. _____ _____
4. _____ _____
5 _____ _____

This is your first list of long-term goals. After you achieve these goals, review your "Principal Symptoms" form. If some symptoms remain on your list, you will again use the "Long-Term Goals" and "Ranking of Long-Term Goals" forms, to set further long-term goals. Additional forms are provided in the Appendix.

Basic Principles of Setting Practice Goals

Now that you have pinpointed your destination—your long-term goals—it's time to establish the means for getting there most efficiently—your practice goals. What follow are the six principles for setting effective practice goals to accomplish each of your long-term goals.

1. Include Exposure and Response Prevention

Just as every complete sentence has both a noun and a verb, every good practice goal should have both exposure and response prevention. As you learned in Chapter 2, exposure and response prevention are the keystones of behavior therapy for OCD. Some practice goals will involve only exposure. But make sure that most of your practice goals include both exposing yourself to something you would normally avoid and also preventing yourself from enacting some compulsion you would normally perform in that situation.

To put it simply, every goal should be written in the form: "I will expose myself to X without doing Y" (where X is a trigger for your obsessions and Y is a compulsion you do to feel better).

2. Put It in Writing

You must write your practice goals down to take them seriously. If you don't write them down, you probably won't accomplish them. Also, having a written practice goal will let you and your helper determine whether you accomplished the goal, since there can be no arguing with a written goal: either you succeeded or you didn't.

3. Ask Yourself the 80 Percent Question

You have a long-term goal, and you need a practice goal to guide your exposure and response prevention practice. But where do you start? You'd like to begin by achieving a practice goal, since doing so makes you feel good and moves you a step toward your long-term goal. Failing at a goal, however, sets you back two steps.

To increase your chances of success, plan a practice goal with your helper and then ask yourself, "If I tried this goal ten times, would I succeed at least eight times?" Of course, you should be honest in assessing your chances of achieving the goal. If your answer is no, then you have chosen a practice goal that is too difficult. Write down an easier one. If you were going to keep from washing your hands for two hours after touching a gasoline can, try a practice goal of one hour. Or, if you were going to check your stove only once before leaving home, try a practice goal of checking twice. When you've written down another practice goal, question yourself again: "Do I have an 80 percent chance of achieving this new goal?" At first you may have to go through this process many times until you come up with a yes answer. You and your helper will need experience and imagination to set up effective practice goals. Work hard, and you'll get the hang of it. I've included examples of practice goals for various problems later in this chapter.

4. Use SUDS Ratings to Guide Your Practice Goals

How do you know when to stop working on a practice goal and move on to a new one? Your SUDS rating will tell you when you have become habituated to a practice goal. First, make a note of your SUDS rating when you begin working on a practice goal. Then, after thirty minutes or so of practice, note your SUDS rating again. The odds are that it has decreased, even if only by 5 points. By the end of the one- or two-hour session, you'll probably notice that your SUDS rating has dropped even more as you get used to the situation. The next time you try this practice goal, make a note of your beginning SUDS rating; you'll probably find that it is lower than the rating you began at the previous time. The last form in this chapter will help you keep track of these changes in your SUDS ratings and show you how habituation is working for you.

When your SUDS rating decreases to a 30 or lower for two practice sessions in a row, it's time to move on to another, more difficult practice goal. You and your helper will have to decide on the rating you will aim for before switching to another practice goal—but it should be a rating at which you feel comfortable.

5. Strive to Achieve, but Be Forgiving

Always try to achieve your practice goals completely. You will get control faster, and have less chance of relapse, if you can do so. If you achieve a practice goal completely, give yourself a pat on the back—you deserve it.

Even though you *try* for 100 percent compliance, there may be times when you don't succeed. Don't be too hard on yourself. As you learned in Chapter 2, some days are more difficult than others. If you don't meet the goal completely, try to figure out why you didn't, but don't get discouraged. You probably just need to set a slightly easier practice goal (remember the 80 Percent Question).

6. Notice Small Gains

Be patient and pay attention to small improvements. By using SUDS ratings in your practice goals, you'll automatically be aware of small gains. Even a reduction of 5 points is encouraging, because it means that habituation is beginning to work. Keep close track of your SUDS rating during practice, as explained in principle 4, and eventually you will see it drop. Don't give up if you don't see *any* improvement on some days; this does happen, but not very often.

Mastering a new skill never happens overnight. Remember what it was like to learn to ride a bike or drive an automobile. You did not wake up one morning doing these things perfectly. Instead, on some days you saw small improvements, and on others, large improvements.

The same thing will happen with behavior therapy for OCD. Don't get discouraged because all your compulsions are not under control in a few hours. Watch for your improvements, no matter how small. They are your road signs that you are on the right course. A major benefit of having a helper is that he or she can point out small improvements that you may not have been aware of. Be patient, and the improvements will build up.

Judge your progress only on how well you met your practice goals. This is very important. One patient told me, "I had a terrible week." When we reviewed his practice, however, we found that he had accomplished all three of his goals completely. After I told him that I thought he had done very well, he replied, "Yes, but I still have so many other problems to work on." Don't let *yes, but*'s get you in trouble. When you discuss your progress with your helper, concentrate only on how well you accomplished your practice goals. If you accomplished them, no matter what they were, then consider that you had a good week in behavior therapy.

Setting Practice Goals

To guide you in setting your own practice goals, I provide here some practice goals that Peggy worked on after each of our early therapy sessions. Try to see how each practice goal applies to one of her long-term goals described earlier. Also notice how each practice goal involves both exposure and response prevention.

Peggy started with her easiest (that is, lowest-SUDS-rated) long-term goal: "Bring food into my house and eat it there." She began with the following practice goal: "Drink a cup of coffee while sitting at my kitchen table for ten minutes without washing or disinfecting the table."

Her SUDS rating began at 50. After two days of practice, it subsided to 20. She then set a new practice goal: "Shop at the supermarket for paper goods with my boyfriend without washing for thirty minutes after getting home."

As Peggy accomplished each practice goal, she moved on to the next one, as shown in the following list of practice goals:

1. Buy canned food and bring it home without washing the cans.
2. Put canned food in cupboards without washing or disinfecting the cupboard.
3. Buy frozen food, bring it home, and for thirty minutes restrain myself from washing the box.
4. Buy frozen food, bring it home, and for one hour restrain myself from washing the box.
5. Buy frozen food, bring it home, and for two hours restrain myself from washing the box.
6. Buy fresh vegetables, bring them home, and for twenty minutes restrain myself from washing my hands.
7. Buy fresh vegetables, bring them home, and for forty minutes restrain myself from washing my hands.

After Peggy accomplished her first couple of practice goals related to her long-term goal of bringing food home and eating it there, she also began working simultaneously on her second long-term goal: "Mix 'clean' and 'dirty' clothes together in the closet" (as mentioned earlier, she considered clothes worn only in her apartment "clean" and those worn outside "dirty"). It's fine to work on two long-term goals at the same time, if you find that this works well for you. Otherwise, stick to one long-term goal at a time. Here are the successive practice goals Peggy set and achieved on her way to accomplishing her second long-term goal:

1. Touch a sweater near the "dirty" jacket in the closet and for one hour restrain myself from washing my hands.
2. Touch the "dirty" jacket in the closet and for one hour restrain myself from washing my hands.
3. Touch the "dirty" jacket in the closet and for two hours restrain myself from washing my hands.
4. Wear the "dirty" jacket from the closet and for two hours restrain myself from washing or showering.
5. Remove the plastic covering from "dirty" jackets in the closet.
6. Put "dirty" jackets next to "clean" jackets in the closet.

Remember that Peggy worked on only one of the practice goals at a time. She moved on to the next one only when the previous goal was accomplished, as judged by decreases in her SUDS rating to a manageable level. You should do the same. If Peggy had tried to work on more than one practice goal at a time, she would have been overwhelmed.

Below are some examples of practice goals for different types of OCD symptoms. These are actual goals that patients have set. Reading them may give you ideas for setting your own practice goals. Be sure, however, that you modify them as necessary to fit your particular long-term goals.

Checking Compulsions

Tom was the teacher described in Chapter 1 who feared that he had attacked or otherwise injured one of his students. As a result, he kept sharp and poisonous things out of his classroom, and he did extensive checking to reassure himself that he had not hurt a student. Here are some actual practice goals that Tom worked on to achieve some of his long-term goals:

1. Bring a stapler to work, and leave it on the desk for one hour.
2. Bring a stapler to work, and leave it on the desk all day.
3. Bring a stapler to work, and leave it on the desk all year.
4. Bring thumbtacks to work, and leave them on the desk for one hour.

5. Bring thumbtacks to work, and leave them on the desk all day.
6. Bring thumbtacks to work, and leave them on the desk all year.
7. When angry with a student, don't draw chalk marks on floor to mark the location of my feet to be sure afterward I haven't pounced on him.
8. Hold a heavy book while patting a student on the back; don't check afterward that I haven't hit him with it.
9. Don't call the parents of children after school hours to check on the students' safety.
10. Write the word "poison" once and stare at it, without performing any rituals.
11. Write the word "poison" ten times and stare at it, without performing any rituals.
12. Write the word "poison" fifty times and stare at it, without performing any rituals.

Repeating Rituals and Counting Compulsions

You remember Ken, the man described in Chapter 1 who had a variety of praying, counting, and repeating compulsions to protect himself from imagined harm. He also feared certain colors and numbers. Here are some practice goals he worked on, first assisted by his roommate, then alone.

1. Wear red-banded underwear for one hour without saying prayers.
2. Walk down stairs without saying "Love God."
3. Step off a curb without tapping my leg or saying "Love God."
4. Say the word "thirteen" repeatedly without saying prayers afterward.
5. Leave the television on channel 13 overnight.
6. Write the number thirteen in red pen.
7. Go to a baseball game on the thirteenth of the month.
8. Resist compulsions while the clock registers thirteen minutes after the hour.
9. Watch TV shows on channel 13.

Compulsive Slowness

Bill was the man described in Chapter 1 who performed activities very slowly and often got stuck in public bathrooms performing his compulsions. Here are some practice goals he worked on in treatment with his behavior therapist:

1. Pick up and put down a spoon within ten seconds while the therapist counts aloud.
2. Pick up and put down a spoon within ten seconds without the therapist counting.
3. Pick up and put down a spoon within five seconds while the therapist counts aloud.
4. Pick up and put down a spoon within five seconds without the therapist counting.
5. Pick up and put down a spoon without hesitation.
6. Follow the same sequence with picking up and putting down a fork.
7. Follow the same sequence with picking up and putting down a knife.
8. Follow the same sequence with taking a sip from a glass of water.
9. Follow the same sequence with taking medication out of a bottle.

Superstitious Obsessions and Compulsions

In Chapter 1 we met Nancy, the woman who had superstitious fears of death associated with certain numbers and activities. Below are the practice goals she worked on during her first few sessions with me.

1. Buy an analog watch [she hadn't been wearing a watch because she feared certain numbers].
2. Wear the watch one hour a day.
3. Wear the watch an entire day.
4. Buy a digital watch.
5. Wear the watch one hour a day.
6. Wear the watch an entire day.

7. Practice doing things "your head says you shouldn't do" for thirty minutes a day.
8. Practice doing things "your head says you shouldn't do" for one hour a day.
9. Eat at regular times on the clock, not only at lucky times.
10. Eat something at thirteen minutes past the hour once a day.
11. Use my computer for thirty minutes a day, without performing repeating rituals with a mouse or keyboard to prevent bad luck.
12. Use my computer for one hour a day, without performing repeating rituals with a mouse or keyboard to prevent bad luck.
13. Say the things I want to say to Mother even if my head says no.
14. Look at a city map without avoiding the cemeteries.
15. Drive by a cemetery and perform no repeating rituals.
16. Go to a cemetery, stay fifteen minutes, think disrespectful thoughts about the dead, and perform no repeating rituals.

Saving or Hoarding Compulsions

You remember the woman I described in the Preface who voluntarily hospitalized herself because she could not throw things away. Her practice goals for this major problem were:

1. Throw away forty empty boxes of laundry detergent.
2. Use index cards to make a list of objects in the house that need to be thrown away.
3. Order the index cards by their degree of difficulty.
4. Spend one hour three days a week (assisted by a helper) throwing out objects listed on the index cards, moving from least to most difficult.

Obsessions Without Compulsions

Paul was the gentleman described in Chapter 1 who was tortured with obsessive thoughts of having molested a child. Because he had only obsessive thoughts with no compulsions, his practice goals were different from those of the patients already discussed in this section.

1. Don't ask my wife for reassurance.
2. Delay thoughts until a designated "worry time."
3. Think obsessive thoughts during this worry time—a full half hour each evening, at the same time, in the same location.
4. Distract myself at the first notice of the obsessions.
5. Produce thoughts for a fifteen-minute period and practice distracting myself or letting them pass naturally through my mind.

Child and Adolescent OCD

A teenage girl was afraid of contamination from poison ivy. As a result, she no longer touched her guitar, portable stereo, or sports equipment, and she avoided the hedges in front of her house. Her first practice goals were:

1. Play my guitar for ten minutes, and for one hour restrain myself from washing.
2. Play my guitar for thirty minutes, and for two hours restrain myself from washing.
3. Touch my portable stereo, and for thirty minutes restrain myself from washing.
4. Touch my portable stereo, and for two hours restrain myself from washing.
5. Touch my tennis racket for ten minutes, and for one hour restrain myself from washing.
6. Touch my tennis racket for thirty minutes, and for two hours restrain myself from washing.
7. Touch the hedges in front of my house, wearing gloves, and for ten minutes restrain myself from washing.
8. Touch the hedges in front of my house, without gloves, and for ten minutes restrain myself from washing.
9. Touch the hedges in front of my house, without gloves, and for one hour restrain myself from washing.

Setting Your Practice Goals

Now it's your turn. Take the easiest long-term goal from the chart "Ranking of Long-term Goals" and enter it on the line provided on the following form. Then, in pencil, enter an exposure and response prevention practice goal for this long-term goal on the line provided. Ask yourself if you have at least an 80 percent chance of achieving this practice goal. If your answer is no, erase the goal and substitute another. Continue this process until your answer to the 80 Percent Question is yes. If you have a helper, he or she should assist you. The form includes spaces for you to record the date of each practice session, along with your beginning and ending SUDS rating for that practice goal. You can use this form to help you track your progress on each practice and to help you decide when to move on to another goal.

RATING YOUR PROGRESS IN PRACTICE GOALS

LONG-TERM GOAL: _____

Practice Date	Beginning SUDS Rating	Ending SUDS Rating
_____	_____	_____
_____	_____	_____
_____	_____	_____
_____	_____	_____
_____	_____	_____
_____	_____	_____
_____	_____	_____

When you have achieved a practice goal—that is, had a low SUDS rating (30 or below) for two consecutive practice sessions—write down another practice goal for that long-term goal. Continue this process until you have achieved the long-term goal. Then move on to the next long-term goal.

Because setting goals is such an important step in controlling your symptoms, you should read this chapter again to make sure you understand it fully before moving on. Once you have your detailed goals, or road map, Chapter 5 will teach you the techniques that will help you accomplish these goals for your particular OCD symptoms.

CHAPTER FIVE

●●

How to Use Behavior Therapy to Get Control of Your Symptoms

●●

> "I believe that anyone can conquer fear by doing the things he fears to do, provided he keeps doing them until he gets a record of successful experiences behind him."
>
> —*Eleanor Roosevelt (1884–1962)*

Mrs. Roosevelt's prescription for reducing fears also works to reduce OCD symptoms. Her simple advice contains the two main tools for successful behavior therapy. First, you must confront the situations that trigger feelings of fear, doubt, dirtiness, or guilt; we call this exposure. Second, you must deny the urge to escape the situations by avoiding them, by washing your hands, by checking door locks, by asking for reassurance, by repeating your actions, by moving slowly, or by distracting yourself; we call this response prevention. If you can do these two things, you will, as Mrs. Roosevelt said, compile a record of successful experiences, and you will begin to conquer your fears and get control of your compulsions.

In this chapter you will learn techniques that will help you apply exposure and response prevention to your OCD problems. These will be your tools to accomplish the goals you set in Chapter 4; although these goals may make sense to you, you may be wondering just how behavior therapy will help you accomplish them.

Not long ago, a medical colleague asked me how we treat OCD with behavior therapy. When I finished explaining all about exposure and response prevention, he said, "Don't tear paper!" At first I was at a loss to understand his comment. But later that day, I recalled an old comedy routine in which Mel Brooks played a famous but eccentric psychiatrist. It seems he was telling a reporter about his toughest patient, a woman who couldn't stop tearing paper. Day and night she spent tearing paper, ruining her life. She had this problem for years until she finally consulted the famous psychiatrist. Miraculously, she was cured after only one session. When the amazed reporter asked the doctor how he had performed such a miracle, he replied matter-of-factly, "I said, 'Don't tear paper, a nice girl like you . . . Go out and meet people, go to a party, go to a social function—don't sit and tear paper." Was this what my colleague thought we did in behavior therapy, tell patients not to tear paper?

Of course, in real life things are not so simple. People don't just stop performing rituals because we tell them to. Their urges are more compelling than that. Instead, behavior therapy involves teaching people the laws their bodies follow in learning and unlearning habits.

Compared with traditional psychotherapy, behavior therapy is mainly an educational process in which we teach people how to change their own bad habits directly. As my colleague Dr. William Minichiello likes to say, what we do as behavior therapists is more teaching than treating. At the OCD Clinic we spend a lot of time during the first one or two therapy sessions explaining the principles of behavior therapy in detail to patients and their families, and responding to their questions and concerns. In essence, we give patients a course in learning and unlearning habits; if it were a college course, we might list it as "Psychology 101: Thoughts, Feelings, and Habits—An Owner's Guide."

Sometimes, simply explaining these principles is enough to send a patient home with the knowledge and motivation to change his or her own symptoms. You may recall the pregnant woman I described in Chapter 2 who avoided many foods and clothes she thought would contaminate her unborn child. With the help of her family she was able to eliminate more than half of her rituals after our first session. Once she learned that she could fight her urges without going crazy, and knowing that they would instead decrease, she had the courage to practice an hour daily to get control of her own behavior. Also, when her family members learned that they were actually adding to her problems by complying with her fears, they returned to their normal routines and also helped her during her daily practice sessions. Not all patients make such rapid progress, of course, but all can control their compulsions to some extent.

Techniques to Assist Exposure and Response Prevention

Patients often ask me, "How will I be able to resist my urges to perform my rituals? They seem so strong." The simplest answer I can give you is "Any way you can." As you've learned, the most important thing is for you to confront the situations you fear without enacting your rituals.

But how will you carry this out? It's one thing to tell yourself "Yes, I'm going to accomplish this practice goal" when you are feeling relaxed a week before the practice session. But when you are actually in the situation, the urges to perform the rituals may be very strong. You therefore should use anything at your disposal to help you resist these urges. The following ten techniques will help you succeed in carrying out your exposure and response prevention.

1. Practice with Your Helper

Having someone around who understands you and your problem can make the difference between giving in to an urge to perform a ritual and resisting it. One of my patients who had hoarding rituals told me that it was much easier for him to resist his urges to take trash out of the garbage can when his helper was there encouraging him not to. Of course, you will eventually have to resist your urges on your own, but at the start, try to have your helper present.

Since your helper will be working with you during very stressful times in your practice sessions, it's important for you both to have rules to smooth the way in working together effectively. To help you along, I offer below some do's and don'ts for you to follow as your part of the contract with your helper. In Chapter 10,

I have included rules for the helper to follow as well. Most of your rules have a counterpart in the rules for your helper.

- *Do* discuss openly all your goals with your helper. Even if a situation seems embarrassing or foolish to you, discuss it with your helper. She must know all your long-term and practice goals to help you achieve them. For example, if your practice goal is to wear clothes that you think are bad luck, your helper must know if you are saying prayers to yourself to prevent a catastrophe while you're wearing these clothes. If your helper doesn't know this, she can't help you perform response prevention effectively.

- *Do* accept encouragement for even partial accomplishment of goals. Part of your helper's job is to encourage you and remind you of progress you may not be aware of. One woman with superstitious fears told me that her husband's encouragement on days when she had difficulty completing her practice sessions kept her from getting discouraged and possibly giving up. Make your helper's job easier—accept his encouragement.

- *Do* ask any reasonable question of your helper. If you have a question about what is normal behavior, then by all means ask your helper. For example, if you wonder whether she would wash her hands after emptying the cat's litter box, go ahead and ask. But if you already know the answer, don't ask your helper just for reassurance. And once your helper answers you, trust her advice. Remember that you selected her because she is someone you can trust. If your helper can't answer all of your questions about exposure and response prevention, reread the section of this book that can help you with the specific problem you are facing.

- *Don't* ask your helper for reassurance. Don't fall into the trap of searching for reassurance to reduce an obsession. If you think you've cut yourself by handling scissors during a practice session, don't keep asking your helper to reassure you that you haven't been injured. If you do this, you'll be putting your helper in an uncomfortable situation: either he gives in and reassures you that you aren't hurt—in which case he defeats the purpose of exposure and response prevention—or he must tell you "We can't discuss that"—in which case he risks getting into an argument with you. Don't put him in this unfair situation.

- *Don't* argue with or get angry with your helper during practice sessions. Your helper has to encourage you to confront situations that make you feel uncomfortable—like throwing away junk you'd prefer to keep—and to resist compulsions that would make you feel better. This is a difficult job. Nobody likes to make a loved one uncomfortable. But she is doing this to help you, because you asked her to. Don't make her job any harder than it has to be. Remember, your helper is enabling you to accomplish the practice goals you *both* agreed to. Don't argue with her or get angry with her for doing her job. If you suspect that your helper is not following the procedures correctly, have her reread the section of this book that discusses the specific procedure.

2. Coping with Anxiety

As you learned in Chapter 2, you *will* feel anxiety if you are practicing exposure and response prevention correctly. In fact, you may think of anxiety as a sign that you are carrying out these procedures correctly. But how do you deal with these unpleasant feelings?

You'll probably find that the anxiety is much less than you expected it to be, as the discussion of the Flat Earth Syndrome in Chapter 4 illustrates. Having your helper working with you will allow you to deal with the anxiety. Adjusting to anxiety is like adjusting to a leg that has fallen asleep. Your first reaction is to not move it, because the feeling of pins and needles is uncomfortable. But you also realize that until you move your leg, and bear with the temporary discomfort as the blood returns to it, you won't be able to walk. It would be wonderful if you didn't have to experience any anxiety at all in exposure and response prevention, but since you do, you can deal with it by telling yourself it is only temporary as your body adjusts to the situation.

You may also find that relaxation techniques can help you cope with anxiety. Two methods of relaxing—relaxing your muscles and controlling your breathing—are described step-by-step in Chapter 7. These methods won't get rid of all the anxiety you feel (that is not the purpose), but they can help you cope with the anxiety that is part of successful exposure and response prevention.

A few people feel severe anxiety during their practice sessions and experience panic or anxiety attacks along with their OCD symptoms. These symptoms of panic or anxiety attacks include shortness of breath, palpitations, chest pain or discomfort, choking or smothering sensations, dizziness or unsteady feelings, tingling in your hands or feet, hot or cold flashes, sweating, faintness, trembling or shaking, the feeling that you or your surroundings are unreal, the fear of dying, and the fear of going crazy.

As alarming as these sensations can be, it's important to realize that they are only symptoms of anxiety. Although they are unpleasant, they are not dangerous. They will go away on their own.

One patient of mine was afraid to eat food that she had touched because she thought it was contaminated and would poison her. But she also had panic or anxiety attacks that would come either out of the blue or when she was under great stress. When she succeeded in touching and eating food during our treatment sessions, therefore, she sometimes felt choking feelings and trembled. At first she misinterpreted these as signs that she was dying. But I immediately corrected this thought and reminded her that her feelings were only symptoms of anxiety. As she repeated this to herself and waited, her anxiety lessened, and she realized that she wasn't poisoned.

You probably will never have such strong anxiety symptoms during your own practice sessions. But if you do, remember to catch any irrational thoughts like "I am dying" or "I am going crazy." Instead, tell yourself "This is only anxiety" or "This feeling will subside by itself." Also try to use the relaxation methods described in Chapter 7. Your helper will be essential in guiding you through these times.

3. Keep Reminders Handy

You may want to photocopy some of the reminders from this book and paste them on index cards for easy reference during your practice sessions. My patients find the graph in Chapter 2, illustrating the rates of change in behavior, feelings, and thoughts during behavior therapy, especially reassuring to look at in practice sessions.

Or you may write down your own reminders and words of encouragement. One man wrote on an index card, "Nothing terrible will happen if I don't check." He carried this card in his wallet wherever he went, and whenever his urges to check became strong, he read the card and felt reassured.

During your first few practice sessions you and your helper should keep this book close at hand in case problems arise and you need to consult it. Mark the pages and the paragraphs that refer to your particular problems so you can easily find them for instruction and encouragement when you need them.

4. Reward Yourself

Give yourself a reward after you complete a practice goal. If you plan a reward, then you can look forward to it during difficult practice sessions. You might reward yourself by buying yourself something you've wanted or by doing something you enjoy; maybe you've been wanting to see that new movie. But play by the rules: reward yourself only if you complete your practice goal. And don't worry about committing bribery. You're using a proven behavior therapy method called self-reinforcement.

One man rewarded himself with either watching sports on television, listening to his favorite music on the radio, or eating his favorite cookies. But he allowed himself these rewards *only* if he achieved his practice goals for that day.

5. Visualize Your Long-term Goals

Seeing yourself in your mind's eye achieving your long-term goals can be a powerful motivator. Visualize specific ways in which your life will be improved by getting control of your problems.

One patient told me that whenever he was tempted to give in to a compulsion during his practice sessions, he would think about his long-term goals of living on his own and returning to work. He found that picturing these momentous things would motivate him to resist his cleaning rituals.

6. Let Obsessions Pass Naturally Through Your Mind

We now know that it is best to let obsessions pass naturally through your mind without trying to resist them. Indeed, fighting your obsessions often has the unwanted result of making them come *more* often. Dr. Daniel Wegner calls this effect "thought suppression" in his book *White Bears and Other Unwanted Thoughts* (New York: Guilford, 1994). In brief, Dr. Wegner has found that when subjects in his psychology experiments are told to resist certain thoughts from entering their mind—such as thoughts of white bears—for a period of time, once they stop resisting, these thoughts come back more often than usual, in a kind of "rebound" effect. Just think—if this happens with unemotional thoughts about white bears, how much stronger might this effect be with your emotionally powerful obsessions?

Because of studies such as these, I now tell all my patients to not give their obsessions any added energy by resisting them, but instead to let them pass naturally through their minds. Another benefit of this approach is that you will probably come to accept that your obsessions are not really dangerous, and that having them does *not* mean that you are a bad person. This will help reduce any guilt your obsessions may cause you, particularly if you have a strong religious background. When the obsessions come, try telling yourself: "Everyone has upsetting thoughts from time to time, but since they don't mean anything, there's no need to feel guilty about having them. Instead I'll let them pass naturally through my mind like people without OCD do."

7. Maintain Standards in Exposure and Response Prevention

When you practice exposure, make sure you are doing it effectively. For example, if you're exposing yourself to an object you believe is contaminated, don't keep one hand "clean" and don't avoid touching anything with the "dirty" hand for the rest of the day. If you have superstitious fears, don't keep your fingers crossed or say a prayer to reduce your anxiety.

You also should make sure that you are practicing response

prevention correctly. If you perform checking rituals, don't spend the practice session trying to remember all your movements to reassure yourself; this is mental checking. Don't say prayers to yourself to prevent something bad from happening while you resist your rituals; this is just another kind of checking.

Remember that exposure and response prevention will be effective only if you practice them correctly. If you have difficulty, discuss this with your helper and review the relevant sections of this book. The two of you will be able to come up with a creative way to help you succeed in your practice.

Once you are certain you're performing exposure and response prevention correctly, make sure you're giving these procedures a fair try. As you learned in Chapter 2, you should practice for at least twenty hours before you decide whether these methods are helping. Use the next form to keep track of how much practice you have done.

PRACTICE SESSIONS OF EXPOSURE AND RESPONSE PREVENTION

Date	What You Practiced	Time Spent	Helped By

8. Hints for Response Prevention

Try breaking your practice goals down into small, achievable steps. Maybe you can only start out by resisting your rituals for three minutes. That's OK. When you can do this easily, extend the time to five or ten minutes. Working toward your goals slowly will make it much easier for you to eventually resist your rituals completely.

Also try getting out of the situation, or environment, after exposure practice. Get out of the room; go for a walk. You can always leave, and usually your urge to perform the ritual will subside if you get away from the situation it's linked with. Later, you can practice gradually staying in the situation for longer periods without performing your rituals.

Sometimes it's helpful to schedule your practice sessions at times of the day that will naturally help you with response prevention. For example, if you always resist your compulsions while at work, maybe you can do your exposure practice early in the morning, right before going to the office. That way, you'll have extra support in resisting your rituals once you get there.

9. Use Audio and Videotapes to Intensify Exposure

The catastrophes that OCD sufferers fear will happen almost never actually do. Obviously I cannot set up real life exposure for your obsessions of your family members being killed in a fiery car crash, or of you accidentally stabbing a baby, or of you being struck dead by God for some mistake you've made! Even asking you to try to imagine these catastrophes happening will probably not be useful exposure treatment, since few of us have a vivid enough imagination, and even if we do, the temptation to turn our attention away from such thoughts is often too strong to resist. Instead, I have helped many of my patients use videotapes to successfully rid them of generic fears and obsessions, and audiotapes to help control idiosyncratic ones.

If you have violent or sexual obsessions you probably go out of your way to avoid seeing any television show or movie that contains strong violent or sexual content. But as you know, avoiding triggers such as these only adds strength to your obsessions. For many of my patients, simply watching videos over and over that contain the particular content that triggers their obsessions leads to habituation of their fears. For example, if you worry that you may inadvertently kill others, you might rent a videotape about a murderer who triggers your obsessions (say, Jeffrey Dahmer, or

Charles Manson); you would then watch it over and over again until you felt your discomfort beginning to go down (of course, you also have to make sure you resist doing any rituals while watching the video). Or if you have superstitious fears you might rent a video that triggers your obsessions about occult or supernatural events (perhaps *The Exorcist*, or *Rosemary's Baby*), then watch it from beginning to end several times until your distress began to go down. I always know this exposure treatment has worked when my patient says: "I couldn't stand to watch that video one more time—it's just too boring!"; then I just smile, congratulate them, and remind them that boredom is the opposite of fear.

On the other hand, the situations that trigger your particular obsessions may be very personal and idiosyncratic. Anna worried that she might kill her infant son by touching him with hands contaminated by bacteria from uncooked meat or eggs. This had all but paralyzed her so that when she came for treatment she was avoiding feeding him or changing his diaper. Although we were able to use standard exposure and response prevention methods to get her to hold her son to feed and change him, this wasn't a comfortable experience because her obsessions about harming him continued. For Anna, only a tailor-made audiotape would provide adequate exposure for her very specific fears.

I told Anna that for her to get the rest of the way better, she would have to expose herself to the *very catastrophe* she was most afraid of. She began by writing out for me, in excruciating detail, precisely what was the worst thing that she feared would happen to her infant. At our next session I reviewed what she'd written on two sheets of yellow legal paper, which I've paraphrased and shortened here to give you a flavor for an effective exposure script:

"I don't wash my hands properly after cooking chicken. I feed my son and later that day I notice he is not breathing right, as if his throat is closing up. I take his temperature and he is getting a high fever. I drive him to the emergency room and tell the doctor what happened. He tells me that I probably gave my son a bacterial infection and that he probably will not survive. I sit next to my baby's crib in the hospital and listen to him wheezing and gasping for breath. He looks up at me with pleading eyes and I know he's asking me to protect him and I know there's nothing I can do to help him. I cry continuously and feel more and more helpless and guilty. Over the next hour I see my son dying from this poison that I put in his body. Finally he dies a horrible death. My husband finally gets to the hospital and when he finds out what happened he yells at me hysterically and blames me for being an irresponsible mother who killed his son. My mother and father and my in-laws tell me they want nothing more to do with me because I was so absolutely irresponsible in taking care of their grandson. My husband leaves me. I become homeless, live in a shelter and become an alcoholic. After several years I realize there is nothing more to live for and I commit suicide."

When I read the actual first draft of Anna's script, I noticed that she had included several mental rituals which I pointed out to her and then crossed out of her script (these were phrases such as "but I tell myself this really isn't happening" or "God forbid this would ever happen to him").[1] I told Anna that I knew that it would be very uncomfortable for her to listen to this script at first; however I assured her that as she listened to it over and over, it would eventually lose its ability to upset her. Then for the first time she could enjoy taking care of her son, which was Anna's original treatment goal. She then read her edited script into a tape recorder, repeating it from beginning to end three or four times until she had filled a thirty-minute side of a sixty-minute audiotape. She then slipped the tape into her Walkman-style portable tape player and listened to it for at least one hour each day. Happily, within two weeks, Anna told me that listening to the tape no longer produced strong discomfort, and soon the fears that accompanied feeding and changing her son were almost gone. It has now been about a year since she first came to see me, she and her son are doing well, and she is enjoying taking care of him and watching him grow up.

1. My colleague Professor Isaac Marks in London has found that before recording a 30-second endless-loop audiotape for exposure it is essential to make sure the script does not contain any phrase that might serve as a mental ritual (that is, one that might artificially reduce distress). He found that before he eliminated these phrases from his patients' scripts they obtained mixed results using these audiotapes for exposure. But after he began to preview these scripts and to cross out any mental rituals prior to letting his patients record the tapes, he found a dramatic improvement in patients' success rates. (Lovell, K., Marks, I. M., Noshirvani, H., O'Sullivan, G., "Should treatment distinguish anxiogenic from anxiolytic obsessive-compulsive ruminations?" *Psychotherapy and Psychosomatics*, 1994; 61:150-155.)

10. Set Aside a Worry Time for Obsessions

A few of my patients will not let their obsessions pass naturally through their mind unless they have a definite time scheduled to think about them later on. Despite my attempts to convince them otherwise, they may feel it is irresponsible not to allow time for their worries, such as mentally reviewing the events of the past day.

If this applies to you, you can use a helpful technique called "worry time," which was developed by Dr. Thomas Borkovek, an expert in the study of worrying: Pick a particular half-hour worry time each day, always at the same time, when you will sit in the same chair, and then, for the entire thirty minutes think about nothing else but your obsessive thought—even if you find it difficult to fill the full time. After a while you may want to decrease your worry time to fifteen minutes. Some people eventually stop worry times completely, while others prefer to continue using them as needed.

11. Helping Children and Adolescents

The same methods of exposure and response prevention are just as important for children as for adults. The major difference in helping children with OCD is that their parents *must* be involved in the treatment. My job as a behavior therapist (and in writing this book) is to teach parents how to help their child participate in the exposure and response prevention needed to get control of their OCD symptoms. Parents must also learn how to reward their children when they succeed in their practice; this is essential.

You might start by helping your child make a list of things he or she would like to do. Then the two of you can set up a system in which, by doing the exposure and response prevention homework, your child earns points that can be redeemed for these rewards. He or she might earn one point for each practice assignment, with the points redeemed at the end of the day or the end of the week.

Be creative in finding rewards for your child; what is rewarding can differ from child to child and from day to day. One eleven-year-old boy desperately wanted to spend time with his father. His parents therefore set up a program of exposure and response prevention for him in which he and his father would go to a ball game together if he worked hard on his problem. With this added motivation, he was able to comply with the treatment.

Parents should also be involved in treating an adolescent with OCD. Freddy was an adolescent boy who was compelled to touch things in his room ritualistically before he could go to sleep. By the time he came to our clinic, he was spending so many hours performing these touching rituals that he would stay up all night if he tried to sleep in his bedroom; instead he slept in the living room. First, Freddy learned how to perform exposure and response prevention. Second, he earned points by carrying out his practice goals, and at the end of each week turned them in to his parents for his reward. With this program he began making progress, first on small goals, then on larger ones. Naturally, adolescents have to want to get better if they are going to participate in exposure and response prevention. In those few cases in which adolescents have been dragged in to see me against their will, we weren't able to make any progress, unless they later decided that they really wanted to cooperate with the treatment.

You should teach your child the behavior therapy techniques in ways that he or she can understand. Also explain why they are important and why they work. For example, you can describe the anxiety he or she feels as a false alarm at a fire station: the firemen hear the alarm and race down the street in a fire engine, but they find there is no fire. Thus your child can ignore his or her anxiety, knowing that it will subside, just as the false alarm soon stops ringing.

Sometimes you can motivate your child to participate in behavior therapy by having him or her pretend to be a warrior (or another popular storybook or cartoon character) fighting a monster, which symbolizes his or her obsessions or urges.

You may get upset and not know what to do if your child throws a tantrum during practice sessions. One girl threw tantrums if she was prevented from performing her rituals and threatened to break all her toys when she got angry. Her parents talked to her and explained that they had to help her learn how to control her temper; if she threw a tantrum, they would have to put her in her room. They explained to her, "We hate to have to do this, but you have to learn to control yourself." At first the parents felt upset and guilty because of their daughter's yelling and throwing things in her room. But after being confined to her room a couple of times she learned to control her temper. Needless to say, this process, which is called time out in behavior therapy, requires a lot of patience on the parents' part to be effective.

Some final words about helping your child control his or her OCD symptoms—be certain that you understand exactly what obsessions and compulsions he or she is having, and how they are related to each other. Do not *assume* that you understand the problem; remember that the symptoms may look very different through a child's eyes.

I have seen many children and adolescents who are so horrified by their obsessive thoughts, thinking this means they are "evil," that they resist admitting to anyone what they are really thinking. This refusal to communicate makes it difficult for family members to understand that the seemingly bizarre behaviors of the young OCD sufferer may be rituals performed to control awful obsessive thoughts.

One example is David, a young boy brought to me by his parents, who were at their wit's end because of his bizarre behaviors of spitting on the floor and shouting obscenities. At first David was silent and refused to tell me what was going on. But several weeks later, after I had assured him that many children have unpleasant thoughts they can't get out of their mind and that, most important, the thoughts were not his fault, he reluctantly admitted that he was having thoughts and images of incest with family members; he was performing spitting and cursing rituals to drive the thoughts from his mind, and also to keep his family members, who triggered these obsessions, away from him. Once David was able to admit these thoughts to me and his parents, we were able to work together to identify all the various rituals he was performing.

David's case illustrates another common feature of OCD in children and adolescents: rituals often pervade and disrupt almost all of their home, play, and school activities. As a result, it is important to carefully (but rapidly) identify as many of the numerous rituals as possible, and to start working with only one or two that are most interfering with the child's life.

Tailoring Behavior Therapy to Your OCD Symptoms

Now let's look at the different OCD symptoms and how we apply the principles and techniques of behavior therapy that you've already learned. As you go through the following section, try to notice how the behavior therapy methods have been modified to suit the particular problem, so that you can do the same for your own OCD symptoms.

Although I sometimes refer in this book to one person as a cleaner or another as a checker, remember that these are only broad generalities. Many people with OCD have more than one kind of symptom. If this is your situation, you will simply choose effective behavior therapy techniques for each type of symptom that you have.

You should read all of the following sections, even for problems different than yours. This will help you get ideas for achieving your own long-term goals from Chapter 4.

Cleaning/Washing Compulsions

Most people will stop washing their hands when they get the feeling that they are clean. But you may have difficulty attaining this feeling. As discussed earlier, you may have lost touch with what normal cleaning involves. Although this may be an embarrassing subject, you should discuss it with at least three other people to get back in touch with what normal cleaning is. Average their answers and use the result to set your long-term goals.

Over the past few years I have asked dozens of patients and their families in what situations they think they really need to wash their hands. The answers I get usually fall into one of the four situations in the list below. Notice that in rules 3 and 4 I emphasize the words "see" and "labeled"; these remind you that you should decide when to wash based only on objective rules, not on vague feelings of dirtiness.

RULES FOR WASHING

1. It's OK to wash after going to the bathroom.
2. It's OK to wash before eating.

3. It's OK to wash when you can *see* something dirty on your body.
4. It's OK to wash when you have touched something *labeled* poisonous.

You should, if you find this list helpful, make photocopies of it, paste the copies onto index cards, and place them in plain sight near all sinks and showers in your home. You can then consult this list each time you want to wash your hands or take a shower. Before you start washing, ask yourself, "Do I really have to wash now?" Then, if you are still in doubt about whether a situation requires washing, always consult your helper first.

If your problem involves excessive showering or bathing, you should begin by asking three people you know well (including your helper) how long their showers are. Then average their answers together. Use this time as your long-term goal.

Begin by asking three people you know well (including your helper) how long they spend getting ready in the bathroom if you have trouble getting your bathroom routines done on time, especially before leaving the house in the morning. Then average these times together and use this as your long-term goal.

In the treatment of cleaning rituals, exposure takes the form of touching an object that triggers feelings of discomfort, anxiety, disgust, or fear; an example might be a garbage can you think is contaminated. Your helper should touch the contaminated or dirty object first, to demonstrate that he or she isn't asking you to do anything he or she wouldn't do. This process, which is called modeling, increases the effectiveness of exposure.

To practice response prevention for cleaning rituals, you have to refrain from wiping, washing, or removing contaminated clothing for the rest of the practice session after you've touched the object. I've found that, despite their fears, almost everyone can refrain from performing cleaning rituals for up to two hours after exposure. During the response prevention phase, remind yourself that it's natural for urges to wash and feelings of contamination to continue for a while but that these will decrease over one to two hours. Keep records of your practice, using the form "Practice Sessions of Exposure and Response Prevention."

The following techniques may help you in your practice sessions. If your problem is excessive showering or bathing, always use a clock or stopwatch to time yourself during your practice sessions. Don't guess at the time; you will be wrong. At first you should always have your helper around to remind you of the time. If you haven't finished your cleaning when he or she tells you there are only a few more minutes to go, you'll have to hurry up. One man had his helper let him know when half the time was up, then again when there were five minutes left. This helped him to pace himself. When your helper tells you that the time is up (this can be from another room), you must turn off the water and get out of the shower or tub immediately. Even if you still feel dirty—and you probably will—you must get out. Remember that all you can control is your actions, like forcing yourself out of the bathroom at the time limit; your feelings and thoughts will follow.

Similarly, if you are trying to control excessive bathroom rituals, you must force yourself to stop when your helper tells you that the time is up. Don't sneak in one more swipe with the toothbrush, comb, or lipstick. Put them down and get out of the bathroom.

People have found various ways of complying with both the exposure and response prevention ends of behavior therapy. One man told me he had devised a foolproof method to keep himself from washing his hands during practice—he learned coin tricks. Now whenever he has an urge to wash his hands, he does a coin trick instead. Another patient was afraid of being poisoned by gasoline, so she made it a point to always use self-service gasoline pumps, then drive around for at least an hour to prevent herself from washing her hands. In the same way, a man afraid of using public rest rooms deliberately used them regularly whenever he was out. But I had to remind him to confront the things he feared. Since he was afraid of touching the water faucets in public bathrooms, he had to touch them directly and resist the urge to use paper towels to turn them on and off.

Use any of the techniques described here to help you carry out exposure and response prevention. Some people find that relaxation techniques help them cope with response prevention after they have touched "contaminated" things. If you find yourself worrying about contamination, you can try both thought stopping and delaying your thoughts, as described previously in this chapter. Reward yourself for success in your practice goals. Visualize yourself in the future; make a list of the things you'll be able to do when you get your cleaning rituals under control, then imagine yourself in the future, doing them.

Incorporate the list "Rules for Washing" into your practice sessions to help you learn how to decide whether you need to wash your hands. Instead of relying on feelings of dirtiness, you will be relying on objective rules in black and white. Try to delay washing for longer and longer periods for each new practice goal.

If you work hard, behavior therapy will help you get your cleaning rituals under control. Your urges and thoughts will subside as well, and you'll probably find the entire process to be much easier than you expected. Don't give in if you find that your urges return in the future in times of great stress. These urges are only temporary and will soon pass.

Checking Compulsions

How do you determine what normal checking is? You should start by asking your helper and one or two other people whether they would check in the situations you fear. Ask them very specific questions related to your problems. If you check your door and windows, ask them if they would check the same things. If you check to make sure you weren't injured, ask them if they would do the same. One woman asked her husband whether, like her, he would call an ambulance to help a man he saw lying under his car. She was surprised that her husband's first thought was that the man was working under his car, and he wouldn't call for help. Once you get your answers, write them down, and refer to them often in setting your long-term goals.

Here is how I try to help people decide for themselves what is obsessional checking. Joyce was a young woman who couldn't leave her apartment without checking. Stoves and faucets had to be turned on and off dozens of times to prevent fire and flood. In our first session of behavior therapy I told Joyce and her mother a fable about a man who painted his house purple with pink polka dots. When his next-door neighbor asked him why, he replied, "Why, to keep away the flying elephants, of course!"

When his neighbor told him that there were no flying elephants, he said, "I know—see how well it's working?"

Then I asked Joyce how she would persuade this man to repaint his house a more conventional color. She said, "I'd tell him that even if his house wasn't purple with polka dots, there would still be no flying elephants." "But," I said, "what if he said that he wasn't willing to take the chance of finding out?" Now Joyce saw the connection between my fable and her problem with checking.

In fact, she and her mother began speaking in terms of this fable when they discussed exposure and response prevention in that first session. "So, dear," her mother explained, "what the doctor is saying is that if I help you stop checking, you'll be like the man repainting his house—after a while you'll find out that no flying elephants will come, and you'll feel safe with the new color." Joyce got the point.

Exposure in the treatment of checking rituals means confronting the situations you fear, like turning off the stove only once; response prevention is resisting the urge to go back and check what you did. You probably check mostly in your home or at work, places where you feel a lot of responsibility. Sometimes, however, you may have the urge to check in places away from your home. One man was afraid to enter stores for fear of closing the door on someone behind him and was afraid of handling objects in the store for fear of dropping them. I accompanied him into stores during our treatment sessions, and I encouraged him to handle merchandise without checking. I have also ridden in a car with a woman who avoided driving because she was afraid she would run over a pedestrian or cause an accident and not know it. I encouraged her not to check her rearview mirror and not to turn her car around to see whether she had hit a pedestrian or another car. She also practiced similar activities between sessions with her husband. Your helper can assist you with the same kinds of practice.

What other techniques can you use to assist you with exposure and response prevention? If you feel the urge to check whether or not anyone else is present, then your helper can stay with you during both exposure and response prevention. But if you feel secure only when someone else is around, then you should perform the exposure alone, and have your helper assist you only in resisting the urges to go back and check. One woman felt unsure only if no one else was there to watch her when she turned off her stove and faucets before leaving her house. Thus, she decided to turn them off only once while alone and to then meet her mother down the street and stay with her for two hours to resist the urge to go back and check that there was not a fire or flood in her apartment. In this case, the woman's mother was not allowed to reassure her while she was practicing response prevention; this would be allowing a form of checking. Instead, she told her daughter, "We weren't supposed to talk about that," and changed the subject.

One woman, a pharmacist who kept re-counting the number of pills in each prescription she filled, turned each bottle upside down after putting the cap on; this helped her reduce the urge to reopen the bottle and pour the pills out to count them. She also read magazines during practice sessions to get her mind off checking. You can come up with your own creative ideas for resisting your urges during practice sessions.

If you find yourself worrying about having caused a dangerous situation after exposure and response prevention, you should refer back to the sections in this chapter titled "Let Obsessions Pass Naturally Through Your Mind" and "Use Audiotapes and Videotapes to Intensify Exposure." If you follow the instructions in these sections, you will probably notice that your obsessions begin to bother you less. If you are not satisfied with your progress, then refer to the section titled "Set Aside a Worry Time for Obsessions."

Rewarding yourself is also a useful technique, for it can help motivate you to control your checking compulsions. Sally had dozens of visual checking rituals she performed every day. She called these brief checks "scanning," since she rapidly scanned her clothes and other objects for dust or dirt. She was carrying out so many of these brief rituals that she wasn't able to practice response prevention effectively. Instead, we counted how many rituals she was performing a day. Then we set a maximum number of rituals she could do each day. If she succeeded in staying below the maximum, she rewarded herself with a movie, or music she enjoyed. If not, she didn't permit herself these activities. With this program she was able to decrease her number of checks by more than three quarters, and is continuing to decrease them.

One man found that keeping reminders handy helped him conquer his checking rituals. He told me that during his practice, he kept reminding himself that I had told him, "The people with OCD who worry most about making mistakes are those who are least likely to make them." With this reminder, and his helper's assistance, he was able to control his four-year-old checking rituals in only two weeks; as a result, he told me, he felt he had been "granted freedom."

Your practice goals should be based on those situations that trigger your fears and worries. You can set your practice goals by slowly decreasing the number of times you check a situation— say, starting from your current number and decreasing by one or two at a time. You can also slowly increase the amount of time you resist the rituals, starting at only a few minutes if you have to and building up to the full one to two hours, the time recommended in Chapter 2 for best results. When working on your practice goals, remember not to ask your helper for reassurance; this is a form of checking. But do accept his or her encouragement for your efforts.

With practice you'll be able to get control of your checking rituals. Concentrate on changing the behaviors themselves; let the urges and thoughts recede in their own time. Urges to check often fluctuate with stresses in your life, so you may feel as if you have good days and bad days. This is normal.

Repeating Rituals and Counting Compulsions

As with all OCD symptoms, in beginning behavior therapy for repeating and counting problems you should get back in touch with what normal behavior is. To help you set your long-term goals, ask two or three people you know well (including your helper) whether they would repeat the things you do or count the things you do. Usually people who don't have OCD repeat or count things only when they are very nervous or distracted. Picture the expectant father pacing back and forth in the waiting room, awaiting news of his newborn baby. He may also count the tiles on the floor, just trying to pass the time or keep his mind occupied. But if his attention is called to them, he can stop these rituals. This should be your goal: to stop excessive repeating or counting if you become aware of it.

The difference is that someone with OCD can't simply stop doing these things. One woman I treated had to wash each part of her body eleven times, with seven repetitions each time, or she would feel dirty. Another patient, after placing his eyeglasses on his night table, had to stare at them while counting to one thousand to reassure himself that he had not thrown them on the floor and broken them.

Exposure and response prevention are straightforward for counting and repeating rituals. First you identify the situations that trigger these rituals, such as reading a book. Then step-by-step, you expose yourself to these situations while resisting the urge to count or repeat actions for increasing periods of time afterward.

Probably the most important technique in exposure and response prevention for repeating and counting rituals is involving a helper in your practice. You'll greatly improve your chances of success if you work with a helper. If, once you confront the situations that trigger your rituals, you get stuck counting objects or repeating actions, your helper can remind you to stop this behavior before you get caught in a loop that is difficult to break out of.

If you find that you go back and reread what you have already read, use the following technique, which was developed to teach speed-reading: point your index finger under the line you are reading and move it across the line; when you get to the end of the line, move your finger down to the next line and begin again. If the urge to reread something hits you, just continue following your finger down and across the page; since your finger is always moving, you won't be able to go back and reread. The urge will slowly subside if you continue this practice. With thought, you and your helper can come up with similar methods to help you with response prevention for your particular problems.

Your early practice goals should involve confronting situations that trigger these urges, while resisting the compulsions for increasing lengths of time. Start out resisting for only a few minutes if this is all you can handle. Later, as you succeed with these early practice goals, you can extend response prevention to the full one to two hours.

The standard procedures of exposure and response prevention should help you get control over your repeating and counting rituals. The woman I described earlier was able to take a shower while washing each part of her body only once after practicing exposure and response prevention. The man was able to put his eyeglasses down and walk away from them within fifteen seconds. As is true for many other OCD symptoms, the urges to perform your rituals are stronger during times of intense stress. It is especially important to resist them at these times; if you do, you'll find they will subside again once the stress is past.

Hoarding/Collecting Compulsions

Your first step in practicing behavior therapy for hoarding and collecting compulsions should be to get back in touch with what is normal. Ask your helper and one or two other people about things that you have trouble throwing away. Ask them how long they keep junk mail or old wrappers and newspapers. Invite them to your house to look through your rooms and advise you as to what they would throw away. You may be surprised at their answers, but you should use them in planning your long-term goals.

In this case, exposure involves throwing away things that you have been saving. Response prevention involves resisting the urge to remove these things from the garbage can afterward.

You will probably need direct supervision from your helper to throw things away at first. After you work with your helper to identify what is junk and can be thrown away, he or she should throw something away first to show you this isn't dangerous. Next your helper should help you throw things away on your own while you resist the urge to take these things out of the garbage. Remember that your goal is not simply to clean your house; you could hire a cleaning person to do that. Your goals are to get used to deciding what is junk and then being able to throw it away. If your problem involves picking junk up from the street, then your helper will work with you to resist these urges while walking around town.

To help him with exposure and response prevention, one man had his sister stay with him for a full week; each day she supervised him as he went from room to room selecting junk and discarding it. He reasoned that if he worked for several hours each day with someone he trusted but who would be firm with him, he would get control of his problem more quickly than by working with someone less familiar and on a less intensive schedule.

Working with a helper is the most important technique for success in exposure and response prevention for hoarding compulsions. You can also use the method of visualizing yourself in the future having accomplished your long-term goals. The man I have just described became so embarrassed with his cluttered house that he allowed no company inside. To motivate himself, he imagined having guests over to celebrate his having thrown away all of his junk.

I have found it helpful for patients to make an inventory of the garbage to be thrown away. This provides them with their practice goals. For example, one woman could not throw away anything from her car. She kept papers, sweaters, bottles, and countless other items in her backseat and trunk. I first had her make a list of all the objects in the car. She then rated each one as to how difficult it would be to throw away, using the SUD Scale. Then, with her helper, she took out several of the items that would be fairly easy for her to discard at a time, threw them away while resisting the urge to take them back, and repeated the process at the next session with items that were harder for her to discard.

Here are some suggestions for reaching your own practice goals. Always work with your helper during your early practice sessions. Make a list of all things that need to be thrown away, and rank these things from easiest to most difficult to throw away. Always begin with items that you rank easiest and that have no sentimental or material value to you. Don't stare at or shake objects before throwing them away, and don't take them out of the trash afterward.

You will find that the anxiety you feel before throwing things away is much worse than the anxiety you feel when actually doing it. Once you've thrown an item away, the worst is over. If you remind yourself that you really do know the difference between junk and valuables, and you continue working with your helper, you will begin to get control of your hoarding compulsions. Because new opportunities to hoard will come to you everyday in the form of junk mail and empty wrappers and containers, you will need to pay particular attention to preventing relapse of your symptoms, as discussed in Chapter 6.

Superstitious Obsessions and Compulsions

We all have some superstitions: fear of black cats, walking under ladders, or Friday the thirteenth. But people who don't have OCD don't let these superstitions control their life. You should begin behavior therapy by asking your helper and one or two other people what they think of your superstitious fears. Once you have their answers, you'll have to rely on them in setting your long-term goals.

The major elements of behavior therapy for superstitious obsessions and compulsions are exposure: confronting situations you fear, whether these are going to "unlucky" places like cemeteries or occult bookstores or wearing clothes in "unlucky" colors; and response prevention: resisting rituals like saying prayers or performing "lucky" actions to undo your "unlucky" actions.

Because your urges to avoid these situations are probably very strong, you will need a helper to work with you. His or her most important functions will be to make sure you expose yourself to "bad luck" situations and to prevent you from performing rituals to counteract these exposures. Your helper should first demonstrate this exposure and response prevention himself or herself to show you that he or she is not asking you to do anything dangerous. It's important to remember that, unfortunately, bad things happen to all of us at times. If misfortune strikes you, discuss this with your helper. Above all, resist your urge to blame your bad luck on your exposure and response prevention practice.

Some people deal with their fears by going out of their way to do "unlucky" things. I asked one man—let's call him John Smith—who was afraid of death and funerals to call a local funeral home and ask if the Smith funeral was being held there today. As he faced these situations repeatedly, his fears subsided.

Rewarding yourself can help motivate you to confront difficult practice goals. If you find that you obsess about bad luck after your practice sessions, use relaxation, thought-stopping, or thought-delaying techniques.

When you set your practice goals refer back to the section in this chapter titled "Use Audio and Videotapes to Intensify Exposure." Try to expose yourself to the objects or situations that are the most difficult for you to confront as soon as possible; because you probably form new associations between "bad luck" objects quickly, this is a way of stopping this spread of superstitious fears—remember the bull's-eye I described in Chapter 4? For example, within the first few weeks of treatment, I asked a woman with fears of death to spend time in a cemetery and a funeral home. A man with superstitious fears of death spent time in an occult bookstore and bought several "bad luck" objects there. Two other people were afraid of apostrophes in books and magazine articles because they signified possession; I asked both to circle all the words they could find with apostrophes in the daily newspaper. All of these patients found that their superstitious obsessions changed slowly as they continued their practice. My role was to provide them with encouragement and reassurance that nothing terrible would happen to them as a result of doing "unlucky" things. This is the same role that your helper will play for you.

If you concentrate only on changing your behaviors, you will get control of your superstitious obsessions and compulsions. Let your urges and thoughts take care of themselves; they will change more slowly, but they will slowly subside as well. Although these urges and thoughts may reemerge in times of great stress, they will subside as the stress passes.

Compulsive Slowness

Begin using behavior therapy on your slowness by asking your helper and one or two other people you trust how long it takes them to do things you have trouble with. Ask them how long it takes them to wash, to eat, to dress, to write a check, or to perform any other activity that is a problem for you. Then average together their answers and use this number as a long-term goal.

Research has found that the standard behavior therapy techniques of exposure and response prevention are very difficult to apply to this problem. Instead, methods called prompting and shaping have shown the most promise in controlling slowness. In prompting, your helper gives you cues or commands to accomplish things in a certain period of time. In shaping, you slowly decrease the amount of time you spend on an activity; in this way your behavior is "shaped" toward normal behavior. For example, to help you go from standing to sitting without getting stuck, your helper would first demonstrate how to do this; then he or she would instruct you to sit down within the agreed-upon number of seconds or minutes, which he or she counted out loud (*prompting*). You would then gradually shorten the interval between standing and sitting until it became a normal length of time (*shaping*).

You will need a helper to encourage you and help you get control of your slowness. Your helper will have to be strict in enabling you to stick to the time limits you set as your practice goals.

To help you work with your helper, you might imagine yourself in a sporting event in which you are trying to beat the clock and set a new record. Each time you set a new practice goal, try to accomplish it as quickly as possible to set a new personal record. This approach will help you distract yourself from time-wasting obsessions. Just as if you were competing in a sporting event, always use a timer or stopwatch to time your activities; never guess at your time.

Having a helper work with you is the most important strategy for success in treating slowness with behavior therapy. You may also give yourself a reward each time you succeed in beating a time limit on a practice goal. One man found that visualizing his long-term goal of living alone kept him motivated to continue his practice.

Before you set your practice goals, begin by timing how long each activity takes you. Then set each practice goal slightly lower. If you now need two hours to get dressed, you may set your first goal at an hour and a half. If this is too difficult, try for an hour and fifty minutes. As you succeed in your early goals, set the time limit lower and lower, until you finally reach your long-term goals. Be patient; getting control of slowness rituals can be a long process.

You should expect to feel anxiety when you begin to speed up your activities—this is natural. If you are willing to accept this, and you work hard with your helper, you should be able to speed up the activities you work on as practice goals. More than with any other kind of OCD problem, however, you must be patient and focus on having a good quality of life *despite* doing some things slowly.

Obsessions Without Compulsions

We all have obsessive thoughts at some time. Research has found that almost everyone has occasional intrusive sexual thoughts or thoughts of driving their car off the road or pushing someone in front of a train. However, the person without OCD feels able to dismiss these thoughts and doesn't worry too much about them. Your long-term goals should include being able to enter situations without experiencing intolerable obsessive thoughts and being able to control whatever obsessive thoughts come into your mind.

If your obsessions are triggered by specific situations, such as homosexual thoughts arising from being around men or women, then exposure will involve entering into these situations, and response prevention will involve staying in them for as long as possible.

Your helper should assist you in placing yourself in the situations that cause your obsessive thoughts. He or she will then help you remain in the situation and cope with your thoughts and anxiety until they begin to subside.

Work with your helper to think of creative ways to confront the situations that trigger your obsessions. One man who was obsessed with "dirty-" or "sleazy-looking" people forced himself to go to bars and other places where he would come in contact with such people. As he continued dong so, his obsessive thoughts decreased.

Try to let your obsessions pass naturally through your mind as described earlier in this chapter. Also be sure to refer back to the section in this chapter titled "Use Audio and Videotapes to Intensify Exposure"; I now use one of these media to help almost all of my patients with upsetting obsessions.

When you set practice goals for obsessions that are solely related to certain diseases, such as getting cancer or AIDS, you can gradually expose yourself to safe materials with your helper. For instance, first your helper, then you, can touch pamphlets about these diseases or sit in chairs that you think people with these diseases have sat in. One patient who had obsessive thoughts about getting cancer exposed himself to reading newspaper and magazine stories about cancer and looked at medical books showing pictures of tumors.

Controlling your obsessive thoughts is hard work, but it can be done. Try to control your thoughts using the techniques described in this section. But if after twenty hours of practice you are not satisfied with your progress, then you should contact a therapist who is familiar with a new technique called cognitive therapy for OCD. Make sure they are familiar with this method.[2] The Obsessive Compulsive Foundation can help provide a referral.

Often treatment with SRI medications can reduce these obsessions. Medication treatment is described in Chapter 8.

Refer back to the techniques in this chapter often during your practice sessions. You may find suggestions that can help you with a particular goal you are working on.

2. This treatment method is described in: Steketee et al., "Cognitive Theory and Treatment of OCD," in Jenike et al., *Obsessive-Compulsive Disorders*, 3rd ed., 1998.

CHAPTER SIX

· ·

Staying in Control

· ·

"Nothing in the world can take the place of persistence."

—Calvin Coolidge (1872–1933)

Linda came to see me for help with her OCD. "Before we start," she said, "I read a pamphlet in your waiting room called 'Learning to Live with Obsessive-Compulsive Disorder'[1] that upset me a lot and I want to discuss it with you. The whole idea upset me— that OCD can't be cured, that I will have to learn to live with it, like some chronic disease, and that it may flare up again in the future."

I told Linda that I understood her concerns but that the point of the pamphlet was not to force her to resign herself to always being troubled by OCD; instead, its purpose was to show that although we can't cure OCD now, through treatment we can reduce the symptoms greatly. In a sense it is true that OCD is like a chronic illness. In times of stress your urges to perform rituals, or your obsessive thoughts, may feel stronger. But, as I told Linda, that doesn't mean that your OCD has to keep on interfering with your life.

Now that you've established some control over your particular OCD problems, it's natural for you to begin to look toward the fu-

1. This excellent pamphlet was written by Barbara Van Noppen, M.S.W., and Steven Rasmussen, M.D., two experts in OCD from Butler Hospital in Providence.

ture. It took hard work to control your symptoms. What will it take to stay in control? The same ingredients—persistence and knowledge.

When I see patients today for behavior therapy, I feel confident telling them what they can expect from the treatment. I can reassure them that their anxiety will subside with exposure. I can reassure them that they will not go crazy from the anxiety. And I can reassure them that their problems will stay under control in the future. How can I be so sure? I suppose that it's a combination of seeing behavior therapy work for hundreds of patients over the last decade and reading the research findings on many other patients around the world.

But twenty years ago, when I was face-to-face with Jack, my first OCD patient, I really wasn't sure what to expect. In some ways I was in the same position you're in now; I had learned the principles of treating OCD with behavior therapy, and they made sense to me. But until you try something for yourself, you never fully believe or understand it. The Japanese have a saying about this: "To know and not to do is not to know."

So I listened to Jack tell me his story. He had fears of becoming contaminated from touching many objects that he considered dirty. He kept his right hand "clean" at all times, refusing to use it to shake hands or even to put it in his pants pocket. To avoid direct contact with "dirty" objects like his laundry, his bed, door handles in public bathrooms, his shoes, or the gas cap on his car, he would cover them with paper towels before touching them. To turn the faucets in a public bathroom, he covered them with paper towels and then held on to the towel to cover the door handle on his way out.

If Jack was forced to touch one of these "dirty" things, he felt vaguely dirty and uncomfortable. He would immediately scrub his hands over and over. Then, as soon as he got home, he would wash the clothes he had been wearing when he had touched the objects.

Because of his OCD symptoms, Jack, a very intelligent and talented young man, was no longer able to work at his full-time job. When I met him, he worked only a few hours a week, and his social life had dwindled since he spent so many hours each day either worrying about being contaminated or washing to remove contamination.

I explained to Jack what I knew about treating his symptoms with behavior therapy. At first I had him touch the "dirty" objects in my office—the chair seats, the faucets and door handles in our bathroom—without washing afterward, and all went well. But he came back the next week without having completed the practice assignments we had agreed he would do at home. After a few weeks of this, we both realized the treatment wasn't working, because Jack couldn't bring himself to touch laundry and other things without washing. I therefore visited his apartment on several occasions to help him touch his laundry, his shoes, his bed, his bathroom fixtures, and other "dirty" objects repeatedly and to prevent him from washing afterward.

Sure enough, this exposure and response prevention worked. After three months of treatment, Jack had almost all of his symptoms under control. I told him that the gains of most patients last for many years. I had a chance to see this for myself. I checked in with Jack six months later, and things were still going well. A year later, the same thing. The last time I saw Jack, his problems had been well under control for more than six years, and he was living a normal life.

The early experience I had with Jack was repeated with many other patients who got better due to behavior therapy and stayed better for years after. But I also found that some types of OCD rituals and thoughts were more difficult to treat than others. Years later, in doing research for a chapter in a scientific textbook, I found that patients with cleaning rituals and checking rituals seemed to have the easiest time with behavior therapy.

Although our patients rarely get 100 percent better with behavior therapy, in most cases they are delighted with their improvements; their OCD symptoms, while still likely to resurface in times of stress, no longer interfere with their work or social life.

To give you an idea of the kind of results you can expect, let's check in with some of the patients you met in Chapter 1 to see how they are doing now. Because these patients had a variety of OCD symptoms, you will probably find some that are like your problems. As a result, you'll learn what *you* can realistically expect from behavior therapy, how to stay in control of your OCD problems, and how to identify and sidestep potential pitfalls along the way.

Long-term Results of Behavior Therapy

Peggy: Cleaning/Washing Compulsions

Peggy had fears of contamination from disease. All of the long-term goals that she worked on have remained under control; that is, three years after her treatment, the problems she worked on no longer interfere with her life. Look back at her long-term goals in Chapter 4 to remind yourself of her situation before beginning behavior therapy.

To be specific, those long-term goals she accomplished were: she washes her hands only when they are really dirty; she washes her hands only once before preparing food; she is able to use shopping carts in the supermarket; she no longer avoids people who look ill; she can go into rooms and use furniture where sick people have been; she can use public washing machines; she can prepare food in her own kitchen; she can mix "clean" and "dirty" clothes together in her closet; her baths now take twenty minutes instead of two or three hours; she bathes once a day instead of four or five times; she can wash her countertops with regular kitchen cleansers instead of feeling she needs to use bleach.

Yet Peggy was not able to achieve all the long-term goals she set. In some cases she was simply not able to comply with the short-term goals she established for herself. She still washes her hands in the process of doing her laundry, she resists shaking hands or brushing against other people, and she prefers not to leave her house after going to the bathroom unless she showers first. Each time Peggy set a short-term goal related to one of these problems, she had good intentions but, for a variety of reasons, was never able to fully accomplish the goal.

Overall, Peggy is very happy with her improvement. Her major compulsions are under control, and her obsessive thoughts are also reduced. She still has some rituals, but these don't interfere significantly with her life.

How tough did Peggy find behavior therapy? Early in her treatment she told me, "I'm amazed at how I've been able to do these things. I've had this obsessive compulsion for at least fifteen years, and I just can't believe how quickly I've been able to shed these obsessions—at least in my apartment." Peggy was pleasantly surprised that she didn't experience much anxiety in her practice sessions and told me that the anxiety she felt anticipating a practice session was much worse than the anxiety she actually felt during exposure and response prevention. She described touching a wheelchair, one of her most feared items, this way: "It really doesn't bother me too much. I'd rather not do it, but I did it. The feeling of accomplishing a goal overcame my reticence."

Finally, she emphasized to me the importance of having a helper assist her: "When I had temptations to avoid things, my boyfriend supported me and said 'You have to do this'—so I stayed there and I survived it."

Overall, Peggy's response to behavior therapy was swift and extensive. By the end of four weeks of practice, she had more than half of her problems under control. Like Peggy, patients with cleaning rituals usually respond rapidly to behavior therapy, and their obsessions and compulsions tend to remain under control in the future.

Peggy now finds that during periods of stress in her family, her urges to clean resurface. However, she is able to refrain from them without washing, and they die down again once the stressful period is over.

Tom: Checking Compulsions

Now let's check in on Tom, the teacher with many checking rituals and fears of hurting his students. How has he fared with behavior therapy? His status is similar to Peggy's: the problems that he was able to work on by successfully meeting short-term goals have gotten better and have stayed under control.

But other symptoms, for which he devised short-term goals that he was not able to meet, are still problems, although somewhat improved. In a few cases, even though he complied with some short-term goals completely, the urges to check did not diminish. In other words, although he reduced his checking for several weeks at a time, he was sometimes still not sure whether he had hurt one of his students.

How difficult did Tom find exposure and response prevention? Here are his comments about attacking various goals as part of behavior therapy. (Review Tom's long-term goals in Chapter 4 to refresh your memory about his problems.)

Tom told me that practicing behavior therapy to learn to use a stapler in his classroom, and around his students, "was very hard. It took me a long while. But it got much easier. Now I can use it without thinking about it."

Another problem for Tom was the need to use carbon paper when correcting students' papers, so he could check afterward that he hadn't written any obscenities on them. Talking about forcing himself not to use carbon paper, he said, "I checked a lot at first. Then I was able to do without it and check only once or twice and feel good."

One of Tom's goals was to resist checking electrical plugs and switches. He found that "it was difficult. I did a lot of counting. My brother helped by saying 'It's off' and I could walk away. My brother also said 'Car is in park' and I could walk away. I took his word for it." (Notice that this time Tom's brother fell into the trap of reassuring Tom and "checking" for him.)

A major goal was to resist checking the position of his feet relative to a chalk mark he drew on the floor to make sure he hadn't attacked a student. This urge, Tom said, "was very hard to resist. I had to have some reference to know I hadn't moved. I found myself staring at something else instead—a piece of lint or a piece of rug, and the urge went away in two seconds."

Finally, Tom talked about his experiences in fighting his urge to call parents to check on the well-being of his students: "This was very difficult. I sometimes gave in. But I tried to tell myself, 'Wait until the next day.' Now I don't do it at all."

Notice that Tom experienced more anxiety than Peggy in resisting his rituals. Many patients with checking rituals feel very unsure and unsafe during response prevention. Having a helper present can make the difference between succeeding and failing in an attempt to reach a particular goal. In Tom's case, the medication fluoxetine (Prozac) helped to reduce his strong urges. The use of medications in combination with behavior therapy is discussed fully in Chapter 8.

Tom has been able to control most of his checking rituals while in his own home. However, his urges to check while at school remain strong, especially when he is feeling angry or anxious. Some people with checking rituals find that even though they have greatly reduced their checking rituals—to the point where they are able to function again—their feelings of uncertainty remain, at a reduced level.

Why didn't Peggy and Tom improve completely? First, this is a common occurrence in OCD. It's easy to say that they did not get completely better because they weren't able to comply with all the short-term goals. OK, but *why* weren't they able to comply with these goals?

I think that the reason lies in the cost-benefit ratio of the activities related to these goals. Briefly, if the benefit you get from some task far exceeds its cost (inconvenience or difficulty), then you will be eager to engage in the activity. But if the benefit and cost are about equal, then you will be in a state of strong indecision about whether to engage in the activity; you may feel paralyzed in trying to decide whether to do it or not. For example, you may happily drive a hundred miles to see an old friend, yet you may think long and hard about driving five miles to visit the dentist.

At first my patients' OCD symptoms dominate their life. They will do almost anything to get help with their problem. At this point, they see the record keeping, exposure, and response prevention as well worth the effort they require. But, as patients get better, their life is affected less and less by their problems.

Finally they reach a point where they have some rituals left that they would rather not have, but that are not interfering with their life. Now the benefits of getting rid of these few remaining rituals no longer seem to greatly outweigh the effort necessary to get control of them. Even though the patients may agree to try behavior therapy for these problems, for a variety of reasons they do not follow through on the practice assignments. They can't explain why, and promise to try harder the next week. But the same thing happens again. In traditional psychotherapy this behavior would be called resisting treatment. But I prefer the nonjudgmental idea of the cost-benefit ratio as an explanation. Pay attention to this in your own practice. If you reach a plateau where your progress slows down, ask yourself why.

Ken: Repeating Rituals
and Counting Compulsions

Next, let's examine what happens with behavior therapy for some less common OCD symptoms. We know less about treating these problems with behavior therapy. However, we've found that most patients are able to control their problems to some extent with behavior therapy. We'll first check back in with Ken, who had numerous rituals involving counting and repeating that constricted his life.

Summarizing his progress, Ken recently told me, "Overall, the things I was able to get 100 percent in practice have not come back." He worked very hard on his short-term goals and as a result achieved almost all of his long-term goals over the course of six months (see Chapter 4 for some of his practice goals). They have remained under control now for three years. Other problems, for which he had set goals that he was unable to comply with, have not remained under his control, a common experience in OCD.

Ken's counting and repeating rituals no longer interfere with his life. But he told me that (like many other patients with OCD) he notices that the urges to perform his rituals increase during stressful periods. At these times, he remembers the techniques I have taught him, and he is able to resist these temporary urges.

Here are Ken's comments about undergoing behavior therapy to get control of his repeating and counting rituals: "I was somewhat skeptical at first of behavior therapy, since I had psychotherapy for six years before, including four years of psychoanalysis. I know all about my childhood, but it didn't help my OCD. The toughest goal was showering with no rituals, while unassisted. It took me a long time to overcome it. And it was much easier in all cases when I was assisted by my friend initially."

The first goal that Ken accomplished was walking down stairs without ritualizing. I helped him do this during our first sessions. His helper accompanied us to learn the techniques to use with Ken in their home practice. "That was the most memorable thing for me. You said, 'Why don't we try it.' When you gave me permission I knew I trusted you and I could do it—it was as if a weight was off my shoulders. You convinced me that everyone else did it. It wasn't difficult the first time, or anytime after that. Then, on my own, once I started, the impulses went steadily down—then they dropped dramatically."

Janet: Hoarding/Collecting Compulsions

Let's see how the woman described in the Preface who was unable to throw things away is doing. With behavior therapy, Janet is starting to throw things away for the first time in more than a decade. When she first started doing her homework practice, she became discouraged upon realizing just what a terrible state she had been living in. But now, as she continues her treatment with me, she is again able to walk from her bedroom door to her bed without having to shovel a path; one by one she's emptying the rooms of her house, filling several trash barrels each week.

Janet hopes to be able to return to work soon, without her hoarding rituals affecting her work. After she gets control of her hoarding problems, we will move on to her other major long-term goal, reducing the need to remember unimportant information.

Here are some of Janet's comments on her subjective feelings about behavior therapy: "I don't feel badly after doing it. But it is very hard to get started doing it. Sometimes it seems overwhelming because I have so much to throw out." "The day before practicing hangs over me like an appendix operation, but when I do start throwing things away I begin to feel great. I really do have a floor! And it's getting easier to throw junk mail away without looking at it. Decisions about what is junk and what is important are coming easier now."

Janet's anxiety was mainly in anticipating throwing things away, not in actually doing it. She probably wouldn't have succeeded as well as she has without having a helper. On this subject she told me, "I can't do it myself as easily without my friend helping me. I'd be inclined to throw fewer things away if Fred weren't there reminding me."

Nancy: Superstitious Obsessions and Compulsions

How do superstitious obsessions and compulsions respond to behavior therapy? Let's check back with Nancy, a woman with a variety of superstitious fears and rituals that affected most areas of her life, to find out.

Nancy worked hard on her short-term goals, and her improvements have proven to be lasting in those areas where she was able to comply with the goals (see Chapter 4 for a discussion of her goals). These problems have now stayed under control for more than two years. However, when she becomes anxious, her obsessive thoughts about superstition come back.

Nancy is now able to work full-time and is back in school. She is dating and socializing with her friends again, and her remaining OCD symptoms do not interfere with her life. Although she is not completely cured, she has control over her behavior again.

Nancy found that she experienced strong anxiety while working toward many of her practice goals. Here are her comments about undergoing behavior therapy to get control of her superstitious fears and rituals: "Even though my rituals are better, I'm still feeling anxious—I'm always fighting the thoughts." "I had a hard time wearing a watch at first" (she was afraid of certain numbers). "I've been resisting repeating things thirteen times, but I'm still obsessing." "I stopped thought stopping because it became a ritual." "When I feel nervous, it is hard not to do repeating rituals." "If you tell me it's safe to do something, then I know it's OK to do it."

Clearly Nancy experienced much more difficulty with exposure and response prevention than the people previously described in this section. Taking clomipramine (Anafranil), an antidepressant medication, helped her reduce her urges and anxiety. Many patients with severe superstitious fears will find behavior therapy much easier if they are taking a medication at the same time.

Bill: Compulsive Slowness

Bill, the man who did everything slowly, made great progress with behavior therapy. But it wasn't easy. Each of his painfully slow activities had to be worked on separately. Needless to say, a great deal of patience and persistence was required. His behavior therapist spent a lot of time working with Bill's family members to teach them how to deal with him to facilitate his treatment.

Originally, some of Bill's thoughts were "Somebody will die if I don't do everything perfectly," "A disaster will occur and I'll be responsible if I don't check and get everything perfect," and "If I don't do this perfectly, I'll be labeled incompetent." His therapist taught him to challenge his obsessions about disastrous things happening if he did not do things perfectly. To this end, he gave Bill index cards inscribed with statements that challenged his thoughts, such as "Nothing terrible will happen if I don't do this perfectly." Then Bill would read one of these cards during his practice sessions to help him finish his activities within the agreed-upon time limit.

Besides participating in behavior therapy, Bill needed to take several medications. Also, because of frequent arguments at his home, it was necessary to persuade him to move out of his parents' house and into a halfway house, which proved a less stressful environment for him. As Bill's case illustrates, the treatment of severe compulsive slowness is frequently more complicated than that of other OCD problems.

Paul: Obsessions Without Compulsions

Finally, let's check in on Paul, the man obsessed with ghastly thoughts of having molested a child. Two months after learning behavior therapy methods, Paul told me, "The thoughts about that incident don't seem to come much anymore. When they do come, they still bother me a lot."

Before seeing me, Paul had been taking fluvoxamine, an experimental antidepressant medication (see Chapter 8), for his OCD symptoms. Although the medication helped his depression and his few checking rituals, it didn't affect his obsessions about having molested a child. But by using the behavior therapy techniques I taught him, Paul has been able to control these thoughts. They still occur occasionally, but they do not intrude as often or as intensely as before, and they no longer affect his work or social life. Interestingly, Paul told me that just knowing techniques that could even partially control these horrible thoughts has made him feel better.

Overall, with a combination of behavior therapy and medication, Paul was able to control his thoughts more than 90 percent of the time—and these gains have lasted for more than a year.

Getting the Odds in Your Favor

By now you will have noticed similarities in these patients. First, you've seen that the improvements they made were likely to last. Because you've probably had your OCD problems for a long time, it is natural to wonder if they will return. Happily, one of the benefits of behavior therapy is that problems that you get under control tend to remain under control. Several research studies have found that improvements at the end of treatment were maintained (or strengthened) at follow-ups of one to five years. However, some patients in these studies needed booster sessions of behavior therapy along the way to hold on to their gains. But these booster sessions involve only a few sessions of practice, and the problems can be controlled much more quickly than the first time you tried behavior therapy. Later in this chapter you will learn how to determine whether you will need booster sessions.

Also, you've seen that you must work on each practice goal individually; that is, accomplishing one long-term goal doesn't guarantee that other goals will automatically be met as a result. As these patients' experiences have shown you, usually only those problems for which you can successfully meet the corresponding goals will improve. This finding has been confirmed by research in OCD. In one study a woman with both cleaning rituals and hoarding rituals was treated with behavior therapy. She cooperated with exposure and response prevention for her cleaning rituals, and these got better. But her hoarding rituals, which were not treated, did not change.[1] Of course, you may be pleasantly surprised to find that some problems change as you get others under control.

1. Rachman and Hodgson, *Obsessions and Compulsions*, 1980.

Finally, you've seen from Peggy's, Tom's, and Ken's experiences that during times of stress, obsessive thoughts and the urges to perform rituals can increase temporarily. One man told me that during these stressful times, "I simply wake up some mornings and I know it's going to be a tough day. These days my anticipatory anxiety seems higher and my motivation seems lower. But I just work harder on these tough days and I keep things under control until the urges go back down again."

At these times it is very important to be persistent in continuing your practice until the urges die down again. This is the best way to guarantee long-term success.

How can you use this information to get the odds in *your* favor for long-term success with behavior therapy? The following are some general principles.

Be Alert to Changes in Stress or Medication

As you've learned, stress can lead to an increase in compulsive urges. If you notice such a change, try to fight the discouragement you may feel; it is only a temporary setback. Jane, the woman you met in Chapter 1, used behavior therapy to get control of her cleaning compulsions and fears of death and germs. The problems for which she set and achieved long-term goals remained under control except in times of extreme stress. During her daughter's illness, she noticed a recurrence of her urges. Two booster sessions of behavior therapy helped Jane get her problems under control again. Eighteen months later, she herself was diagnosed with a serious physical illness and noticed a recurrence of her symptoms. Again I saw her for behavior therapy, for two sessions. In her case, the recurrence of the symptoms was probably a result of a combination of the increased stress on her body and mind, and of her tendency to stop doing her practice activities (and to resume avoiding things) when under stress.

One particular kind of stress needs particular emphasis because it is such a frequent cause of relapse in OCD: stress due to a troublesome marriage or family situation. Sadly, I have seen patients whose OCD symptoms improved greatly while at our residential treatment program near Boston, only to see these symptoms come back gradually after they return home to a stress-ful family or marital situation that has not been corrected.

If you find your OCD symptoms returning after you've made good progress using the methods outlined in this book, you should ask yourself: "Do members of my family criticize each other excessively? Are we overinvolved in each other's problems?[2] Do we ignore important emotional issues that need to be talked about?" If the answer to any of the three questions is yes, then you should seek professional counseling to help you and your family deal with these problems, not only to maintain your gains, but also to live a happier life.

Some patients who have been taking an antidepressant med-ication during behavior therapy and discontinue it may find that their symptoms return. If this is your experience, your doctor may recommend that you return to your medication, try a new medication, or try behavior therapy. Our clinic patients find that their symptoms usually are brought under control with one of these approaches.

An interesting example of relapse after stopping medication was Peggy, the woman with fears of contamination. She began taking clomipramine after she had most of her OCD symptoms under control, and the medication helped reduce her thoughts even more. But when she came off the clomipramine six months later, urges and rituals that she had had under control before be-ginning on the medication increased in strength temporarily. Booster sessions of behavior therapy helped her get control once again.

Make Behavioral Practice Part of Your Everyday Life

Have you ever started an exercise program and found that the only way to stick with it was to make it a part of your daily routine? If you neglected to exercise every day, you probably found that, despite your good intentions, you slowly stopped doing the exer-

2. This family pattern is called "high expressed emotion," and is a common cause of relapse of OCD symptoms, as described in detail in Steketee and Van Noppen, "Group and Family Therapy for Obsessive-Compulsive Disorder," in Jenike et al., *Obsessive-Compulsive Disorders*, 3rd ed., 1998.

cises. Behavior therapy, too, must become an established part of your day. The new behaviors you've learned will then become second nature to you.

To accomplish this with your practice for your OCD symptoms, look back over your long-term goals and see how you can work your techniques for achieving each of them into your everyday routine. As you have learned, the symptoms for which you can accomplish your practice goals are likely to remain under your control.

For example, Peggy's goals of bringing food into her house, mixing "clean" and "dirty" clothes in her closet, and being able to use public laundromats are things she will be doing as part of her daily routine for the rest of her life. After a while, she will no longer think of these as practice activities, but just as daily routines. As a result, the benefits and convenience she receives from doing them will help her maintain them in the future. You should, therefore, set up practice goals that will lead to behaviors that fit easily into the kind of life-style you want to lead someday. By doing this, you'll be avoiding one of the major pitfalls—not working on your practice goals. I have found that most patients who do not keep up with practice goals do so for one of two reasons. The first is that they do not have a helper. It is much more difficult to accomplish a goal without the aid of a helper. It can be done, but why not get the odds on your side, instead of against you? The second reason is that they have set goals that are too difficult. Remember the 80 Percent Question? If you set goals that you have little chance of achieving, you will be setting yourself up to fail at that goal. Conversely, if you set only very easy goals for yourself, you will probably achieve them but you won't advance toward your major long-term goals. Your goals should become more challenging as you get more control. Keep the image of the bull's-eye in mind. You should always be moving toward the bull's-eye, not simply around one of the outer rings.

Check Up on Yourself Periodically

To make sure you are maintaining your gains, you should periodically check up on yourself. After your problems have been under control for six months or so, you need to check up on yourself only about twice a year.

At this time, you should retake the tests in Chapter 3 to make sure you haven't unknowingly slipped back into any old bad habits. You should also monitor yourself after a particularly stressful time in your life. Such a period may have included bad things (illnesses or deaths), or good things (moving to a new location, taking a new job, or getting married), which are also stressful to the body and mind. Women with a tendency to develop OCD should check up on themselves frequently during and after a pregnancy. Finally, if you have been idle for a long time, you should monitor yourself to make sure you haven't fallen back into your bad habits to fill the empty time.

Give Yourself a Behavior Therapy Booster

If your follow-up shows any slipping back, you should immediately give yourself a booster of behavior therapy. Don't be discouraged by this; about one in four OCD patients need brief boosters of behavior therapy to maintain their improvement.

Here is how to go about it. First, reread Chapters 4 and 5, which deal with setting goals and practicing exposure and response prevention for your particular problems. Then, with your memory refreshed and your goals set, resume your practice sessions with a helper. You will find that you'll quickly get your problems back under control—it always takes much less time than when you began behavior therapy.

What if you have controlled your compulsions but your urges and thoughts haven't changed? If you have tried the behavioral techniques for at least twenty hours, as suggested, had a helper, and complied with your short-term goals, and your urges and thoughts have not decreased *at all*, then you should contact a qualified psychiatrist or psychologist to see what can be done to help you further.

Do not feel as if you have failed! As we discussed earlier, all you can control is your behavior, and you have done this. The quality of your life has probably already improved somewhat just from your having reduced your compulsions and avoidance. Keep resisting them while you are getting in touch with a therapist. The odds are good that a professional therapist will help you get more control over your problems.

CHAPTER SEVEN

•••

Getting Control of Problems Related to OCD

•••

"The unfortunate thing about this world is that good
habits are so much easier to give up than bad ones."
—W. Somerset Maugham (1874–1965)

Maybe you've patiently read the previous chapters looking for
help for your particular problem, but although it seems like
OCD, it doesn't fall into one of the categories I've been describing. Can behavior therapy help you? In many cases, the answer is
still yes. But behavior therapy is applied differently to the disorders discussed in this chapter—trichotillomania, Tourette Disorder, and excessive bodily worries—than it is to the classic OCD
symptoms I described in Chapter 1. This chapter will explain approaches in getting control of these problems.

First, a word of warning. Many of the problems reviewed in this
chapter are severe disorders. The behavior therapy methods used
in treating them, moreover, may be difficult to apply because of
the strong impulses involved; thus, you should always try to get a
helper to assist you with these methods. You can try to use the
techniques described in this book to get control of your problems, but you should get professional help as soon as possible if
you find they are not working. Finally, if you suffer from the disorders described in this chapter, you will probably require treatment with a medication to help you improve as much as possible.

Trichotillomania

Sarah was a young woman who came to me for help. She explained that she was subject to periods when she could not stop pulling out her hair. It began with her eyelashes. Once these were plucked smooth, she progressed to her eyebrows, until, finally, the hair on her scalp was the target of her rituals. She told me that she pulled her hair when she was under emotional stress.

Sarah admitted to me that it felt good to pull the hair out; in fact, it was one of the few ways she could get relief from the pressures in her life. But once she began, she felt unable to pry her hand from her scalp. Minutes turned to hours as she plucked out her hairs one by one. The results of her habit were obvious: there was a two-inch bald patch at the crown of her head and one above each temple, and her original hairline had all but disappeared.

When she came to my office, Sarah showed the telltale signs of trichotillomania: she wore a kerchief around her hair during the first session and her hair pulled up in a bun during the second. These were attempts to hide the evidence of her destructive habits from the world. If her habits continued untreated, her final refuge would be to wear a wig. (We have seen patients who have plucked their entire scalp smooth—one hair at a time.)

If you pull your hair out—from your eyelashes, eyebrows, scalp, or pubic region—then you may suffer from trichotillomania.[1] The name comes from the Greek word *trichos*, which means "hair." Dr. Judith Rapoport believes that the occurrence of trichotillomania, like that of OCD, has been vastly underestimated. In fact, she believes that a large proportion of women who buy wigs do so to cover up the evidence of their hair-pulling habit. Unlike OCD, which is equally common in males and females, trichotillomania is found almost exclusively in females.

Behavior therapy for trichotillomania was originally used mainly to treat children and adolescents with this problem. Although no carefully controlled scientific studies of behavior therapy for trichotillomania have yet been conducted, there are many

---

1. You may instead twirl your hair between your fingers and wear it away by constant manipulation. Trichotillomania is sometimes called "trich," for short.

reports of children and adults who got better and stayed better with behavior therapy.

Several methods of behavior therapy and hypnosis have been tried for trichotillomania, with varying degrees of success. But the method that has proven most helpful is called habit reversal and was developed by Dr. Nathan Azrin for use in controlling bad habits. It is a safe method you can use to get control of your own hair-pulling habit. Let's examine what it involves.

Habit Reversal

Habit reversal is composed of five steps: awareness training, learning a competing response, relaxation training, contingency management, and generalization training. Each of these steps is necessary for the method to succeed. I will describe the steps exactly as I would to a patient who came to me with a hair-pulling problem. We usually go over these steps during the first session.[2] Because habit reversal is also the preferred behavior therapy method for the tics of Tourette Disorder, I will describe each of the steps in detail.

1. Awareness Training

The first component in awareness training is to keep track of each time you pull out your hair. Have a small notebook handy at all times. Each time, *immediately* after you pull out your hair, make a note of the date, time, situation, your feelings, and how long you spent pulling out your hair. Write down all this information right after you finish pulling out your hair, don't rely on your memory. Some people find that the simple act of recording this information sometimes reduces the frequency of the habit. This procedure is often called self-monitoring or mood monitoring by behavior therapists.

The next part of awareness training, and of controlling any habit, is to become acutely aware of the first movement of the habit. When you have a habit for a long time, you are no longer aware of it. In fact, that's what a habit is—something you do without conscious awareness. You should focus on your first move-

2. For a more detailed description of these methods, look for the simple but effective book *Habit Control in a Day*, by Drs. Azrin and R. G. Nunn, 1977.

ment, because once you give in to the habit, it is exceedingly difficult to stop yourself. And you have a much better chance of stopping the habit right at the start; as the saying goes, nipping it in the bud.

You must become *acutely* aware of the first movement of your hand. If you pull out your eyebrows or eyelashes, you should pay close attention to the first movement of your hand toward your eyes. If you pull out only your scalp hair, then instead you will be attentive to any movement of your hands toward your head.

What do I mean by becoming acutely aware? By the end of the second session, I expect my patient to be able to tell me all the situations in which she (or, rarely, he) begins to pull out her hair. You will probably be surprised to learn that there are usually only a few situations in which you perform this habit.

For example, Beth, a ten-year-old girl with long hair, was surprised to find that she pulled out her hair (from the back of her head) in only two situations. In the first, she was lying on the floor watching television, with her head propped up by her right arm and hand. By having her and her parents pay close attention to her habits, we learned that she always started twirling her hair with the fingers of her right hand; this led to plucking the hair out. In the other situation, Beth was sitting in a chair doing schoolwork, again resting her head on her right hand and arm. She would begin to twirl her hair with the fingers of this hand and then would start pulling the hair out. Beth told me that these situations were those in which she was most aware of feeling bored. Once she was able to identify these situations and feelings, she became acutely aware of any movement of her right hand toward her hair in these two circumstances. For Beth, the problem was no longer an unconscious habit, but now a series of conscious movements that occurred in certain situations that she was able to look out for.

How do you go about becoming as acutely aware of your habits as was Beth? Here are the questions that I want my patients to find answers for. Ask them of yourself. If you can't answer each one, then you must pay more attention, or ask someone who lives with you to observe you. In any case, don't go on with habit reversal until you can answer all these questions:

- Which hand do you usually use to pull out your hair?
- In what situations do you usually pull out your hair (looking in a mirror, watching television, reading, sitting in school)?
- What position is your body usually in when you begin to pull out your hair?
- Do you usually begin by pulling your eyelashes, eyebrows, or scalp hair?
- What emotions do you usually feel right before you begin to pull out your hair?

Once you can answer these questions, you are well on your way to being acutely aware of when your problem occurs. Now you're ready for the second critical step in controlling your hair pulling: learning a competing response. This is the heart of the habit reversal method.

2. Learning a Competing Response

The basic principle of habit reversal is deceptively simple: when you have the urge to give in to your habit, force yourself to engage in a behavior that physically inhibits you from performing the habit. This is called a competing response because the muscles involved in the preventive activity *compete* with those involved in the habit. For example, if you had the habit of quickly jerking your head backward, you would force yourself to instead tighten your neck muscles and pull your chin slightly down and in, to maintain your head in an eyes-forward position. You would then keep your neck tensed in that position for two minutes, or until the urge had died down. Thus, in habit reversal you are retraining your muscles to execute a different movement in response to your urges, *a movement that will prevent you from performing the habit.*

For a competing response to trichotillomania, simply make any movement that will prevent you from moving your hands toward your head, face, or eyes, and stay in that position for two minutes. If you feel the urge to pull out your hair, clasp your hands together and keep them in that position for two minutes, or until the urge passes. If you are reading a book when the urge strikes, simply squeeze the edges of the book for two minutes. If driving a car, tighten your grip on the steering wheel for two minutes, or until the urge passes.

For the first few times, you should practice this component of habit reversal while looking at a clock until the two minutes are up. If at the end of this time you still feel a strong urge to pull out your hair, continue the habit reversal for another two minutes, and then another, if necessary, and so on. After you have practiced this a few times, you will be able to estimate how long two minutes is without looking at a clock. Then there will be no need to be a clock-watcher; a few seconds here or there won't make any difference.

If you are performing a competing response properly, you will find that you cannot pull out your hair: it will be simply impossible for your muscles to engage in these two competing responses at the same time. As you practice, your muscles will gradually un-learn their old habits in response to your urges, and you will be able to stop the movement of your hand toward your face, eyes, or head. Some of my patients reduced the frequency of their hair pulling by more than 90 percent after our first session, merely by learning to be acutely aware of developing a competing response.

I suggested to Beth, for example, that she sit up straight while doing her homework or watching television. If she became aware of an urge to move her hand toward her head to pull out her hair, she was to squeeze her hands together and hold them that way for two minutes. When she came back the next week she told me, "Most of the time the urge was gone when the time was up. When it wasn't, I did it again, and the feeling was gone."

3. Relaxation Training

Once Beth learned to perform the competing response effectively, I taught her the third component of habit reversal, relaxation. Relaxation helps to reduce the urge that led to her plucking out her hair. You remember from Chapter 2 that your OCD urges will subside if you resist your rituals, but problems like trichotillomania and Tourette Disorder are different—the urges in these disorders usually don't subside without a relaxation technique. For this reason relaxation is a critical part of habit reversal.

The following example illustrates why reducing this urge with relaxation is so important. Sarah, the young woman already mentioned in this chapter, told me in our first session that a doctor had previously taught her to use a competing response and that she subsequently had controlled her hair pulling for the first time in many years. Unfortunately, he did not also teach her to use relaxation to reduce the urges that led to her hair pulling. As a result, when she began having arguments with her boyfriend several months later, she didn't know how to control her feelings of anxiety and anger, and she began to pull out her hair again.

Practicing a competing response breaks the actual habit, while relaxation reduces the urge that triggers the habit. In this way the two techniques are analogous to response prevention and exposure, which also have to be used together.

The first method of relaxation I use with habit reversal is muscle relaxation. In muscle relaxation training, you will first make yourself aware of feelings of tension in your muscles. You will do this by tensing a particular group of muscles, holding the tension for about ten seconds, and then allowing the muscles to relax. You should then be able to feel the contrast between the feelings of tension and relaxation in that muscle group.

Try this yourself now. Begin by tensing the muscles in your right hand by making a fist. Squeeze hard, and pay attention to the feelings in your hand and arm. Count to ten and let your right hand relax. Compare the way your right arm feels now with the way it felt while you were tensing it into a fist. Now try it again, and pay close attention to the different feelings.

Most people don't realize that to relax, you don't have to actively do anything. When I asked you to make a fist, you automatically knew which muscles to tense to do this. But when I told you to let your hand relax, what did you do? Nothing—you simply let go of the tension that was in your hand. You knew how to do this automatically, and it just happened. Never try to *make* your muscles relax; it won't work. Instead, do the opposite of whatever you did to tense them in the first place.

Next you'll practice tensing and relaxing other key groups of muscles in your body. As you learn to relax these muscles, feelings of tension in your body should subside.

1. Right hand and arm—make a tight fist
2. Left hand and arm—make a tight fist
3. Right shoulder—shrug shoulder toward right ear
4. Left shoulder—shrug shoulder toward left ear
5. Right foot and leg—point toes and foot toward the ceiling

6. Left foot and leg—point toes and foot toward the ceiling
7. Stomach and chest—pull stomach in and hold it in
8. Eyes and forehead—squeeze eyes tightly shut
9. Mouth and jaw—squeeze lips together tightly

To do these nine exercises, which make up the relaxation procedure, sit in a comfortable position, with your feet flat on the floor and your arms in your lap. Use the movement listed next to each muscle group to produce the tension. Hold the tension while you count to ten. As you count, pay attention to the feelings in each muscle group. At ten, let the muscles return to normal; just do the opposite of whatever you did to tense them. If any movement causes you pain, try to do it less vigorously; skip that movement if you still feel strong discomfort.

Practice this method of tensing and relaxing these muscles daily for at least two weeks. After the first week, you'll have memorized the order of the procedure and will be able to do the exercises without looking at the list. To use muscle relaxation as part of habit reversal, do these tense/relax exercises during the two minutes you are doing the competing response. Of course, if you are using your hands as part of the habit reversal (as when you squeeze them together), you will not be able to do steps 1 and 2 of the relaxation procedure. Skip those steps you can't do and continue with the others.

You should feel a reduction in feelings of anxiety and urges to perform your ritual when you've finished this procedure. You can prove this to yourself by using the SUD Scale (described in Chapter 4) to rate how you feel before and after relaxation.

After you've learned muscle relaxation well and have practiced it for several weeks, you can try to bypass the step of tensing your muscles—instead, concentrate on the level of tension within each muscle group and let it become more relaxed.

The second valuable method of relaxation training that I teach my patients is diaphragmatic breathing. With it, you learn to breathe using your diaphragm instead of your rib cage. You may have heard of diaphragmatic breathing before; many actors and singers use it to help them project their voice better in a large theater.

Before you learn diaphragmatic breathing, you should understand how your body breathes. Picture a large bird cage. The steel bars of the cage are like your rib cage, and the floor of the cage is like your diaphragm, the muscle that is stretched across the bottom of your rib cage.

There are two ways of breathing. One is to use your rib cage to expand your lungs. This is how you breathe when you feel out of breath. You can easily tell that you're breathing this way, because your chest will heave as you inhale and relax as you exhale. This kind of breathing is also associated with your body's anxiety or fear response.

A better way for you to breathe is to use your diaphragm to help move air in and out of your lungs. You can tell when you're breathing this way, because your chest barely moves. Most of the movement is in your stomach, which will slowly expand when you inhale and relax when you exhale. Diaphragmatic breathing is associated with relaxation.

Try this yourself now. Put your left hand on your chest and your right hand on your stomach, just above the navel. Take a deep breath and pay attention to the movement in both hands. Most of my patients find that their left hand (the one over their chest) moves more. It heaves when they inhale and relaxes when they exhale. If this also happens to you, then you tend to breathe using your rib cage.

Now try to breathe diaphragmatically. Keep your hands in the same positions. As you take a deep breath, imagine that you're filling your stomach with air. You might also imagine your stomach being like a balloon, which you inflate with air as you inhale and deflate as you exhale. Watch your hands as you breathe. If you see that the hand over your stomach is moving more than the hand over your chest, you are doing it correctly. Try to continue diaphragmatic breathing for two or three minutes.

If you are having trouble getting the knack of diaphragmatic breathing, try this trick: stretch both arms back over your head as far as they will go. Now take a deep breath, keeping your arms above and behind your head, still stretching. You probably noticed that you were able to breathe diaphragmatically that time, for the simple reason that you were preventing your ribs from helping you breathe by keeping the muscles between them stretched. Try breathing this way for a minute or so, or for as long as you can hold your hands above your head. When this rhythm seems natural to you, put your hands back over your chest and stomach and try to breathe diaphragmatically in that position.

If you are still having trouble breathing diaphragmatically, don't worry. Remember, you've been breathing using your rib cage for many years; now you're learning a new habit, and it takes time. Many people find it easier to learn diaphragmatic breathing while lying down, since they are no longer working against gravity. Try this, going through all the steps I've just described.[3]

Once you are able to breathe diaphragmatically, keep your mouth closed[4] and breathe using only your nose; this will automatically help you breathe more slowly and concentrate better. There is no need to hold your breath between inhaling and exhaling; breathe naturally at a speed that is right for you. How can you tell if the speed is right? Listen to yourself breathing—if you can hear the air rushing in and out of your nostrils, then slow down a little until your breathing is silent. This will be the correct speed for you.

Finally, think of the word "relax" during your diaphragmatic breathing practice. Slowly say to yourself the syllable "re" as you inhale. Then slowly say "lax" as you exhale. (Pronounce the syllables silently, not out loud.) The word will sound something like this to you: "(begin to inhale) *reeeeeeeeee*, (begin to exhale) *laaaaaxxxxxxxxx*."

Now practice the entire procedure, making sure you're following all the steps:

1. Put one hand over your stomach and the other over your chest.
2. Breathe so that the hand over your stomach rises as you inhale and falls as you exhale.
3. Breathe silently through your nose.
4. Think of "re" as you inhale, "lax" as you exhale.

3. A book that explains these methods in detail is Albert Forgione and Frederic Bauer's *Fearless Flying*, 1980. Don't be put off by the title. Although the book is about overcoming fears of flying, the authors' clear descriptions of diaphragmatic breathing and muscle relaxation can help you with your OCD problems too.
4. If you find it difficult to breathe with your mouth completely closed, you can leave it open slightly.

Once you are familiar with the procedure, you can remove your hands from your chest and stomach. Finally, you can practice diaphragmatic breathing while standing, until you can do it comfortably in this position.

To incorporate this technique into habit reversal, breathe diaphragmatically during the full two minutes during which you do your competing response. You will probably be more relaxed if you close your eyes while doing this, but if you can't (because other people are around or because you are driving), just keep your eyes open.

4. Contingency Management

For your new habits to last, it is important for them to be rewarded, either by you or by family or friends. "Contingency management" means arranging conditions, or contingencies, so that this will happen often. For example, to reward yourself, first write on an index card examples of the inconvenience, embarrassment, and suffering that came from your hair pulling, along with the advantages you will get from controlling it. Then review this index card frequently to keep motivated, and also to reward yourself whenever you successfully resist an urge to pull your hair. As you improve, you should also plan to take part in enjoyable activities that you would have avoided in the past because of your hair pulling.

Your friends and family can also reward you, by commenting positively on your improved appearance whenever they notice periods when you have controlled your bad habit. This is especially important with children, who usually need encouragement from parents and teachers to continue using habit reversal. Children can earn points, which can be accumulated and then exchanged for activities of their choice, by using habit reversal and by controlling their hair pulling (this method is described in Chapter 5).

5. Generalization Training

It is critical for you to learn how to resist the urges to indulge in tics or hair pulling in many different situations in your life. To do this, after you have learned how to use habit reversal effectively in one situation (say, in your room), then make a list of other situations in which you commonly feel the urge to pull your hair. Then try to *imagine* yourself using habit reversal successfully in each of these situations.

Here is an example of the successful use of habit reversal for trichotillomania.

Sarah was the young woman I described earlier. Although her hairstyle helped to cover the evidence of her hair-pulling rituals, it couldn't disguise her eyebrows and upper eyelashes, which she had plucked smooth.

She told me that she had had this habit since she was seven years old. At that time, she started pulling out her eyelashes. As she got older, when she was feeling angry or afraid, she also began to pluck out her eyebrows, and later her scalp hair. Her problem had escalated over the past two years until it was totally out of control and she came to see me for help. At this point she was pulling her hair out in at least one bout each day.

Sarah learned habit reversal quickly. As I described previously, she had already learned the competing response method. But now I taught her the complete habit reversal method, including awareness training, habit reversal, relaxation (through diaphragmatic breathing), contingency management, and generalization training. By the end of our first session, she knew the procedure well and went home to practice it. When she returned for her second session, she told me she had used the method effectively. As a result, she did not pull out any hair over the next three weeks.

At our third session, Sarah said she had felt increased stress due to arguments with her boyfriend and family and searching for a job. This caused a renewed urge to pull out her hair. We reviewed the habit reversal procedure again, and I gave her advice about more effective ways of dealing with the stresses in her life. After continuing to use the habit reversal techniques effectively, she had only two five-minute episodes of pulling out her hair over the next two months, despite continued stress in her life. She was pleased to see her hair growing back in areas that had been bald before, and she had increased her social activities.

When you use habit reversal for trichotillomania, you should try for complete compliance with the habit reversal procedure. Even if you resist all urges to pull out your hair except for one occasion, on that one occasion you could end up stuck in your ritual for two hours, pulling out large patches of hair. Each time you pull out a particular hair, you increase the chances of damaging the hair follicle and preventing the hair from growing back. Even if the hair does grow back, it will not reach its previous length for a long time, and initially it may look like peach fuzz.

In trichotillomania, as in OCD, the best way to improve your chances of complying with your goals completely is to enlist the aid of a helper. First, have your helper read the sections of this book that relate to your problem. Then ask him or her to let you know whenever you start your ritual. Tell your helper how you are doing each day, and listen to his or her advice and encouragement.

Even though you will aim for 100-percent compliance with habit reversal, don't be too discouraged if you slip up once in a while. This happens to most people at some time or other; as happens with OCD, you'll probably have easy days and difficult days. But don't give up on the difficult days. Discuss your problems with your helper, and try to figure out what caused you to slip up this time and how to prevent it from happening next time. Also pay attention to improvements you have made. Have you reduced the number of times you pulled out your hair by 10 percent or more? Have you noticed any hair growing back? If so, these are signs of progress.

After several weeks of practicing the habit reversal method, your urges should begin to subside. Despite the improvement, you should continue to use the method for several months until you are sure that your problem is under control.

Many patients who cannot control their hair pulling completely can benefit from the combination of habit reversal and SRI medications.[5] After four to twelve weeks on these medications, most people begin to notice a drop in the strength of their urges to pull out their hair. They also find it easier to resist the urges. Details about dosage and side effects of these drugs are included in Chapter 8.

---

5. My colleagues Drs. Nancy Keuthen and Richard O'Sullivan followed many patients for more than a year after treatment and found the majority continued to do very well.

Skin Picking

As publicity about trichotillomania has become more common, more and more patients come to our clinic asking us for help with a related problem: They want us to help them stop their compulsive picking of skin blemishes, pimples, blackheads, or sores. Skin picking (the technical term is "neurotic excoriation") is usually done on the face, upper back, or chest, but may occur almost anywhere—one woman picked through the skin on the soles of her feet until she had dug nearly to the bones and tendons. Like trichotillomania, skin picking often occurs in "bouts" of intensive picking, and it usually occurs in response to a feeling of tension or boredom, but usually without any associated obsessions. Fortunately, the similarity between skin picking and trichotillomania appears to extend to both responding to similar treatments: Many of our patients respond well to treatment with habit reversal, often in addition to taking an SRI medication. If you pick excessively at pimples, blackheads, blemishes or sores, you should first try to apply the habit reversal method described in the preceding section. But if your skin picking problem is very severe, or if you are not able to get it under control with habit reversal, then you should see a psychiatrist experienced with such problems for a trial of an SRI medication (possibly in combination with other medications if this is not successful).

Tourette Disorder

As a young boy, Steven had hated to go to church ever since the day he first shouted bad words in front of all those people. But his parents realized it wasn't his fault: the doctor had told them their son had Tourette Disorder, and he couldn't control the many twitches, grunts, and obscenities he produced.

As Steven grew up, his symptoms changed, and by the time he came to see me he no longer shouted obscenities, although he still had the urge from time to time. Instead, he described to me dozens of twitches, or tics (rapid bodily movements), that he was compelled to enact almost constantly. He couldn't explain rationally why he did these "weird" things—hopping in place, grunting, sniffing, tearing his shirt pockets, or tensing his stomach muscles—which robbed him of so much of his time and energy; he simply felt he had to do them. He was able to resist them for a while, but the urges would build up, like a pressure cooker over an open flame. Eventually unleashed, the tics spilled out, one after another, until Steven felt satisfied.

One day I read Steven a description of Tourette Disorder written by another sufferer,[6] who described his movements and sounds as desperate attempts to "scratch" a "psychic itch." Although scratching the itch could be delayed, the itch built into a supreme tension, an "exquisite torture," which could be relieved only by one of the tics. Steven told me this described his experiences perfectly.[7]

Here are a few of the behaviors that, over the years, Steven felt compelled to perform repeatedly to satisfy this psychic itch: blinking his eyes; grimacing and twitching his face; jerking his head; jerking his shoulder; tensing or jerking his stomach; making various finger or hand movements; kicking his legs; making grunting noises; making animal noises, like barking; making snorting sounds; sniffing or clearing his throat; repeating other people's words; shouting obscene words; and hurling insults at both strangers and friends.

If you have a number of these symptoms or had them in the past, you may also have Tourette Disorder, which is named for Georges Gilles de la Tourette, the French neurologist who first described it, in 1885. If these problems are interfering with your life, you should see a neurologist with experience in treating this disorder to determine if you have it.

One difference between OCD and Tourette Disorder is that OCD patients may feel urges to shout obscenities or insult others, but they never do so, while Tourette Disorder sufferers often act on these urges. In fact, some researchers have suggested that

6. J. Bliss, "Sensory Experiences of Gilles de la Tourette Syndrome," 1980.
7. One way of visualizing the distinction between the tics of Tourette Disorder and the compulsions of OCD is to refer back to the figure on page 53 called "Sample Rates of Change with Behavior Therapy of an OCD Ritual." If you suffer from tics, and resist the behaviors (as shown by the decreased "behaviors" line in the figure), you'll probably find that the "feelings" and "thoughts" lines will instead move *upward*, and stay very high until you finally do the tic behavior.

"one major difference between patients with OCD and TS [Tourette Syndrome] is that whereas patients with OCD ruminate about shouting out obscenities in church, the unfortunate TS patients do so!"[8]

Another major difference between OCD and Tourette Disorder is that patients with OCD can normally give an explanation of why they are performing some ritual. If I ask "Why did you do that?" they may answer, "I checked the lock so that my house wouldn't be robbed." The person with Tourette Disorder, in contrast, usually can't explain why he clears his throat repeatedly, jumps in place, twitches his shoulder, or turns his head to one side. Often he rapidly runs through a series of tics until one is successful at scratching the itch.

This distinction is fascinating to witness in a patient with both OCD and Tourette Disorder symptoms. Besides having Tourette Disorder, Steven, like many other Tourette Disorder sufferers, also had several symptoms of OCD. At our first interview, he told me that he could easily tell which were OCD symptoms: "I know that when I have to wash my hands to keep from getting a disease, or check to make sure noting terrible happens, that this is an OCD symptom." Here is how he described his Tourette Disorder symptoms to me: "Sometimes I just feel like I have to hop, or maybe tear the pocket on my shirt, or throw the car in reverse. I know there is no reason to do these things, but I have to. These are my Tourette symptoms."

When a patient has both OCD and Tourette Disorder symptoms, he or she can usually get control of the OCD symptoms by using the standard behavior therapy techniques of exposure and response prevention. If a doctor diagnoses you as having both Tourette Disorder and OCD symptoms, then you should follow the methods of exposure and response prevention outlined in the previous chapters.

You will probably also benefit from an SRI medication to help reduce your urges to ritualize. But these medications probably won't help your Tourette Disorder symptoms, which require other behavior therapy and medication approaches.

8. Green and Pitman, "Tourette Syndrome and Obsessive-Compulsive Disorder: Clinical Relationships," 1990.

Dr. Nathan Azrin and his associates have successfully used habit reversal to control the tics of patients with Tourette Disorder.[9] Here are a few of his recommendations for competing responses you can use to prevent the tics from occurring. For barking, he suggests you use slow rhythmic breathing through the nose (similar to the diaphragmatic breathing you've learned), with the exhalation slightly longer than the inhalation. For eye squinting, he suggests you blink softly at a rate of one blink every three to five seconds, shifting your gaze downward about every five to ten seconds. For forward shoulder jerking, he suggests you push your hands down and backward against some object, like the arms of a chair if you are sitting, or your thigh if you are standing.

As you can see, patients with this disorder usually have a large number of motor tics (movements) and vocal tics (barking, or pronouncing obscenities). As a result, behavior therapy is a complex process for them. It is important to pick one or two tics to work on, and devise a competing response for each one. While performing the competing responses the patient would also use relaxation to reduce the urge (the psychic itch) that triggers the movement. If you would like to try habit reversal to get control of your Tourette Disorder symptoms, you should look for a behavior therapist with experience in this disorder.

As mentioned earlier, the drugs that help OCD symptoms do little for Tourette Disorder symptoms. But other medications, such as haloperidol (Haldol) and pimozide (Orap), which affect the neurotransmitter dopamine, can provide help. These medications can have serious side effects, and therefore it is necessary for a doctor to monitor your dosage carefully and to discontinue the drugs if they are not helpful. If you would like to try medication for this problem, you should find a psychiatrist (or neurologist) with extensive experience in treating it.

9. Azrin and Peterson, "Behavior Therapy for Tourette's Syndrome and Tic Disorders," 1988.

Excessive Bodily Worries

The following disorders have a common element: The patient has the obsessive thought that there is something wrong with his or her body, either its appearance (body dysmorphic disorder), its normal functioning (bowel or urinary obsession), or a particular medical problem (hypochondriasis).

Body Dysmorphic Disorder

Some patients become convinced that there is something terribly wrong with their appearance. No matter how many times they are reassured by others that they look fine, they stick to their belief.

Imagine getting up one morning, looking in your bathroom mirror, and noticing for the first time that your nose is hideously proportioned, or your ears, or your head. You wonder why you never noticed it before, and you suddenly become conscious of it twenty-four hours a day. Your spouse must be sparing your feelings by not bringing it up at the breakfast table, you think. How, you ask yourself, can they bear to look at me day after day? Surely the Elephant Man was less disfigured.

One such patient was Linda. One day she looked in the mirror and noticed that her face was lined with hideous deep wrinkles. Not ordinary wrinkles, but horrible wrinkles, around her eyes and forehead. How, she asked herself, could a woman of thirty have such wrinkles? Her husband tried to reassure her that her appearance was perfectly normal, but she couldn't be consoled.

This disorder is called body dysmorphic disorder (or BDD for short; until recently it was referred to by its older name, "Dysmorphic phobia") which comes from a combination of the Greek *dys*, a prefix meaning "bad," and *morphe*, for "form." In other words, the person becomes convinced there is something bad about his or her form, or appearance.

Patients with BDD are similar in some respects to OCD patients with pure obsessional thoughts, as mentioned earlier. In both cases, there are no behavioral compulsions or rituals. However, BDD differs from OCD because the content of the thoughts is not sexual, violent, or blasphemous; instead, it always involves the delusional belief that something is wrong with one's body.

Can behavior therapy help BDD? Recent research at our clinic, led by Dr. Sabine Wilhelm, suggests the answer is yes. Dr. Wilhelm recently found dramatic improvements in a group of BDD sufferers having attended her behavioral group treatment program for this problem (it seems there is something therapeutic about being in a group with others who have the same problem). The most important elements in treatment of BDD appear to be: (1) learning how to correct automatic irrational thoughts about your appearance (such as, "I am the ugliest person on earth" or "I will never find a mate because I am so hideous"), (2) being able to look in a mirror for extended periods while describing your appearance *objectively* (for example, rather than focusing immediately on a thought like "my nose is hideous," learn to start with objective facts like "my hair is dark brown and curly, my forehead is mostly smooth with a few shallow creases," etc.), (3) practice exposure by going into the social situations you have been avoiding (perhaps attending parties, dating, or simply walking down the street, or going into busy malls).

BDD can be a serious disorder, and you should try to work with a qualified behavior therapist who has experience with it. You should also see a psychiatrist to determine whether you should try an SRI medication in addition to behavior therapy for this disorder. Dr. Katherine Phillips, a pioneer in the treatment of BDD, has found that SRI medications are effective for many BDD sufferers.[10]

Bowel or Urinary Obsession

We have seen some patients become obsessed with their body's elimination functions. A few become convinced that they are emitting a foul anal odor, which other people can surely smell, when really there is no odor at all. Other patients fear having to have a bowel movement when out of the house and being unable to reach a bathroom; they obsess about this and may spend hours in their bathroom before leaving the house to make sure they are "perfectly empty." Finally, some patients have developed rituals to make sure that all the urine is out of their bladder. As a result,

10. Katherine Phillips' excellent book on BDD (*The Broken Mirror*, New York: Oxford Press, 1996) contains a wealth of information about the treatment of this often disabling disorder.

they may have to stand in a certain way or think certain thoughts while they are urinating. For all these patients, obsessions about normal body functions can come to control their whole life.

Although little research has been done in this area, some patients are able to get control of their symptoms with a combination of behavior therapy and medication, as the following case illustrates.

Diane was a fifty-seven-year-old woman who came to our clinic to be evaluated for agoraphobia and anxiety. She had first developed symptoms twenty years earlier, when, while shopping, she felt an overwhelming urge to defecate. From that time on, she feared losing control of her bowels, particularly in stores. She was unable to leave home without going to the bathroom first. She developed panic attacks a few years before coming to our clinic and avoided situations where these attacks might occur. She appeared anxious but denied having depressive symptoms.

When her symptoms first began, Diane underwent barium enema and psychiatric evaluation, and was told that her problems were all in her head. She was then treated unsuccessfully with medications for her anxiety. She denied having any prior psychiatric symptoms or family history of psychiatric disorder, except for her thirty-one-year-old daughter, who suffered from agoraphobia with panic attacks.

Diane became free of agoraphobic, bowel-obsessive, and panic symptoms after taking 50 to 75 milligrams of imipramine daily for two weeks. At the same time that she started taking imipramine, she began behavior therapy, which consisted of relaxation, correcting her irrational thoughts, and exposure therapy, in which she took increasingly longer walks and entered stores either accompanied by her therapist or alone. At the latest follow-up, she had been seen for twenty-one sessions of behavior therapy and was still free of bowel obsessions.[11]

If you are subject to any rituals or obsessions connected with elimination, you can try to use the exposure and response pre-

11. This case was reported in Jenike et al., "Bowel Obsessions Responsive to Tricyclic Antidepressants in Four Patients," 1987.

vention methods outlined earlier, preferably with a helper. But many patients with these problems refuse the assistance of a helper, since they are dealing with subjects that are extremely private. If you find that you are not able to carry out exposure and response prevention on your own, you should contact a behavior therapist who has experience in treating your kind of disorder.

SRI medications and some of the older antidepressants, like imipramine, are very effective in reducing these obsessions. In our clinic we refer patients for a trial of medication for their problem, whether or not they undergo behavior therapy. Because these problems can dominate a person's life, we want to help get them under control as rapidly as possible.

Hypochondriasis

What if you were sure that there was something terribly wrong with your body? Even though the doctors tell you your tests are perfect, you know they are wrong. You are convinced that your heart is defective. Soon you will have a heart attack. Did you just feel your heart skip a beat? That proves it. You're sure you're going to die.

This was what happened to Robert. In addition to performing several OCD rituals involving checking and repeating, Robert was convinced that he was very ill. He usually worried that he was going to have a heart attack. But sometimes he also became convinced that he had oral cancer, or bowel cancer, or AIDS.

Although Robert was able to get good control of his OCD rituals with behavior therapy, his fears about his health remained. This is hypochondriasis. Remember that Robert had no reason to believe he was ill. Although he worried about every ache and pain, all his medical tests were normal, and he got reassurance from all his doctors. Whether hypochondriasis is related to OCD can only be determined by further research

Monosymptomatic hypochondriasis is slightly different from hypochondriasis, which is a general concern about one's health. Hypochondriacal patients, like Robert, may be worried about many different aspects of their health, and their concerns may change over time. But "monosymptomatic" refers to one symp-

tom. The patient with this disorder is convinced there is something wrong with *one part* of his or her body only. If Robert worried *only* that a *particular* part of his body was decaying or emitting
a foul odor, then he would have monosymptomatic hypochondriasis.

Can behavior therapy help with hypochondriacal fears? This is
a difficult question to answer. On the one hand, behavior therapy
will not *cure* this problem; on the other hand, behavior therapy
can help keep your worries in check so that you live and enjoy
your life despite having these worries. Unlike the large majority
of OCD sufferers, if you have hypochondriasis you probably *really*
believe that there truly is something wrong with your body, which
the doctors have not yet been able to find. As you know, fixed beliefs such as these often prove resistant to exposure techniques
because the next time a new physical symptom appears (and it
will, since we all have sensations in our body that could cause us
concern if we focused our attention on them full-time!), it will
strengthen your conviction that you are really very sick. If you
then go off to check this out with yet another doctor or to have
yet another medical test, the worries will probably return in full
strength. Dr. Paul Salkovskis at Oxford believes that cognitive
therapy, by teaching you how to examine and correct your irrational automatic thoughts about your health, may be helpful in
dealing with hypochondriasis.

I have found that it is most important that you find *one* doctor
whom you like and trust, who understands about your hypochondriacal concerns, and who will be able to give you honest information in a caring way, without providing you with excessive
reassurance—for which you will almost certainly beg at some
time.

If you think you have hypochondriasis, and you have been
thoroughly checked out physically, you should find a psychiatrist
or psychologist with experience in this field.

In any case, whether using behavior therapy or medication,
you will need to have a therapist working with you to help get
control of your problem.

A final note about behavior therapy for hypochondriasis: several patients I have seen with hypochondriasis also suffered from
panic disorder (the symptoms of panic are listed in Chapter 5).

These patients misinterpret their anxiety symptoms as signs of a serious disease.

If you have both hypochondriasis and panic attacks, a behavior therapist can help teach you how to control your panic attacks as well as how to correctly interpret your body's signals. This approach is usually called cognitive-behavioral treatment for panic attacks. You may also probably benefit from trying a medication that controls panic attacks; some effective medications are alprazolam (Xanax) and donazepam (Klonopin).

CHAPTER EIGHT

• •

Medications for OCD

• •

"Hast Thou, pellucid, in Thy azure depths, medicine for case like mine?"

—*Walt Whitman (1819—1892)*

If you walked into any large OCD clinic today to ask for help with your symptoms, the chances are good that your doctor would suggest both behavior therapy *and* an antidepressant medication. Why is this? When behavior therapy for OCD was first developed, in the 1960s and 1970s, there were no other proven treatments offering relief for this chronic disorder. Various medications had been tried for OCD, but none was consistently effective. However, over the last decade, with our recognition that an estimated 2 to 3 percent of the population may suffer from OCD at some point, there have been many experimental studies of more effective antidepressant medications, like clomipramine (Anafranil) and fluoxetine (Prozac).

Medications like these have both advantages and disadvantages when compared with behavior therapy. On the positive side, taking a medication is easier than behavior therapy, which requires a great deal of hard work. On the negative side, medications used for OCD produce side effects, as do most drugs. Although these medications are usually mild and tolerable, patients occasionally experience unwanted side effects and have to stop taking them. In addition, many patients relapse soon after discontinuing these medications.

Millie, the woman I described in Chapter 2 who truly believed she would be contaminated and eventually develop cancer, provides a good example of the need for the combined use of medication in patients who are not able to succeed with behavior therapy alone. I could treat Millie successfully with behavior therapy only after she began taking medication for these thoughts.

After a few weeks on fluoxetine, Millie's thoughts began to change. Although still wary, she was no longer certain that she would contract cancer. She was then able to make progress confronting her fears with the combination treatment of behavior therapy and fluoxetine, and within two months was back living in her apartment and working. When I last spoke to her she was still taking fluoxetine, and she proudly told me how, on her own, she had successfully completed the behavior therapy she was unable to do months before.

Patients with pure obsessions often respond quickly to medications when behavior therapy alone cannot control their thoughts. I learned this firsthand from one of my first patients with OCD. This young woman woke up one morning and found that she was obsessed with the thoughts "Am I a homosexual?" and "Could I become a homosexual?" She had no homosexual urges and was upset by these thoughts. She performed no rituals but worried day and night about these questions, to the extent that they ruined her life.

Soon after I first saw this young woman, her psychiatrist prescribed phenelzine (Nardil). When I saw her again two weeks later I was amazed by the remarkable change—her thoughts had simply stopped. She told me that her life was back to normal. As long as she stayed on the medication, her thoughts remained under control. When she stopped taking the medication, her thoughts returned.

In this chapter you'll learn about the role of medications in treating OCD, which medications are proven effective and in what doses, and what side effects are usually experienced. Common questions about medication for OCD are answered, and the combination treatment of behavior therapy and medication is discussed. When you finish this chapter, you should be an informed consumer about medication for OCD, and you'll have an idea as to whether it may help your OCD problems. Of course, all medication should be taken under the close supervision of your physician or therapist.

SRI Medications

Over the past ten years several medications have come on the market which can greatly reduce the symptoms of OCD. Before describing each drug individually, I want to encourage you to think about the serotonin-reuptake inhibiting (SRI) medications *as a group* (this is how many of us who treat OCD think about them today). Clomipramine (Anafranil) was the first such medication available, and was the first medication formally approved by the U.S. Food and Drug Administration (FDA) to be advertised for the treatment of OCD. Next to become available was fluoxetine (Prozac), a popular antidepressant drug that was also found to help reduce OCD symptoms. (Despite never having been specifically approved by the FDA to be advertised for treating OCD, it is widely used by doctors for this purpose.) Next to become available was fluvoxamine (Luvox), followed by sertraline (Zoloft) and paroxetine (Paxil), and most recently citalopram (Celexa).

These six SRI medications have two very important things in common: (1) all help reduce (but not eliminate) OCD symptoms in most patients who take them, and (2) all increase the availability of the neurotransmitter serotonin in the brain. Although there are differences of opinion about which of these SRI drugs is *most* effective for OCD, it is probably best to consider all of them as being about equally effective in treating OCD,[1] while differing mainly in their side effect profile.

If you see a physician for medication for your OCD symptoms, you should expect to be prescribed one of these six SRI drugs. If instead of these drugs, your doctor prescribes some other medication for your OCD, you should politely ask him or her to explain why they are not recommending that you start with what is generally agreed upon as the first line drug treatment for OCD

1. Michael A. Jenike, "Drug Treatment of Obsessive-Compulsive Disorders," in Jenike et al., *Obsessive-Compulsive Disorders,* 3rd ed., 1998.

today. Your doctor will decide which SRI drug to prescribe for you after talking with you about your particular situation. If the first SRI drug you take is not effective (after you've taken a sufficient dose for at least three months), then your doctor will probably suggest that you switch to one of the other SRI medications for a second trial, which is then often effective.

How much do patients improve with SRI drugs? The results are similar to those in behavior therapy—most patients are greatly improved, but almost none will get 100 percent better. Using the YBOCS score as a guide, any patient whose score improves between 25 percent and 35 percent or more after taking an SRI drug is usually considered a "drug responder," and more than half of those participating in our studies of these drugs have been responders.

Now let's examine separately each of these six first-line medications for treating OCD.

Clomipramine

As you learned in Chapter 2, the early 1970s saw a breakthrough in the medication treatment of OCD with the use of clomipramine. Clomipramine is very similar to other tricyclic (meaning the chemical structure has three rings) antidepressants, like imipramine (Tofranil) and amitriptyline (Elavil). The only structural difference between clomipramine and imipramine is the substitution of a single chloride atom. But this small change in structure alters the way clomipramine affects the brain neurotransmitter serotonin. One effect of clomipramine is to keep more serotonin available in the spaces, or synapses, between nerve cells, enabling these cells to transmit signals. Studies indicate that this is important for a medication to help alleviate OCD symptoms.

Although clomipramine was not approved by the FDA for marketing in the United States until January 1990, it had already been a popular antidepressant drug in Europe, South America, and Canada for two decades. European psychiatrists, including Dr. J. J. Lopez-Ibor in Spain, first noticed that clomipramine helped many patients with OCD, and in 1982 Dr. Marie Asberg and her associates in Sweden confirmed that it was effective in reducing OCD symptoms. Their research suggested an initial treatment of five to ten weeks. They further recommended that, once a patient's symptoms had been alleviated by this treatment, the medication be taken for a prolonged period, probably several years. But even at that early stage of research in OCD, Dr. Asberg and her colleagues were already advocating the combination of clomipramine with behavior therapy.

In the decade since Dr. Asberg's research, there have been many studies at OCD centers like our own indicating that clomipramine is an effective treatment for OCD.

Side Effects and Dose Range

The most common side effects are dry mouth, dizziness, constipation, and sexual difficulties (total or partial inability to experience orgasm). There is a small risk of seizures at doses of over 250 milligrams. But we now know that seizures are very unlikely if the total daily dosage of clomipramine is kept at 250 milligrams per day or lower for adults.

Patients are often uncomfortable discussing sexual issues, and as a result they rarely volunteer information about sexual side effects. We have found, however, that when we *specifically* ask patients whether they are having sexual problems as a result of taking clomipramine, perhaps as may as 50 percent of both sexes admit having such problems. Like all the side effects of clomipramine, sexual problems will disappear within a few days after either decreasing the dose or discontinuing the medication.[2] Most of our patients tolerate clomipramine well, and few discontinue the medication because of side effects.

Occasionally, low dosages of clomipramine given over short periods may result in significant improvement in symptoms. But to demonstrate a full effect, treatment should continue for at least ten to twelve weeks, at dosages up to 250 milligrams per day. Improvements in OCD symptoms may not be seen until after four to eight weeks of treatment with clomipramine.

2. Ibid.

Fluoxetine

Fluoxetine, a cyclic antidepressant, became available in the United States in February 1987 and has been approved in the United States by the FDA for treating depression. Because fluoxetine, like clomipramine, affects the brain neurotransmitter serotonin,[3] it has also been prescribed for patients with OCD at our clinic and other clinics, with encouraging results. A number of studies now suggest that fluoxetine has strong effects on the obsessions and compulsions of OCD.

Side Effects and Dose Range

Dr. Jack Gorman, in his recent book, *The Essential Guide to Psychiatric Drugs*, uses a simile to convey the side effects of fluoxetine (referred to here by its trade name):

> The side effects can be likened to drinking too much black coffee at once: jitteriness, nausea, stomach cramps, and diarrhea. Some patients get a headache and have trouble falling asleep while on Prozac. There are scattered reports of difficulty achieving orgasm while taking Prozac. Overall, however, these side effects are usually very mild and often do not occur at all. . . . Almost everybody can safely take Prozac.

Keep in mind that Dr. Gorman, among others, also advises that, "with few exceptions, patients who have obsessive-compulsive disorder should also have behavioral psychotherapy."[4]

As was the case with clomipramine, if we specifically asked patients about sexual side effects, the percentage of patients reporting a problem was fairly high. All of these side effects are reversible; they go away soon after the person stops taking fluoxetine.

---

3. Fluoxetine has the effect of making more serotonin available in the synapses between nerve cells. Normally, serotonin is quickly reabsorbed by the transmitting nerve cell (this is called reuptake). Fluoxetine (as well as other SRI drugs) delays this reuptake so the serotonin remains in the synapse longer, and brain signals can pass through. As a result, these drugs are called serotonin reuptake inhibitors.
4. Gorman, *The Essential Guide to Psychiatric Drugs*, 1990.

From our clinical experience, it appears that 40 to 80 milligrams per day is required for optimal outcome in OCD patients, compared with dosages of 20 to 40 milligrams for treatment of depression. But some patients with OCD seem to respond to the lower doses as well. If patents have a good response to fluoxetine, then they may be able to take lower maintenance dosages.

Fluvoxamine

Fluvoxamine is a cyclic antidepressant medication that has been shown to be effective in treating OCD. Like fluoxetine and clomipramine, it affects serotonin, allowing more serotonin to remain in the synapses between nerve cells.

Several studies at OCD centers like ours have indicated that fluvoxamine is an effective treatment for many patients with OCD. Patients may have to wait between six and twelve weeks until fluvoxamine's positive influence on obsessions and compulsions becomes apparent.

Side Effects and Dose Range

Side effects are mild and consist mainly of insomnia, nausea, fatigue, and headache.

In our study of fluvoxamine the maximum dose was 300 milligrams per day, and seventeen of the eighteen patients in the group were able to take this dose. The remaining patient was unable to take more than 200 milligrams per day.

Sertraline

Sertraline has been approved by the FDA for the treatment of depression and OCD. It works by slowing the removal of serotonin from the synapses between nerve cells in the brain, thus making more serotonin available. Several studies have found sertraline to be more effective than a placebo pill in treating OCD.

Side Effects and Dose Range

Studies have used various doses of sertraline between 50 to 200 milligrams a day, and have found all doses to be effective and to produce mild side effects that are tolerated well.

Paroxetine

Paroxetine has been approved by the FDA for the treatment of depression and panic disorder. However, it has also been found effective in the treatment of OCD. It is thought to work by slowing the reabsorption of serotonin.

Side Effects and Dose Range

A large study found that doses of 40 to 60 milligrams per day of paroxetine are effective for OCD. Side effects are generally mild and similar to those of other SRI medications.

Citalopram

Citalopram has been approved by the FDA for advertisement in the treatment of depression. However, it has been found to help reduce OCD symptoms, and like the other drugs listed here, it works by slowing the reabsorption of serotonin by nerve endings in the brain, so that the neurotransmitter stays available longer to transmit impulses between the cells.

Side Effects and Dose Range

Citalopram is prescribed in dosages of 40 to 60 milligrams per day. Its side effects are generally mild, and similar to the other SRI medications.

MAOIs

If SRF drugs are not effective for you, some other medications that may help OCD symptoms are MAOIs (monoamine oxidase inhibitors), which are available by prescription. These are a group of antidepressant drugs that have been successfully used for many years in treating depression and panic attacks. The most common MAOIs are phenelzine and tranylcypromine (Parnate). We recently found that MAOIs may only be helpful for a subgroup of OCD sufferers with symmetry, or other atypical obsession.[5]

When we first established our OCD clinic, before clomipramine and fluoxetine were available, Dr. Jenike often prescribed an MAOI for patients with OCD. The case history at the beginning of this chapter, of the patient whose homosexual obsessions disappeared soon after starting to take phenelzine, shows how dramatic improvement can be in some cases. Today, these medications are sometimes used as a second- or third-line treatment, if a patient doesn't respond to SRI drugs.

Side Effects and Dose Ranges

MAOIs have few side effects when they are used correctly, but there are dietary restrictions that must be followed. Patients on MAOIs must not eat foods containing large amounts of tyramine, a substance found in many fermented foods like aged cheese, beer, and sour cream; a rapid, dangerous increase in blood pressure can result if foods containing tyramine are eaten in combination with MAOIs. If your doctor prescribes an MAOI, make sure he or she gives you a full list of foods and drugs to avoid and also discusses the procedures involved in taking the medication. If you follow your doctor's recommendations carefully, MAOIs have few side effects.

The other caution is that *it is critical to wait at least five weeks* after stopping another serotonergic antidepressant (like clomipramine or fluoxetine) before starting an MAOI. Deaths have resulted when these drugs have been used at an interval of less than five weeks.

In our clinic, phenelzine usually is prescribed in doses of 15 to

5. Jenike, "Drug Treatment of Obsessive-Compulsive Disorder," 1998.

90 milligrams per day (with 60 to 90 milligrams per day most common). Tranylcypromine usually is taken in doses of 10 to 60 milligrams per day (with 40 to 60 milligrams per day most common).

What Other Medications Can Help OCD?

Almost every antianxiety, antidepressant, and antipsychotic drug has been tried at one time or another for OCD. Although there are one or more case reports of many of these drugs working in individual patients, there is no strong evidence that they can help most patients with OCD.

In rare patients, OCD symptoms are obviously the result of depression. These patients had no OCD symptoms before becoming severely depressed but developed them soon after their depression set in. Traditional antidepressants like imipramine (Tofranil) or amitriptyline (Elavil) can usually reduce this depression, and OCD symptoms then either decrease on their own or with brief behavior therapy, as was illustrated by the case of Martha in Chapter 2, the woman who was successfully treated for her compulsion to write down and remember meaningless bits of information. Newer antidepressants like buproprion (Wellbutrin) and venlafaxine (Effexor) are sometimes used to treat OCD.

Some other medications seem to help improve OCD symptoms when *added* to a medication like clomipramine or fluoxetine, but not when given *alone*. When used with other drugs, these medications are called augmenters, since they augment, or enhance, the effect of the anticompulsive medication

Some medications that show promise as augmenters include lithium, clonazepam (Klonopin), trazodone (Desyrel), buspirone (Buspar), alprazolam (Xanax), methylphenidate (Ritalin), haloperidol (Haldol), pimozide (Orap), and the neuroleptics: clozapine (Clozanil), risperidone (Risperdal), and olanzapine (Zyprexa).[6]

If your doctor prescribes one of these medications as an augmenter, make sure you ask about the proper way to take the medication and about side effects. Some of these medications, such as

---

6. Neuroleptic drugs decrease the amount of the neurotransmitter dopamine in the brain, which appears to help OCD sufferers who also suffer from tics (or from very strong beliefs that their obsessions are true).

haloperidol and pimozide, can have serious and long-term side effects if used incorrectly or for a long period of time.

Common Questions About Medications for OCD

In conversations with patients, and some colleagues, certain questions about medications come up over and over. To clarify these issues, I collected the most common questions and posed them to my colleague Dr. Michael Jenike, a psychiatrist at Massachusetts General Hospital. Dr. Jenike and I have worked closely together for almost ten years, studying various treatments for OCD. He was a pioneer in testing many of the drugs now in common use for OCD and is an internationally known expert on medication treatment of OCD.

Q. What do antiobsessional medications have in common?

A. Most medications that are effective in the treatment of OCD are thought to have effects on a brain chemical called serotonin. Clomipramine, fluoxetine, fluvoxamine, sertraline, paroxetine, and citalopram all block reuptake of serotonin at the points where nerves connect in the brain—the synapses— and allow serotonin to remain in these important areas for a longer time. We think that this increased serotonin produces changes, over a period of a few weeks, in receptors (areas where serotonin attaches) in some of the membranes of the nerves. We also believe that these receptors may be abnormal in patients with OCD and that the changes that occur in them due to these medications at least partly reverse the abnormalities. This is only part of how drugs work; it is very likely that other brain chemicals in addition to serotonin are involved.

*Q. Who should **not** take antiobsessional medications?*

A. In general, we don't give antiobsessional medications to women who are pregnant or are breast-feeding. Since we do not clearly understand the effects of these drugs on a fetus or infant, this is the wisest course of action. If severe OCD cannot be controlled any other way, these medications seem to be quite safe, however.

In very elderly patients, it is best to avoid some of the medications like clomipramine, which have side effects that can interfere with thinking and can cause or worsen confusion in the elderly. Some of the other antiobsessional drugs, like fluoxetine, can be used by the elderly, but greatly reduced dosages are usually needed.

Although these drugs can be taken by patients with heart disorders, special caution is required, and close monitoring with frequent cardiograms is necessary.

Q. Will I have to take antiobsessional medications forever?

A. No one knows yet how long patients should take these medications once they have been effective. Many patients are able to discontinue medications after a six- to twelve-month treatment period. But it is likely that about half of OCD patients will need to be on at least a low dosage of medication for years. We are now studying which patients can discontinue the medications, and what is the best way to help patients withdraw from them. It seems likely that the risk of relapse will be lower if patients learn to use behavior therapy techniques while they are doing well on medications. These techniques may then enable patients to control any symptoms that return when they stop taking medication.

Q. Do antiobsessional medications cause long-term, irreversible side effects?

A. As far as we know there are no irreversible side effects caused by the SRI drugs or the MAOIs. Many patients have used them for years without difficulties. Some of the drugs that are occasionally used—such as the antipsychotic, or neuroleptic drugs, like haloperidol, chlorpromazine (Thorazine), thioridazine (Mellaril), and trifluoperazine (Stelazine)—*can* produce irreversible neurologic problems, such as shaking or tongue thrusting. These drugs are best avoided in patients with the usual forms of OCD; if they are used, it should generally be for only a few weeks. Occasionally patients need to remain on these potentially dangerous drugs for longer periods of time.

Q. Should I take antiobsessional medications only when I am feeling stressed?

A. No. This is a common mistake. These medications are meant to be taken on a regular basis to maintain a constant level in your bloodstream. Take them at the times your doctor tells you to, and try never to miss a dose.

Q. What kind of doctor should I look for to prescribe these antiobsessional medications?

A. Although any licensed physician can legally prescribe these drugs, it is probably best to deal directly with a board-certified psychiatrist who understands OCD. A list of psychiatrists with special interest in OCD can be obtained from the OC Foundation, a national organization based in Connecticut (the foundation's address is given in Chapter 9). It is important to find a psychiatrist who is also a psychopharmacologist; that is, one who has special knowledge about the use of drugs to treat psychiatric disorders.

Q. What if I feel as if I've failed because I need a drug to help me?

A. A helpful way of thinking about the use of medication for severe OCD is to compare your illness with a common medical disorder such as diabetes. There is growing evidence that OCD is, in fact, a neurological or medical illness and not simply a result of some problem in the environment or of inadequate upbringing. As with the diabetic who needs insulin to live a normal life, some OCD patients need anticompulsive medication to function normally; diabetics also often feel angry and upset about having to take insulin. There is no evidence that OCD is a result of anything that the patient has done, and it is best to consider it a chemical disorder in a part of the brain.

Q. What if I'm afraid to take medications because of my obsessional fears about drugs?

A. Usually with reassurance from a doctor that you trust, your fears can be overcome. If you still refuse to take medication, behavior therapy can be started first, and part of the therapy can focus on your reluctance to take medication. Our experience indicates that the combination of medication and behavior therapy will maximize your improvement.[7]

Q. How long does it take antiobsessional medications to work?

A. Don't give up on a medication until you have been taking it at a therapeutic dose for ten to twelve weeks. Many patients feel no effects for the first few weeks of treatment, but then they improve greatly. We don't know why the medications take so long to work for OCD. Even many psychiatrists give up on the medications after four to six weeks, since this is the time it takes for depressed patients to improve. Thus, you may have to remind your psychiatrist to keep you on the medication longer.

Combining Medication with Behavior Therapy

Patients often ask me whether they can or should take medications while engaged in behavior therapy. Although a good number of patients with mild OCD symptoms, or rituals like compulsive cleaning or checking, can get control of their symptoms with behavior therapy alone, many others benefit from the combination of behavior therapy and the medications described in this chapter.

Like Dr. Jenike, most psychiatrists and behavior therapists today believe that combining behavior therapy and medication is an efficient approach to treating many patients—adults, children, and adolescents—with moderate or severe OCD. I tell my patients that taking antidepressant or antiobsessional medications cannot interfere with their progress with behavior therapy; if anything, it will only help them more.

---

7. One woman was unable to take a pill no matter how much reassurance and support I gave her; she was sure it would poison her. As part of behavior therapy, over several visits I helped her get used to taking fluoxetine in these small steps: (a) having the bottle of pills on the table in front of her; (b) touching the bottle; (c) holding a pill in her hand; (d) dissolving the pill in water, after receiving instructions from the drug manufacturer. She then drank one sip the first day, building up slowly over several weeks to an effective dose.

Often, SRI drugs can reduce strong obsessional thoughts and urges, and also control any strong depression or anxiety that may interfere with behavior therapy. As a result, many patients who had difficulty with behavior therapy at first are able to participate in it easily after responding to a medication. The following case history illustrates just such an instance.

Mary had severe OCD. She worried constantly that she had said the wrong thing. She feared contamination from touching her own body, and washed her hands over and over. Mary would not touch the floor, trash can, or anything that had touched either.

She asked for reassurance from her parents many times each hour. She was so unsure of herself that, although in her late twenties, she slept at night with her mother. She did not even trust herself to handle cooking utensils when her parents were out of the house.

When Mary came to our clinic she was unable to function on her own. She could no longer work and had stopped driving. She couldn't stand to be away from her parents. At first it was impossible to have a conversation with her; she continually worried that she had said something wrong and had hurt my feelings, so she repeatedly apologized profusely. As a result, she was unable to concentrate on our conversation.

Mary did try behavior therapy with me. But because of her extreme anxiety and poor concentration, she couldn't complete her home practice assignments. Although she did succeed in learning to sleep alone, she wasn't able to control any other obsessions or compulsions

At Dr. Jenike's recommendation, Mary made an appointment with a colleague of ours in Canada to be evaluated for clomipramine, which at that time wasn't available in the United States. During the first month of taking the drug, she noticed only the side effects of dry mouth and constipation.

But, after two months on the medication, Mary's condition began to change dramatically. Her worries about having said the wrong thing decreased, she felt more sure of herself, and she became less dependent on her parents. Her fears about contamination also decreased. Overall, Mary's symptoms improved by more than 50 percent. Although not perfect, she was now able to function on her own. She soon moved into her own apartment and enrolled in college.

When we again tried behavior therapy, this time with Mary still taking clomipramine, she was able to work hard and reduced her symptoms even more. She has now remained on the medication for more than three years and continues to do well.

As you can see, behavior therapy and medication should not be considered mutually exclusive treatments for OCD. In our OCD clinic, we may treat patients either with medications alone, behavior therapy alone, or a combination of the two.

When should you consider trying medication for your OCD symptoms? If you have less severe cleaning and checking rituals, you'll probably do very well with behavior therapy alone. But if you spend eight or twelve hours a day performing rituals, or you are severely depressed or anxious, or you strongly believe in your obsessions, or you have only obsessions without compulsions, or your compulsions are more like tics, then you should probably try a medication in addition to behavior therapy.

In the event that you are unable to carry out the necessary exposure and response prevention practice either with a helper or with a behavior therapist, SRI drugs can make it easier for you to get control of your problems.

CHAPTER NINE

●●

Your Questions Answered

●●

"Come to the edge, He said.
They said, We are afraid.
Come to the edge, He said.
They came.
He pushed them . . . and they flew."
—Guillaume Apollinaire (1880–1918)

Despite my best efforts in the previous chapters to give you all the information you'll need to get control of your OCD symptoms, you probably still have some questions. This chapter answers the most common ones I've been asked by my patients and those who have been part of our support groups.

To help me answer these queries, I've tapped the collective wisdom of my past and present behavior therapy colleagues in the Massachusetts General Hospital OCD Clinic: Drs. William Minichiello, Nancy Keuthen, Deborah Osgood-Hynes, Sabine Wilhelm, John Hurley, and Joseph Ricciardi. Our group of psychologists has had as much experience treating OCD with behavior therapy (with and without medication) over the years as any other group in the world. I've incorporated their answers in the following responses to actual questions from our patients.

Q. I've tried to stop these rituals on my own—what will be different in behavior therapy?

A. Our answer is simple: with behavior therapy you'll approach your problems in a *systematic* way for the first time, using scientific principles to help you change your behaviors for the better. You'll approach your problems gradually, and your behavior therapist will teach you how to cope with the anxiety you will feel.

All patients have tried on their own to control their symptoms before coming to see us for behavior therapy. The fact that they are now seeing a behavior therapist indicates that they've failed in their many attempts.

Trying to get control of OCD symptoms on your own, without behavior therapy, is like trying to get a college degree on your own, without enrolling in a program. You can have all the books you need for your degree just sitting there in a library. But if you don't have a teacher to assign lessons and give you feedback on your work, you're not going to make much progress.

Q. *Don't I have to understand* why *I have these obsessions and compulsions instead of learning about behavior therapy? It seems so simple and mechanical.*

A. There is rarely a single underlying cause for a particular behavior. Some actions are the results of complex causes and others are simply habits. In either case, behavior therapists try to change the problem behavior directly. If along the way the person also understands why he or she was performing the action, that's wonderful. But we've seen too many patients who come to us after years of therapy who "understand" why they are performing their rituals but still can't stop them. More important, we believe, is to help you identify current problems (anxiety or depression, or specific situations) that are triggering your OCD symptoms. Identifying these problems then helps you control your own habits.

Behavior therapy may appear mechanical, but it is important to understand the principles underlying this treatment so you can apply the technique with confidence and without fear of causing any harm.

Q. *Don't I have to clear up my family, marriage, or work problems before I can work on my OCD symptoms?*

A. Like everyone else, people with OCD commonly have problems in several areas of their life: finances, marriage, family, or job. They often ask me whether they can successfully work on their OCD symptoms while they still have these problems. As you already know, stress of any kind can increase the severity of OCD symptoms—most people have more obsessive thoughts or stronger urges when they are depressed, angry, or anxious. It therefore only makes sense that you should try to resolve your other problems *at the same time* that you are getting control of your OCD symptoms. If you don't, you may run the risk of a return of your OCD symptoms during stressful periods in the future. For example, if someone I'm treating is not working, I encourage the individual to get a part-time or volunteer job as he or she starts to control the OCD symptoms. Many patients find that when they stay at home all day with nothing to occupy their mind, their OCD symptoms become worse. If there is anything else you can do to reduce the major stresses in your life, do it. This will make it easier for you to get control of your OCD symptoms.

Other kinds of therapy focus on marriage or family problems first, rather than directly on the OCD symptoms. But behavior therapists find that by changing OCD symptoms first, personal relationships usually improve automatically. I tell my patients, "Why not assume that your relationship with your spouse [or other family member] will get better as you get control of your OCD symptoms? If there are really problems in your relationship, these will become crystal clear to you, either as you try to work with the other person in practice sessions, or once you are functioning normally again."

Q. Won't relaxation, meditation or hypnosis help my OCD?

A. Although we use these methods very successfully in treating other anxiety problems, like phobias or panic attacks, we have found that they have little use in the treatment of OCD. In fact, relaxation training by itself seems to do so little to help OCD symptoms that some researchers have used relaxation as a placebo treatment against which to compare the effects of exposure and response prevention.[1] As I described in Chapter 5, however, these techniques can be used *along with* exposure

1. Rachman and Hodgson, *Obsessions and Compulsions*, 1980.

and response prevention to help you deal with any anxiety you feel during this treatment. These techniques can also be used *along with* habit reversal in treating trichotillomania or Tourette Disorder, as you learned in Chapter 7.

The one exception seems to be the use of hypnosis in treating trichotillomania. There are several reports of hypnosis alone helping adults and children with this disorder who were very hypnotizable after only a few sessions. The subject hasn't been studied extensively, but you might want to see a qualified hypnotist if other methods are not successful in stopping your hair pulling.

Q. If my OCD is very severe, can behavior therapy help me?

A. Yes. We have successfully treated many patients with severe OCD in our clinic. But most of these patients have taken medications while practicing behavior therapy. Chapter 8 describes the medications that are helpful for OCD symptoms. The chances are that if your OCD is very severe (as assessed in Chapter 3), you will have to see a behavior therapist for professional help in getting control of your symptoms, and your therapist probably will recommend drugs as part of your treatment.

But be optimistic: even though behavior therapy may take longer for severe symptoms than for mild symptoms, you can be helped. Dr. Minichiello once told me, "I have yet to come across a patient who was strongly motivated to work hard (either doing the exposure and response prevention with me, a family member, or alone) who didn't get better."

Q. My problem is hair pulling. How much improvement can I realistically expect, and how long will it take?

A. If you are strongly motivated to work on your problem, you can expect rapid and dramatic improvement with behavior therapy. But if you are not willing to work hard, then you probably won't improve much. This is true for all compulsive behaviors. Getting control of the problem must be one of the most important priorities in your life.

I've found that patients with trichotillomania whom I've

treated with behavior therapy have fallen about equally into one of two categories: those who, regardless of their age, are very motivated to work hard and are able to control all or almost all of their hair pulling after only a few sessions (like some of the patients described in Chapter 7, many are able to stop after the first or second session), and those who are less motivated and have trouble complying with the habit reversal procedure from the first session on. Many of these patients become frustrated, embarrassed, or angry, and drop out of treatment.

Work hard and stay optimistic. There's no reason not to expect that you can learn how to inhibit this behavior. One patient with a severe case of trichotillomania always wore a hat or scarf, and she would even pull the hair out of wigs. She learned that for her, pulling out her hair meant she was overstressed and needed to reduce her commitments. Now she uses her occasional urges as a *signal* to stop and reduce the stresses in her life. She has a stylish haircut and has pulled out only a few hairs over the last four months.

Q. Are there any support groups I can join?

A. Yes. As I described in Chapter 1, many of our patients find that talking to someone else with similar problems can be helpful. Often this is the first time they have even met anyone else with OCD. Before joining a support group, some patients had trouble believing that anyone else even had the same problem.

In these groups, patients exchange information about behavior therapy, medications, and dealing with family and friends who don't fully understand OCD. Getting support from others with problems like your own will give you added motivation to get control of your own symptoms. You will also have a chance to share the knowledge you gain to help someone else with OCD.

The OC Foundation (337 Notch Hill Road, North Branford, CT 06471; Telephone (203) 315-2190; email: info@ocfoundation.org; website: www.ocfoundation.org) provides information about support groups in many areas of the country. If there is no group in your area, the foundation can give you information on how to get a support group started.

Q. Isn't it dangerous to suppress rituals?

A. Not at all. This fear comes from Freudian theories that performing rituals prevents potentially dangerous anxiety from coming to the surface. We now know that this is not true. In fact, research with hundreds of patients shows that the worst result of suppressing rituals is a temporary increase in anxiety. But most patients tell me that the anxiety they felt during response prevention was much less than they expected. Although some people do experience strong anxiety during behavior therapy, this is not dangerous, and no one has ever gone crazy from resisting OCD rituals. Don't forget that having OCD causes patients plenty of anxiety already, just in dealing with their everyday life. Of the hundreds of patients we've treated, we've never seen anyone who was harmed by resisting rituals in response prevention.

Q. Isn't the relationship with the therapist the important thing?

A. It's true that it is important to find a therapist or a helper whom you can trust and work with. But behavior therapy puts much less emphasis on the relationship between the therapist and the patient than do more traditional therapies. I find that my relationship with my patients is important to the extent that I am supportive and understanding of their suffering, and I can increase their chances of doing the necessary exposure and response prevention practice.

As you've learned, a trusted adviser or helper can enable you to overcome your bad habits with behavior therapy. Naturally, your helper should be someone who has the same qualities you would look for in a behavior therapist. In one study it turned out that an understanding college professor could help his students with advice about problems to the same extent as a professional therapist. Although this was a study of less serious problems than OCD, it does show that there is nothing magical about having a therapist to work with, at least not for less severe problems.

Therefore, although the relationship with the therapist is not really *the* important factor in behavior therapy, it is important because it can determine whether a patient will comply with exposure and response prevention. The therapist and client have to feel comfortable with each other, and the therapist must not be mechanical. Instead, he or she must convey a sense of warmth, empathy, and confidence about his or her skills and must not make the patients feel that their OCD symptoms are foolish, bizarre, or weird. The therapist with genuine warmth, respect, empathy, and confidence will increase the chances that the patient will listen to his or her advice and allow the behavior therapy techniques to be effectively employed.

Q. How can I be certain that what I fear will happen will never really happen?

A. Sadly, the answer is you can't be certain! If you suffer from OCD you probably want a 100 percent guarantee that you will *never* do anything dangerous or that no harm will ever come to you or your family members. Unfortunately, life does not work like this. If I think about it, I know that there is no guarantee that I won't be hit by a car coming home from work today—but somehow my brain automatically accepts the very small chance of this happening and so permits me to go on living my life.

More than two thousand years ago the Buddha (a great psychologist besides being a religious teacher) warned that one of the key things that makes us suffer is that we always want more than we will actually get—whether what we want is material like gold and jewels, or (my addition) in the case of OCD, more certainty than you will ever achieve. Thus the solution the Buddha might have offered you in northern India those hundreds of years ago might have been something like this: "To stop suffering you must learn to accept that you will never achieve as much certainty as you want, no matter how much you pursue it; so it is up to you to choose: Either accept this truth and live your life happily, or fight against this truth and continue to suffer."

Let me say it again for emphasis: You will never be certain that you won't act on the urges you have, or that the terrible things you fear will happen will not actually happen—but I can assure you that the odds of these things actually happening are small enough that it is not worth wasting your life trying (in vain) to get 100 percent certainty. Better to trust in yourself, your religious beliefs, or in evolution having prepared us well for surviving in this world.

If evidence from brain studies better helps to convince you this is true, brain imaging studies of OCD sufferers now suggest that there really is something wrong with these peoples' "certainty system"; whatever automatically lets someone without OCD feel that things are OK does not function correctly in the OCD sufferer's brain (who then tries to convince himself that everything is OK, eventually becoming tired and frustrated when he cannot use other brain functions to achieve 100 percent certainty).

Q. I've heard a lot about cognitive therapy—can this help my OCD?

A. Exposure and response prevention, as described in this book, remain the first-line behavioral treatment for OCD. They are supported by dozens of studies with hundreds of subjects. On the other hand, some people are unwilling to do exposure therapy, and others don't fully respond to this kind of treatment. We have been very interested in whether cognitive therapy techniques (which are undeniably effective in treating depression) could be modified to treat OCD. Happily there has been recent progress on this front: Several studies now prove that if cognitive therapy is carefully tailored to identify and challenge the particular thought errors that an OCD sufferers makes, this treatment can reduce OCD symptoms. These errors include being over-responsible for bad consequences, being too perfectionistic, and overestimating the true probability of dangerous events happening. If you would like to try cognitive therapy techniques, you should find a behavior therapist who is trained in these methods and who is familiar with the *specific* OCD cognitive therapy treatment programs that are being used in various parts of the United States, Canada, and the Netherlands.[2]

Q. Can a computer help OCD sufferers do behavior therapy?

A. Yes. Over the past five years, my colleagues, Drs. John Greist and Isaac Marks, and I have developed and tested a computer-assisted behavior therapy program (called BT STEPS) that OCD sufferers can access from their homes via a Touch-Tone telephone and use along with a detailed manual. A very large study we conducted in many clinics in the United States found that OCD sufferers who used BT STEPS improved nearly as much as those who were treated by expert behavior therapists, and much more than those who only learned relaxation. The results of this study are hopeful news for those OCD sufferers who do not have access to expert behavior therapists. If you are not able to get your OCD symptoms under control using the methods outlined in this book and you would like to find out more about BT STEPS, you can contact Healthcare Technology Systems in Madison WI, by telephone at (608) 827-2440 or on the Internet at www.healthtechnologysyst.com. (*Note:* BT STEPS is a trademark of Healthcare Technology Systems, LLC.)

Q. How can I tell if the things I do are compulsions or tics?

A. This can be a hard distinction to make, and even experts in OCD and Tourette's Disorder have difficulty in making this distinction—in fact the first time that I heard the term "complex motor tics" used was by a neurologist describing the actions of his patient with Tourette's Disorder who, in addition to his obvious shoulder shrugging and grunting (that is, simple tics), also spent hours lining up his shoes perfectly on his closet floor (which he was calling a "complex motor tic," but which can equally be considered a "compulsion").

OCD symptoms and tics almost certainly overlap in the circuits within the brain that underlie these problems. In general

2. Gail S. Steketee, et al., "Cognitive Theory and Treatment of Obsessive-Compulsive Disorder," in Jenike et al., *Obsessive-Compulsive Disorders*, 3rd ed., 1998.

if you find that (1) you do a particular action to reduce an urge or tension, (2) if you resist doing the action you feel tension building until you finally do the action, and (3) you feel compelled to do the action over and over again, perhaps dozens of times, you are probably suffering from a tic (especially if there's no rational reason you can think of for having to do it).

The easiest way to tell is simply to try to do response prevention for the action: If you find you *can* totally resist doing the action, and the urge to do it decreases, then it is best to consider it a compulsion. On the other hand if you find that no matter how hard you try you cannot resist doing the action, or if while resisting it, the urge to do it builds more and more, than it is best to consider it a tic (and you should then try the habit reversal technique to try to get control over it).[3]

Q. Do the terms "compulsion" and "ritual" mean the same thing?

A. When talking about OCD, the answer is yes. These terms are usually used interchangeably, with "ritual" used more commonly in Europe. I personally prefer the term "compulsion" because many rituals are helpful to us—religious rituals or a Japanese tea ceremony for example—in that they relax our minds by freeing them from having to think about the comforting actions we have performed over and over in the past. On the other hand, "compulsion" almost always connotes something we don't want to do but are forced to do against our will (the technical term for this is "ego dystonic").

Q. What if I'm not able to do a homework assignment—should I just give up?

A. This question is frequently asked in OCD support groups by patients who have run into problems with behavior therapy. They have failed on a particular homework assignment and are feeling either too frustrated or embarrassed to continue with treatment. If they are seeing a behavior therapist, they may be tempted to simply never go back.

3. Barbara J. Coffey, et al., "Tourette's Disorder: Clinical Similarities and Differences," in Jenike et al., *Obsessive-Compulsive Disorders*, 3rd ed., 1998.

Of course, this would be a terrible mistake. In behavior therapy, as in life, things don't always go smoothly, and as Murphy's Law states, if anything can possibly go wrong, it will—and at the worst possible time. If you have trouble applying the methods from earlier chapters, don't give up; this is only a temporary setback. You probably made the mistake of trying to meet a practice goal that was too difficult.

Recently we treated a man who would repeatedly wash his hands if he accidentally touched the bottom of his pants while hanging them up (he thought they were contaminated). So we set him the homework assignment of hanging his pants up and then not washing afterward until an hour had passed. But he found that he wasn't able to keep from washing. As he tried over and over, he became more frustrated. He asked himself, "I'm doing so well not washing after doing other things; why am I having so much trouble with this problem?" We told him, "Hold on. Don't feel guilty. Obviously you're not ready for this homework yet. We need to help you to have more successful experiences first." So we shortened his time for response prevention. First we told him to resist washing for five minutes after hanging up his pants, and he was able to do this. Then he resisted for ten minutes, and then fifteen. Finally he was able to build up to a full sixty minutes, the time recommended in Chapter 2 for exposure and response prevention.

The moral of this story is that if you can't accomplish a particular goal, it doesn't mean that you are not capable enough. It just means that you and your therapist need to be more clever in establishing a goal that you can accomplish.

Q. My child is performing a few OCD rituals—what should I do?

A. Patients with OCD become very worried if they see their children performing any ritual. But they forget that most children go through stages in which they enact various rituals. Dr. Minichiello told me that he remembers as a little boy developing a ritualized way of walking on the tips of his toes up the iron stairs at his school; he called this ritual "tips to iron." But as he got older, the ritual disappeared on its own.

We tell parents that unless the problem interferes with the child's life in a major way, it's best not to worry about it. Give your child reassurance and support, and wait and see if he or she outgrows it. If the rituals continue and they interfere with your child's life, then you should take him or her to an expert in OCD to verify the diagnosis.

Q. How can I find a behavior therapist for OCD?

A. The OCD sufferer in search of a behavior therapist must be a wise consumer and shop around for the most qualified clinician. Despite the fact that OCD can be successfully treated with certain behavioral techniques, not all behavior therapists are proficient with these techniques, and not all behavior therapists are experienced in treating OCD.

Most behavior therapy is done by psychologists, usually at the doctoral level (Ph.D., Psy.D., or Ed.D.), although some psychiatrists (M.D.) and some clinical social workers (M.S.W.) provide behavior therapy too. When consulting a mental health professional, it is important to specifically ask for a behavior therapist, since many of these professionals do not offer behavior therapy. Your behavior therapist should be licensed by the state in which he or she practices. Licensure is your assurance that this therapist has met certain recognized standards of training and supervision in his or her particular field. Each of these health care specialties has different licensure requirements, which vary from state to state.

At this time we know that the most effective behavioral treatment of OCD is based on exposure and response prevention. When you consult a behavior therapist, ask him or her to describe his or her treatment approach. If the therapist does not mention exposure and response prevention, then you should ask why. Other behavior therapy techniques used to treat anxiety and avoidance behaviors are systematic desensitization, relaxation training (or stress management), and assertiveness training. As described in an earlier answer, these techniques may occasionally be called for, since in behavior therapy the treatment plan is often altered to meet the needs of each unique patient; however, a therapist should be able to justify why he or she is deviating from the procedures that have proven successful in controlling OCD symptoms.

You should also ask a prospective behavior therapist about his or her experiences with other OCD sufferers. Most behavior therapists belong to the Association for Advancement of Behavior Therapy (305 Seventh Avenue, 16th floor, New York, NY 10001; (212) 647-1890; www.aabt.org), which publishes a directory of its members. You can contact AABT to inquire whether a particular therapist is a member and whether he or she lists OCD as a specialty. But AABT is not a certifying organization, and not all its members offer behavior therapy.

The OC Foundation provides information about behavior therapists in many areas of the country. You may also contact the Anxiety Disorders Association of America (11900 Parklawn Drive, Suite 100, Rockville, MD 20852; (301) 231-9350; www.adaa.org) to get the names of behavior therapists in your area who treat OCD.

If you cannot find a therapist in your area who specializes in behavior therapy, contact the university psychology department, social work department, or medical school nearest you and ask for a referral. Ask to speak to the chairperson of either the department of clinical psychology, counseling psychology, psychiatry, or social work. Finally, you can contact your local community mental health clinic; it may have a behavior therapist on the staff or may be able to give you a referral.

CHAPTER TEN

• •

For Family, Friends, and Helpers

• •

> "I get by with a little help from my friends."
> —John Lennon (1940–1980)
> and Paul McCartney (b. 1942)

Your friend or family member has OCD and you'd like to help. But you don't know how to do it and at the same time avoid arguments and family discord. Or, a friend has asked you to serve as a helper for her as part of her behavior therapy treatment, but you're not sure you can handle the role. This chapter will teach you how to use the behavior therapy principles in this book to live amicably with an OCD sufferer (even if you won't be working as a helper) or to be a successful, supportive helper.

If you haven't already read the previous chapters, do so now before trying to use the following suggestions. You will need to understand the principles of treating OCD to be able to apply them in an effective, nonthreatening way. As you read these chapters, also keep in mind that OCD sufferers can't "just stop doing it." The fact that they suffer from OCD doesn't mean that they are weak, or that they have no willpower, or even that they are lazy. Although *you* may have been able to break a habit like smoking or nail biting just by gritting your teeth and stopping it, the OCD sufferer has terrible thoughts and overpowering urges that you've probably never experienced.

Still, OCD sufferers *do* have to begin resisting their rituals. The difference between them and you is that they must do it in a graduated way that is acceptable to them. Otherwise they may fail and give up completely.

One couple told me they were sure that their eleven-year-old daughter was performing rituals and making frequent requests for reassurance on purpose. "If she *really* wanted to stop doing these stupid things," they told me, "she'd just stop. She's only doing them to drive us crazy." The first thing this couple had to learn in order to help their daughter was that she *couldn't* control her rituals as easily as they believed she could; her failure to control them did not stem solely from spite. While still frustrated by their daughter's problems, once they realized this, they were more understanding and reacted less often with anger to what they before saw as merely stubborn behavior.

People with OCD are often able to hide their rituals and obsessions from even their closest relatives. One woman I treated had somehow managed to hide most of her rituals from her husband of twenty years. When she finally got up the courage to discuss her cleaning rituals with him, he was stunned to learn that she had these problems.

Try to be supportive and discuss the OCD sufferer's problems with him or her. If he or she agrees, the two of you can review the completed YBOCS Symptom Checklist from Chapter 3. As you discuss each problem you can ask, "How will I know if you're doing that?" or "How do you want me to respond if you start doing that?" Being open and honest about his or her problems is often the OCD sufferer's first step toward getting control. This process will also alert you to the OCD sufferer's problems. For example, the husband of one of my patients was relieved to finally understand why his wife would never eat in certain restaurants, would never walk down certain streets, and would refuse to do certain things. Solving the complex riddle of her superstitious fears was his key first to understanding and then to compassion.

No matter how odd a ritual or obsession may seem to you, don't make OCD sufferers feel that their thoughts or actions are crazy or dangerous. Instead, put yourself in their shoes by trying to imagine how you would feel if you told someone about sexual or violent thoughts that you couldn't push out of your mind, no matter how nonsensical you thought they were.

Dealing with Family Members or Friends Who Have OCD

The following are specific tactics to guide you in helping a family member or friend who suffers from OCD. Some of the advice in this section is adapted from the excellent pamphlet "Learning to Live with Obsessive-Compulsive Disorder," by Barbara Livingston and Dr. Steven Rasmussen of Butler Hospital in Providence, and is used by permission of the authors.

Help by Not Helping

The single most important rule to follow in living with an OCD sufferer is to not perform his rituals for him—in other words, you can help by not helping. The Old Testament commands us to honor our father and mother. But what happens when the father is afraid of contamination, and commands his children to strip off their clothes in the garage and don "germ-free" clothes before entering the house? What should his children do when he demands that no shoes be worn in the house, that no visitors be allowed in, and that not a crumb of food be eaten in the house?

For the Jones family, what happened was that Sam's wife and children went along with his commands; in effect, they helped him carry out his OCD rituals. Of course, they didn't realize they were doing this. They were only trying to avoid terrible arguments and the heartbreaking sight of Sam in tears, which would ensue should they disobey his orders. Finally, the family took a stand when Sam wanted to move to a new house to outrun the contamination of their present house: they insisted that he get treatment for his OCD.

Another patient, Marsha, found two ways to relieve her anxiety, either by carrying out a checking ritual herself or by having her husband carry out the ritual for her. As I worked with her in behavior therapy, we would get one checking ritual under control and then move on to the next one on her list. Finally we arrived at her last ritual: checking the doors, locks, and stove before bedtime. The records I had asked her to keep showed that for several weeks she had resisted her urges to check these objects, as we had agreed. I therefore couldn't understand why her urges to check were not subsiding, as I expected they would.

One day, while I was talking with Marsha and her husband, Ted, it came out that, each night, she insisted Ted get out of bed to check the doors, locks, and stove and then return to bed and reassure her before she would go to sleep. Why did Ted go along with this? He told me that it was easier than "fighting and screaming with her about it." Once again, a family member was actually harming a loved one by helping in the wrong way. Once I explained this, Ted stopped checking for Marsha and instead helped her in a constructive way by reminding her to resist urges to check and by encouraging her to deal directly with her anxiety.

These two examples illustrate the conflicts that can develop from having a family member with OCD. But rather than taking the easy way out and giving in to the patient's rituals, family members—and the OCD patient—must recognize that the only way to really help the patient is to stop helping him carry out his rituals. This approach is based on the same principles of exposure and response prevention described in Chapter 2.

Avoid Day-to-Day Comparisons

Often OCD sufferers feel as if they are back at the start at times when their symptoms are strong. You may also have made the mistake of comparing your friend or family member's status with the way she functioned before developing OCD. Due to the waxing and waning course of OCD, it is important to look at *overall* changes since treatment began. Day-to-day comparisons are misleading, because they don't accurately reflect improvement. On the days that the sufferer slips, you can remind her that "tomorrow is another day to try," so that she won't interpret her relapse as a failure. Feeling as though one is a failure is self-destructive; it leads to feeling guilty, feeling imperfect. These distortions create stress, which can exacerbate symptoms and cause the patient to feel less in control. You can make a difference if you remind the sufferer of how much progress she has made since her worst episode and since beginning treatment.

Pay Attention to Small Improvements

People with OCD often complain that family members or friends don't understand what it takes to cut down a shower by five minutes or resist asking for reassurance one more time. While these accomplishments may seem insignificant to relatives or friends, they represent very big steps for the patients. Acknowledgment of these seemingly small accomplishments is a powerful tool; it encourages the person with OCD to keep trying and lets him know that his hard work is recognized by you. *Praise is a strong positive reinforcer.* Don't hesitate to use it!

Be Supportive

The more you can avoid personal criticism, the better. It is the OCD that gets on everyone's nerves, not the OCD patient. Your family member or friend still needs your encouragement and your acceptance of her as a person, not criticism. Remember, however, that acceptance and support do not mean ignoring compulsive behavior. Without hostility, explain that compulsions are symptoms of OCD and that you won't help her with them, because you want to help her resist. This projects more of a nonjudgmental attitude, which reflects acceptance of the person.

Keep Communication Clear and Simple

Avoid lengthy explanations. This is often easier said than done, since most people with OCD constantly ask those around them for reassurance: "Are you sure I locked the door?" "Can I be certain that I cleaned well enough?" You have probably found that the more you try to prove that the sufferer need not worry, the more he disproves you. Even the most sophisticated explanations won't work; there is always that lingering "what if."

In your efforts to help the sufferer reduce his compulsions, you may easily be perceived as mean or rejecting, although you are trying to be supportive. It may seem obvious that family members, friends, and sufferers are working toward the common goal of symptom reduction, but the ways in which people do this vary. First, there must be an agreement between the relatives or friend and the sufferer that it is in the sufferer's best interest for the family or friend *not* to participate in rituals (this includes responding to incessant requests for reassurance). It is ideal for the family members or friend and the sufferer to reach this agreement. Often attending a family educational support group for OCD, or seeing a family therapist with expertise in OCD, facilitates family communication.

Be Firm but Also Sensitive to Mood

With the goal of working together to decrease compulsions, family members and friends may find that they have to be firm with the OCD patient about prior agreements on assisting with compulsions, how much time should be spent discussing OCD, how much reassurance should be given, and how much the compulsions should be allowed to infringe upon other's lives. OCD sufferers commonly report that mood dictates the degree to which they can divert obsessions and resist compulsions. Likewise, family members and friends have commented that they can tell when the sufferer is having a bad day. Those are the times when family or friends may need to back off, especially if conflict escalates to a potentially violent situation. On good days, sufferers should be encouraged to resist compulsions as much as possible.

Use Humor

The ability to distance oneself from irrational fears and laugh is healthy, especially when done in company. Both sufferers and family members (or friends) report this to be a relief. Again, you should consider the sufferer's mood before gently poking fun at OCD. Although humor has been recognized for its healing properties for ages, it may not be best to joke when the OCD symptoms are acute.

Stay Flexible

These are, above all, guidelines, not iron-clad rules. Always consider the severity of the OCD symptoms and the sufferer's mood as well as level of stress when making decisions about enforcing limits. Be reasonable and try to convey caring in your actions.

Dealing with Family Members or Friends Who Won't Get Help for Their OCD

What if a friend or a relative either refuses to get treatment or denies that he has OCD? Since you know that OCD can be effectively treated, this is a very difficult situation, and it usually produces feelings of hopelessness and anger in people close to the sufferer.

Sometimes you will have no choice left but to carry on with your life, while reminding the sufferer periodically that you are willing to help, that you recognize his shame and distress, and that people can get better from OCD if they get treatment. Sometimes a person with OCD will not seek help until he hits rock bottom. Of course, watching someone you care for suffer when he could be getting help is very painful. In the meantime, you and other friends or relatives should learn more about OCD and seek support to reduce your feelings of helplessness.

Remember, if the OCD victim is not motivated to get control of his symptoms, you are not going to be able to motivate him. In other words, if his OCD symptoms bother you more than they bother him, the outlook for behavior therapy is poor. The old joke goes, "How many psychologists does it take to change a light bulb? One. But the bulb really has to want to change!" Nowhere is this joke closer to reality than in behavior therapy for OCD.

In any case, you should still try to follow the advice in this chapter about not helping the OCD sufferer carry out his rituals. It is the sufferer's right to not yet want help, but you should explain that you simply can't knowingly assist him in making his problem worse.

If You Are Asked to Be a Helper

I have found that the help of a family member or friend often means the difference between success and failure with behavior therapy. Most of my patients who have not succeeded with behavior therapy have had no one at home to help them with practice assignments.

As a helper you will assist the OCD sufferer in setting goals and carrying out practice assignments, and you'll also give encouragement when the going gets tough. These are the very same functions frequently carried out by a behavior therapist. Because the obsessions and compulsions you will be dealing with are often of a very personal or embarrassing nature, the OCD patient must have a strong degree of trust and respect for you.

Being a helper can be a difficult job. You are usually not an expert in behavior therapy, and the practice sessions can be as frustrating for the helper as for the OCD patient. The following guidelines are a sort of job description to help you find your way in this difficult but rewarding job.

Your first step is to be honest about your ability to be a helper. If an OCD sufferer asks you to be a helper, you should first read carefully the preceding chapters. Familiarize yourself fully with OCD and with behavior therapy. It is important that you always know exactly why you are following a particular procedure. Reread sections of this book often if you forget.

Next ask yourself, "Can I function effectively as a helper?" and "Do I have the patience and interest to help this person?" If you think your answers may be no, it is best to be honest now. Simply explain to the OCD sufferer that you don't think you are the best person to help her right now. And suggest that it may be better for her to find someone else, who can help her more.

I've found that my patients often either eliminate or are turned down by several people from their list of potential helpers before they find one whom they can work with. So if you decline to be a helper, there should be no hard feelings. If, however, it turns out that you are the *only* person available to be a helper, you should agree to the role, despite your doubts, and then you and the OCD sufferer should closely follow the guidelines in this chapter to avoid problems in working together.

If you have decided that you can work as a helper, you should of course also follow all the suggestions given earlier for dealing with family members or friends with OCD. But you will also need extra knowledge, since you will be working closely with the patient while she is in some of the most stressful situations possible: confronting things she is terribly afraid of, and resisting rituals that would reduce her anxiety.

If the OCD sufferer has asked several other people to serve as helpers along with you, you should decline, because the more people that are involved, the greater the chances of misunderstandings and confusion. You can merely point out that it is best to keep things simple, and one way of doing this is to have only one helper at a time.

Before the patient and the helper begin any home practice, I ask the helper to agree to the following rules, and the patient to agree to the corresponding rules, in Chapter 5. They should serve as ground rules for both parties as they carry out behavior therapy on their own.

- *Do* encourage the OCD sufferer as much as possible. Remember that resisting rituals and obsessions is very frightening and difficult, especially in the beginning. Always use praise and keep the overall tone positive. One patient explained to me what a difference it made to have her husband's support: John continually praised Ann's accomplishments and supported her during difficult practice sessions.

- *Do* encourage even partial accomplishment of goals. In Chapter 4 you learned how important it is to set achievable goals. But sometimes OCD sufferers don't accomplish a goal completely, despite their best efforts. John told Ann, "That's OK, honey, so you didn't keep from washing your hands for the whole two hours, but the hour and a half you did was a big improvement over last week." Seemingly small comments like this can make a big difference in outcome.

- *Do* answer all reasonable questions. As you learned in Chapter 4, OCD sufferers have often lost touch with what people normally do in certain situations. Add to this the strong anxiety they feel when confronting their problems, and you can begin to see why they frequently ask you whether some activity is safe. If you think the question is reasonable, then answer it fully and honestly, but answer it only *once*. If the OCD sufferer later asks you the same question again, just say, "You already know the answer" or "We can't discuss that anymore."

- *Do* use humor. Ann told me that she found it very helpful for her husband to use humor to keep things light during their practice sessions. For example, John told her that they'd probably be able to take a trip to Europe with the money she would save on soap as she got better.

Though he made it clear that he took her problems seriously, at the same time he made light of the consequences she feared. When Ann told him she still thought there was a small chance he would die if she didn't wash her hands properly, he said, "Don't tell the insurance company that or they'll raise the premiums on my life insurance policy." Ann told me that John's attitude made resisting her rituals seem less like a life-threatening risk on her part, and she was even able to laugh at some of the imagined deaths and illnesses she had previously feared would result from resisting washing rituals.

But whenever you use humor, be careful. Make sure that the OCD sufferer doesn't think you are making fun of him or his problems. Once lost, his trust and respect will be difficult to regain.

- *Don't* use harsh criticism. A young man in our clinic asked his father to help him resist his contamination rituals. But after one session it became clear that they couldn't work together: the first time he had difficulty with a practice assignment, his father remarked, "What's the matter with you? You're just weak and lazy, otherwise you'd be able to do it!"

Luckily this young man was able, with the encouragement and praise of an understanding behavior therapist, to successfully complete many practice assignments on his own, and he improved markedly. His father later told him, "Sure you're better, but look how sick and crazy you still are!" This kind of criticism can lead an OCD sufferer to give up behavior therapy before he has a chance to see improvement in his symptoms. Please don't let this happen to your family member or friend.

- *Don't* provide reassurance for obsessions. As you learned earlier, you should answer a reasonable question once and only once. After that, simply say, "We already discussed that." Some patients, looking for continual reassurance, ask, "Did I really shut off that light?" or "Did I say anything obscene without knowing it?"

Resist your own urge to take the path of least resistance

and give in by reassuring the OCD sufferer. Instead, say pleasantly but firmly, "We agreed not to discuss that again" or "You already know the answer to that question." After you say this, ignore any further requests for reassurance. With practice, you can do this politely by repeating one of the preceding statements and then simply changing the subject. If you get frustrated with this process, don't worry—that response is normal. It takes a lot of patience to be an effective helper, but it's worth it in the end.

• *Don't* get into arguments during practice assignments. Your role is to help the OCD sufferer, not to get into arguments with him. But neither should you have to stand idly by and absorb his anger. When I meet with both the patient and his helper for the first time, I always tell the patient, "If you are going to get angry at anyone, then get angry at me, because I gave you the assignment." To the helper I say, "At the first sign of an argument, walk away. You are doing him a favor by helping—you don't need to get involved in an argument for your trouble."

If the OCD sufferer becomes angry with you during a practice session or tries to argue, simply remind him that this is a goal you *both* agreed to work on. Try working on another goal if this doesn't help. Should he remain angry or argumentative, simply tell him that you are stopping the practice session for that day, and you'll both pick up where you left off at your next scheduled practice session.

But in the event that you have to prematurely end more than two practice sessions due to arguments or anger, you should try to sit down together and find out what is causing your conflicts. You both should reread the relevant sections of this book.

If after this you still can't resolve the problem, it may be time to find a new helper. Should this problem continue with a second helper, the OCD sufferer probably will need help from a professional behavior therapist.

Don't try to convince the OCD sufferer that his obsessions are wrong; he will always win the argument. He may well have called a poison control division and the Centers for Disease Control for information; he may have done research at a library about which cleaning fluids can be poisonous and where asbestos can be found. You won't be able to convince him that it is very unlikely that he *will* leave his stove on. Unlike people without OCD, he can't see that the risk may be one in a hundred thousand; he may see it as one in two. Remember also that your reassurances can become a kind of checking for the OCD sufferer—what you see as reassuring may in fact be maintaining his problem. Since you can't win these arguments, avoid them and instead say "We can't discuss that" or "You already know the answer."

Once you and the OCD sufferer have agreed to these rules (and in some cases it's helpful to get this agreement in writing), then you're ready to begin your work as described in the preceding chapters.

The case of Ann and her husband illustrates how smoothly exposure and response prevention practice can go with your helper. John worked with Ann during most of her daily hour-long practice sessions. First they reviewed the practice goal to be worked on that day—for example, touching dirty clothes she thought were contaminated. John stayed close by and encouraged Ann as she touched these things and then as she went about her normal routine while resisting her urges to wash. From time to time he asked her what her SUDS rating was, to keep in touch with her declining level of discomfort. When Ann occasionally asked him for reassurance that nothing terrible would happen, John was supportive yet firm in telling her that she already knew the answer. At the end of each practice session, John pointed out Ann's improvements to her, and the two discussed whether to continue working on the same practice goal the next day or move on to a more difficult one. Over the weeks they worked together, although there were ups and downs, Ann was able to accomplish her long-term goals. Since she and her husband had worked closely together, their success was cause for celebration for both—one time dinner in a favorite restaurant, another time a weekend trip.

If you are acting as a helper for a family member, before you get to work, here is an important final reminder: you did not cause the symptoms. Especially if you are a parent helping your child with OCD symptoms, keep this in mind. I recently saw a mother trying to help her young daughter control her hair pulling. But every time the girl had trouble in her behavior therapy practice, her mother became angry and yelled at her, and the girl then lied about her hair pulling. Later, the mother admitted to me that she believed that she had caused her daughter's problem in some way, and because of her guilt she could not stand to be patient and allow her daughter to get control of her problem in gradual steps.

There is no research showing that anything you did caused OCD, or that you could have done anything to have prevented the OCD. You are helping the OCD sufferer, whatever his age, as much as you can *now* by using effective treatment methods for his problems. If the two of you can't get them under control in your practice together, the next step is to see a professional.

This goes for husbands and wives as well. You did not cause your spouse's OCD by anything you did. Stress does make OCD worse, so try for both your sakes to keep your interactions on an even keel, but don't feel guilty for having caused these problems in the first place—you didn't.

Keep in mind that the most important qualities in a helper are knowledge, compassion, firmness, and patience. Good luck in helping your loved one or friend get control.

Bibliography

American Psychiatric Association. *Diagnostic and Statistical Manual of Mental Disorders,* 4th ed., Washington, D.C.: American Psychiatric Association, 1994.

Azrin, Nathan H., and R. G. Nunn. *Habit Control in a Day.* New York: Simon and Schuster, 1977.

Azrin, Nathan H., and Alan L. Peterson. "Behavior Therapy for Tourette's Syndrome and Tic Disorders." Ch. 16 in Donald J. Cohen et al., *Tourette Syndrome and Tic Disorders: Clinical Understanding and Treatment.* New York: John Wiley, 1988.

Baer, Lee, and William E. Minichiello. "Behavior Therapy for Obsessive-Compulsive Disorder." Ch. 17 in Michael A. Jenike et al., eds., *Obsessive-Compulsive Disorders,* 3rd ed.

Bliss, J. "Sensory Experiences of Gilles de la Tourette Syndrome." *Archives of General Psychiatry* 37:1343–1347 (1980).

Boswell, James. *The Life of Samuel Johnson.* New York: Random House, 1968.

Diagnostic and Statistical Manual of Mental Disorders, 4th ed., revised. Washington, D.C.: American Psychiatric Press, 1994.

Drosnin, Michael. *Citizen Hughes.* New York: Holt, Rinehart and Winston, 1985.

Forgione, Albert, and Frederic Bauer. *Fearless Flying: The Complete Program for Relaxed Air Travel.* Boston: Houghton Mifflin, 1980.

Gorman, Jack. *The Essential Guide to Psychiatric Drugs.* New York: St. Martin's Press, 1990.

Green, Robert, and Roger Pitman. "Tourette Syndrome and Obsessive-Compulsive Disorder: Clinical Relationships." Ch. 5 in Michael A. Jenike et al., eds., *Obsessive-Compulsive Disorders,* 2nd ed.

Greist, John H. "Obsessive Compulsive Disorder: A Guide." University of Wisconsin: Lithium Information Center, 1989.

Jenike, Michael A. "Somatic Treatments." Ch. 5 in Michael A. Jenike et al., eds., *Obsessive-Compulsive Disorders,* 1st ed.

————. "Drug Treatment of Obsessive-Compulsive Disorder." Chap. 17 in Michael A. Jenike, Lee Baer, and William E. Minichiello, eds., *Obsessive-Compulsive Disorders: Theory and Management,* 2nd ed. Chicago: Year Book Medical Publishers, 1990.

————. "Managing Sexual Side Effects of Antiobsessional Drugs." *OCD Newsletter* 4:3, 1990.

————. "Psychotherapy of Obsessive-Compulsive Personality Disorder." Ch. 27 in Michael A. Jenike et al., eds., *Obsessive-Compulsive Disorders,* 3rd ed.

Jenike, Michael A., Lee Baer, and William E. Minichiello. "Bowel Obsessions Responsive to Tricyclic Antidepressants in Four Patients." *American Journal of Psychiatry* 144 (10): 1347–1348 (1987).

————. "Cingulotomy for Refractory Obsessive-Compulsive Disorder: A Long-Term Follow-up of Thirty-three Patients." *Archives of General Psychiatry* 48: 548–555 (1991).

————, eds. *Obsessive-Compulsive Disorders: Theory and Management,* 1st ed. Littleton, Mass.: PSG Publishing, 1986.

————, eds. *Obsessive-Compulsive Disorders: Theory and Management,* 2nd ed. Chicago: Year Book Medical Publishers, 1990.

————, eds. *Obsessive-Compulsive Disorders: Practical Management,* 3rd ed. St. Louis: Mosby, 1998.

Jenike, Michael A., Scott L. Rauch, Lee Baer, and Steven A. Rasmussen. "Neurosurgical Treatment of Obsessive-Compulsive Disorder." Ch. 26 in Michael A. Jenike et al., eds., *Obsessive-Compulsive Disorders,* 3rd ed.

Livingston, Barbara, and Steven Rasmussen. "Learning to Live with Obsessive Compulsive Disorder." New Haven, Conn.: OC Foundation, 1989.

March, John S., and Karen Mulle. *OCD in Children and Adolescents: A Cognitive-Behavioral Treatment Manual.* New York: Guilford, 1998.

Marks, Isaac M. *Living with Fear.* New York: McGraw Hill, 1978.

————. "Review of Behavioral Psychotherapy, I: Obsessive-Compulsive Disorders." *American Journal of Psychiatry* 138(5): 584–592 (1981).

Phillips, Katherine A. *The Broken Mirror.* New York: Oxford University Press, 1996.

Rachman, S. J., and R. J. Hodgson. *Obsessions and Compulsions.* Englewood Cliffs, N.J.: Prentice-Hall, 1980.

Rapoport, Judith L. *The Boy Who Couldn't Stop Washing.* New York: E. P. Dutton, 1989.

Rasmussen, Steven, and Jane Eisen. "Epidemiology and Clinical Features of Obsessive-Compulsive Disorders." Ch. 2 in Michael A. Jenike et al., eds., *Obsessive-Compulsive Disorders,* 2nd ed.

Rasmussen, Steven, and Ming Tsuang. "Epidemiology and Clinical Features of Obsessive-Compulsive Disorder." Ch. 3 in Michael A. Jenike et al., eds., *Obsessive-Compulsive Disorders,* 1st ed.

Steketee, Gail S., Randy O. Frost, Josee Rheaume, Sabine Wilhelm. "Cognitive Therapy and Treatment of Obsessive-Compulsive Disorder." Ch. 18 in Michael A. Jenike et al., eds., *Obsessive-Compulsive Disorders.* 3rd ed.

Steketee, Gail S., Barbara L. Van Noppen. "Group and Family Treatment for Obsessive-Compulsive Disorder." Ch. 21 in Michael A. Jenike et al., eds., *Obsessive-Compulsive Disorders,* 3rd ed.

Appendix:
Self-Rating Forms

The following is a collection of all the self-rating forms found in the preceding pages, for you to photocopy and use as you progress through the different stages of behavior therapy. The forms will allow you to determine the nature and severity of your particular OCD problems, to set and rank your goals in behavior therapy, and to assess your gradual improvement.

For a detailed explanation of the significance of the forms and how to use them, please refer to the chapter indicated on each form.

....

YALE BROWN OBSESSIVE-COMPULSIVE SCALE
SYMPTOM CHECKLIST
(GOODMAN, RASMUSSEN, ET AL.)

(See Chapter 3, "Test Yourself," for further information.)

Check only those symptoms that are bothering you right now. Items marked with an asterisk (*) may or may not be OCD symptoms. To decide whether you have a particular symptom, refer to the description or examples of each item in the right-hand column.

OBSESSIONS

Aggressive Obsessions

____ 1. I fear I might harm myself.

Fear of eating with a knife or fork, fear of handling sharp objects, fear of walking near glass windows.

____ 2. I fear I might harm other people.

Fear of poisoning other people's food, fear of harming babies, fear of pushing someone in front of a train, fear of hurting someone's feelings, fear of being responsible by not providing assistance for some imagined catastrophe, fear of causing harm by giving bad advice.

____ 3. I have violent or horrific images in my mind.

Images of murders, dismembered bodies, or other disgusting scenes.

____ 4. I fear I will blurt out obscenities or insults.

Fear of shouting obscenities in public situations like church, fear of writing obscenities.

____ 5. I fear doing something else embarrassing.

Fear of appearing foolish in social situations.

____ 6. I fear I will act on an unwanted impulse.

Fear of driving a car into a tree, fear of running someone over, fear of stabbing a friend.

____ 7. I fear I will steal things.

Fear of "cheating" a cashier, fear of shoplifting inexpensive items.

____ 8. I fear that I'll harm others because I'm not careful enough.

Fear of causing an accident without being aware of it (such as a hit-and-run automobile accident).

____ 9. I fear I'll be responsible for something else terrible happening.

Fear of causing a fire or burglary because of not being careful enough in checking the house before leaving.

Contamination Obsessions

____ 10. I am concerned or disgusted with bodily waste or secretions.

Fear of contracting AIDS, cancer, or other diseases from public rest rooms; fears of your own saliva, urine, feces, semen, or vaginal secretions.

____ 11. I am concerned with dirt or germs.

Fear of picking up germs from sitting in certain chairs, shaking hands, or touching door handles.

____ 12. I am excessively concerned with environmental contaminants.

Fear of being contaminated by asbestos or radon, fear of radioactive substances, fear of things associated with towns containing toxic waste sites.

____ 13. I am excessively concerned with certain household cleansers.

Fear of poisonous kitchen or bathroom cleansers, solvents, insect spray, or turpentine.

____ 14. I am excessively concerned with animals.

Fear of being contaminated by touching an insect, dog, cat, or other animal.

_____ 15. I am bothered by sticky substances or residues.

Fear of adhesive tape and other sticky substances that may trap contaminants.

_____ 16. I am concerned that I will get ill because of contamination.

Fear of getting ill as a direct result of being contaminated (beliefs vary about how long the disease will take to appear).

_____ 17. I am concerned that I will contaminate others.

Fear of touching other people or preparing their food after you touch poisonous substances (like gasoline) or after you touch your own body.

Sexual Obsessions

_____ 18. I have forbidden or perverse sexual thoughts, images, or impulses.

Unwanted sexual thoughts about strangers, family, or friends.

_____ 19. I have sexual obsessions that involve children or incest.

Unwanted thoughts about sexually molesting either your own children or other children.

_____ 20. I have obsessions about homosexuality.

Worries like "Am I a homosexual?" or "What if I suddenly become gay?" when there is no basis for these thoughts.

_____ 21. I have obsessions about aggressive sexual behavior toward other people.

Unwanted images of violent sexual behavior toward adult strangers, friends, or family members.

Hoarding/Saving Obsessions

_____ 22. I have obsessions about hoarding or saving things.

Worries about throwing away seemingly unimportant things that you might need in the future, urges to pick up and collect useless things.

____ 23. I am concerned with sacrilege and blasphemy.

Worries about having blasphemous thoughts, saying blasphemous things, or being punished for such things.

____ 24. I am excessively concerned with morality.

Worries about always doing "the right thing," having told a lie, or having cheated someone.

Obsession with the Need for Symmetry or Exactness

____ 25. I have obsessions about symmetry or exactness.

Worries about papers and books being properly aligned, worries about calculations or handwriting being perfect.

Miscellaneous Obsessions

____ 26. I feel that I need to know or remember certain things.

Belief that you need to remember insignificant things like license plate numbers, the names of actors on television shows, old telephone numbers, bumper sticker or T-shirt slogans.

____ 27. I fear saying certain things.

Fear of saying certain words (such as "thirteen") because of superstitions, fear of saying something that might be disrespectful to a dead person, fear of using words with an apostrophe (because this denotes possession).

____ 28. I fear not saying just the right thing.

Fear of having said the wrong thing, fear of not using the "perfect" word.

____ 29. I fear losing things.

Worries about losing a wallet or unimportant objects, like a scrap of notepaper.

....

____ 30. I am bothered by intrusive (neutral) mental images.

Random, unwanted images in your mind.

____ 31. I am bothered by intrusive mental nonsense sounds, words, or music.

Words, songs, or music in your mind that you can't stop.

____ *32. I am bothered by certain sounds or noises.

Worries about the sounds of clocks ticking loudly or of voices in another room that may interfere with sleeping.

____ 33. I have lucky and unlucky numbers.

Worries about common numbers (like thirteen) that may cause you to perform activities a certain lucky number of times or to postpone an action until a certain lucky hour of the day.

____ 34. Certain colors have special significance to me.

Fear of using objects of certain colors (e.g., black may be associated with death, red with blood and injury).

____ 35. I have superstitious fears.

Fear of passing a cemetery, hearse, or black cat; fear of omens associated with death.

Somatic Obsessions

____ 36. I am concerned with illness or disease.

Worries that you have an illness like cancer, heart disease, or AIDS, despite reassurance from doctors that you do not.

____ *37. I am excessively concerned with a part of my body or an aspect of my appearance (dysmorphophobia).

Worries that your face, ears, nose, eyes, or another part of your body is hideously ugly, despite reassurance to the contrary.

COMPULSIONS

Cleaning/Washing Compulsions

____ 38. I wash my hands excessively or in a ritualized way.

Washing your hands many times a day or for long periods of time after touching, or thinking you have touched, a contaminated object. This may include washing the entire length of your arms.

____ 39. I have excessive or ritualized showering, bathing, toothbrushing, grooming, or toilet routines.

Taking showers or baths or performing other bathroom routines that may last for several hours. If the sequence is interrupted, the entire process may have to be restarted.

____ 40. I have compulsions that involve cleaning household items or other inanimate objects.

Excessive cleaning of faucets, toilets, floors, kitchen counters, or kitchen utensils.

____ 41. I do other things to prevent or remove contact with contaminants.

Asking family members to handle or remove insecticides, garbage, gasoline cans, raw meat, paints, varnish, drugs in the medicine cabinet, or kitty litter. If you can't avoid these things, you may wear gloves to handle them, such as when using a self-service gasoline pump.

Checking Compulsions

____ 42. I check that I did not harm others.

Checking that you haven't hurt someone without knowing it. You may ask others for reassurance or telephone to make sure that everything is all right.

_____ 43. I check that I did not harm myself.

Looking for injuries or bleeding after handling sharp or breakable objects. You may frequently go to doctors to ask for reassurance that you haven't hurt yourself.

_____ 44. I check that nothing terrible happened.

Searching the newspaper or listening to the radio or television for news about some catastrophe you believe you caused. You may also ask people for reassurance that you didn't cause an accident.

_____ 45. I check that I did not make a mistake.

Repeated checking of door locks, stoves, electrical outlets, before leaving home; repeated checking while reading, writing, or doing simple calculations to make sure you didn't make a mistake (you can't be certain that you didn't).

_____ *46. I check some aspect of my physical condition tied to my obsessions about my body

Seeking reassurance from friends or doctors that you aren't having a heart attack or getting cancer; repeatedly taking your pulse, blood pressure, or temperature; checking yourself for body odors; checking your appearance in a mirror, looking for ugly features.

Repeating Rituals

_____ 47. I reread or rewrite things.

Taking hours to read a few pages in a book or to write a short letter because you get caught in a cycle of reading and rereading; worrying that you didn't understand something you just read; searching for a "perfect" word or phrase; having obsessive thoughts about the shape of certain printed letters in a book.

___ 48. I need to repeat routine activities.

Repeating activities like turning appliances on and off, combing your hair, going in and out of a doorway, or looking in a particular direction; not feeling comfortable unless you do these things the "right" number of times.

Counting Compulsions

___ 49. I have counting compulsions.

Counting objects like ceiling or floor tiles, books in a bookcase, nails in a wall, or even grains of sand on a beach; counting when you repeat certain activities, like washing.

Ordering/Arranging Compulsions

___ 50. I have ordering or arranging compulsions.

Straightening paper and pens on a desktop or books in a bookcase, wasting hours arranging things in your house in "order" and then becoming very upset if this order is disturbed.

Hoarding/Collecting Compulsions

___ 51. I have compulsions to hoard or collect things.

Saving old newspapers, notes, cans, paper towels, wrappers, and empty bottles for fear that if you throw them away you may one day need them; picking up useless objects from the street or from garbage cans.

Miscellaneous Compulsions

___ 52. I have mental rituals (other than checking/counting).

Performing rituals in your head, like saying prayers or thinking a "good" thought to undo a "bad" thought. These are different from obsessions, because you perform them intentionally to reduce anxiety or feel better.

___ 53. I need to tell, ask, or confess things.

Asking other people to reassure you, confessing to wrong behaviors you never even did, believing that you have to tell other people certain words to feel better.

___ *54. I need to touch, tap, or rub things.

Giving in to the urge to touch rough surfaces, like wood, or hot surfaces, like a stovetop; giving in to the urge to lightly touch other people; believing you need to touch an object like a telephone to prevent an illness in your family.

___ 55. I take measures (other than checking) to prevent harm or terrible consequences to myself or others.

Staying away from sharp or breakable objects, such as knives, scissors, and fragile glass.

___ *56. I have ritualized eating behaviors.

Arranging your food, knife, and fork in a particular order before being able to eat, eating according to a strict ritual, not being able to eat until the hands of a clock point exactly at a certain time.

___ 57. I have superstitious behaviors.

Not taking a bus or train if its number contains an "unlucky" number (like thirteen), staying in your house on the thirteenth of the month, throwing away clothes you wore while passing a funeral home or cemetery.

___ *58. I pull my hair out (trichotillomania).

Pulling hair from your scalp, eyelids, eyelashes, or pubic area, using your fingers or tweezers. You may produce bald spots that require you to wear a wig, or you may pluck your eyelids or eyebrows smooth.

YALE BROWN OBSESSIVE-COMPULSIVE SCALE (GOODMAN, RASMUSSEN, ET AL.)*

(See Chapter 3, "Test Yourself," for further information.)

OBSESSIVE THOUGHTS

Review the obsessions you checked on the YBOCS Symptom Checklist to help you answer the first five questions. Please think about the *last seven days* (including today), and check one answer for each question.

1 How much of your time is occupied by obsessive thoughts? How frequently do the obsessive thoughts occur?

___0 = None[1]
___1 = Less than 1 hour per day, or occasional intrusions (occur no more than 8 times a day)

1. If you checked this answer, also check 0 for questions 2, 3, 4, and 5, and proceed to question 6.

* This self-report version of YBOCS, used by permission of the authors, has been modified for computer administration by Dr. John Greist, a leading researcher in OCD at the University of Wisconsin. I have modified the wording of questions 4 and 5 to clarify their meaning and to emphasize the goal of successful behavior therapy treatment for OCD: obsessions are *not* to be resisted; compulsions are *always* to be resisted.

__2 = 1 to 3 hours per day, or frequent intrusions (occur more than 8
     times a day, but most hours of the day are free of obsessions)
__3 = More than 3 hours and up to 8 hours per day, or very frequent
     intrusions (occur more than 8 times a day and during most
     hours of the day)
__4 = More than 8 hours per day, or near-constant intrusions (too
     numerous to count, and an hour rarely passes without several
     obsessions occurring)

2. How much do your obsessive thoughts interfere with your social or
   work functioning? (If you are currently not working, please think
   about how much the obsessions interfere with your everyday
   activities.) (In answering this question, please consider whether
   there is anything that you don't do, or that you do less, because
   of the obsessions.)

__0 = No interference
__1 = Mild, slight interference with social or occupational activities,
     but overall performance not impaired
__2 = Moderate, definite interference with social or occupational
     performance, but still manageable
__3 = Severe interference, causes substantial impairment in social or
     occupational performance
__4 = Extreme, incapacitating interference

3. How much distress do your obsessive thoughts cause you?

__0 = None
__1 = Mild, infrequent, and not too disturbing distress
__2 = Moderate, frequent, and disturbing distress, but still manageable
__3 = Severe, very frequent, and very disturbing distress
__4 = Extreme, near-constant, and disabling distress

4. How often do you *try* to disregard these thoughts and let them
   pass naturally through your mind? (Here we are *not* interested in
   knowing how successful you are in disregarding your thoughts but
   only in how much or how often you *try* to do so.)

__0 = I always let the obsessions pass naturally through my mind.

__1 = I disregard them most of the time (i.e., more than half the time I
      try to resist)
__2 = I make some effort to disregard them
__3 = I rarely try to disregard the obsessions
__4 = I never try to disregard the obsessions

5. How *successful* are you in disregarding your obsessive thinking?
   (*Note:* Do not include here obsessions stopped by doing *compulsions*.)

__0 = Always successful
__1 = Usually successful in disregarding obsessions
__2 = Sometimes successful in disregarding obsessions
__3 = Rarely successful in disregarding obsessions
__4 = I am rarely able to even momentarily disregard the obsessions

COMPULSIONS

Review the compulsions you checked on the YBOCS Symptom Checklist
to help you answer these five questions. Please think about the *last seven
days* (including today), and check one answer for each question.

6. How much time do you spend performing compulsive behavior?
   How frequently do you perform compulsions? (If your rituals
   involve daily living activities, please consider how much longer it
   takes you to complete routine activities because of your rituals.)

__0 = None[2]
__1 = Less than 1 hour per day is spent performing compulsions, or
      occasional performance of compulsive behaviors (no more than
      8 times a day)
__2 = 1 to 3 hours per day are spent performing compulsions, or
      frequent performance of compulsive behaviors (more than 8
      times a day, but most hours are free of compulsions)
__3 = More than 3 hours and up to 8 hours per day are spent
      performing compulsions, or very frequent performance of
      compulsive behaviors (more than 8 times a day and during
      most hours of the day)

2. If you checked this answer, then also check 0 for questions 7, 8, 9, and 10.

__4 = More than 8 hours per day are spent performing compulsions, or near-constant performance of compulsive behaviors (too numerous to count, and an hour rarely passes without several compulsions being performed)

7. How much do your compulsive behaviors interfere with your social or work functioning? (If you are not currently working, please think about your everyday activities.)

__0 = No interference
__1 = Mild, slight interference with social or occupational activities, but overall performance not impaired
__2 = Moderate, definite interference with social or occupational performance, but still manageable
__3 = Severe interference, substantial impairment in social or occupational performance
__4 = Extreme, incapacitating interference

8. How would you feel if prevented from performing your compulsion(s)? How anxious would you become?

__0 = Not at all anxious
__1 = Only slightly anxious if compulsions prevented
__2 = Anxiety would mount but remain manageable if compulsions prevented
__3 = Prominent and very disturbing increase in anxiety if compulsions interrupted
__4 = Extreme, incapacitating anxiety from any intervention aimed at reducing the compulsions

9. How much of an effort do you make to resist the compulsions? Or how often do you try to stop the compulsions? (Rate only how often or how much you try to resist your compulsions, not how successful you actually are in stopping them.)

__0 = I make an effort to always resist (or the symptoms are so minimal that there is no need to actively resist them)
__1 = I try to resist most of the time (i.e., more than half the time)
__2 = I make some effort to resist

__3 = I yield to almost all compulsions without attempting to control them, but I do so with some reluctance
__4 = I completely and willingly yield to all compulsions

10. How much control do you have over the compulsive behavior? How successful are you in stopping the ritual(s)? (If you rarely try to resist, please think about those rare occasions in which you *did* try to stop the compulsions, in order to answer this question.)

__0 = I have complete control
__1 = Usually I can stop compulsions or rituals with some effort and willpower
__2 = Sometimes I can stop compulsive behavior but only with difficulty
__3 = I can only delay the compulsive behavior, but eventually it must be carried to completion
__4 = I am rarely able to even momentarily delay performing the compulsive behavior

Add up your scores for questions 1 to 10, using the numbers next to the answer you checked for each question.

Assessing the Strength of Your Belief in Your Obsessions or Compulsions

(See Chapter 3, "Test Yourself," for further information.)

The following question is adapted from YBOCS experimental questions by Goodman, Rasmussen, et al.

Check the one statement that best describes what you believe right now. Do you think your obsessions or compulsions are reasonable or rational? Would there be anything besides anxiety to worry about if you resisted them? Do you think something would really happen?

__0 = I think my obsessions or compulsions are unreasonable or excessive

___1 = I think my obsessions or compulsions are unreasonable or
excessive, but I'm not completely convinced that they aren't
necessary
___2 = I think my obsessions or compulsions may be unreasonable or
excessive
___3 = I don't think my obsessions or compulsions are unreasonable or
excessive
___4 = I am sure my obsessions or compulsions are reasonable, no
matter what anyone says

Assessing Avoidance Due to OCD

(See Chapter 3, "Test Yourself," for further information.)

The following question is adapted from YBOCS experimental
questions by Goodman, Rasmussen, et al.

Check the one statement that best describes how many things you
have avoided in the past week.
Have you been avoiding doing anything, going anyplace, or being
with anyone because of your obsessional thoughts or because you
were afraid you would perform compulsions?

___0 = I haven't been avoiding anything because of OCD
___1 = I have been avoiding a few unimportant things because of
OCD
___2 = I have been avoiding some important things because of OCD
___3 = I have been avoiding many important things because of OCD
___4 = I have been avoiding doing almost everything because of OCD

Assessing Depression

(See Chapter 3, "Test Yourself," for further information.)

The following two questions have been modified on a ten-item depression screening scale called the "Harvard Department of Psychiatry/National Depression Screening Day Scale"* (HANDS, for short).

For each question, carefully read each of the four choices. Check the number next to the statement that best describes the way you've been feeling over the past week.

1. How often have you been feeling blue over the past week?

__0 = None or a little of the time
__1 = Some of the time
__2 = Most of the time
__3 = All of the time

2. How often have you thought about suicide over the past week?

__0 = None or a little of the time
__1 = Some of the time
__2 = Most of the time
__3 = All of the time

* Baer, L., Jacobs, D. G., Meszler-Reizes, J., Blais, M., Fava, M., Kessler, R., Magruder, K., Murphy, Kopans, B., J., Cukor, P., Leahy, L., O'Laughlen, J., "Development of a Brief Screening Instrument: The HANDS." *Psychotherapy and Psychosomatics* 69:35–41 (2000).

PRINCIPAL SYMPTOMS

(See Chapter 4, "Setting Your Goals," for further information.)

Include only items marked with a *P* on the YBOCS Symptom Checklist.

Date: _____

OBSESSIONS

Symptom   *General Area*

_____   _____

_____   _____

_____   _____

_____   _____

COMPULSIONS

Symptom   *General Area*

_____   _____

_____   _____

_____   _____

_____   _____

LONG-TERM GOALS

(See Chapter 4, "Setting Your Goals," for further information.)

Date: _____

PRINCIPAL SYMPTOM: _____

_____

Most important things you do too much or avoid because of this problem:

1. _____
2. _____
3. _____
4. _____
5. _____

Change to *long-term goals* you want to accomplish by the end of treatment:

		SUDS Rating
1.	_____	_____
2.	_____	_____
3.	_____	_____
4.	_____	_____
5.	_____	_____

RANKING OF LONG-TERM GOALS

(See Chapter 4, "Setting Your Goals," for further information.)

Date: _____

Arrange your long-term goals based on their difficulty, from easiest to most difficult:

SUDS
Rating

1. _____ _____
2. _____ _____
3. _____ _____
4. _____ _____
5. _____ _____

RATING YOUR PROGRESS IN PRACTICE GOALS

(See Chapter 4, "Setting Your Goals," for further information.)

LONG-TERM GOAL: _____

PRACTICE GOAL: _____

Practice Date	Beginning SUDS Rating	Ending SUDS Rating
_____	_____	_____
_____	_____	_____
_____	_____	_____
_____	_____	_____
_____	_____	_____
_____	_____	_____
_____	_____	_____

PRACTICE SESSIONS OF EXPOSURE AND
RESPONSE PREVENTION

(See Chapter 5, "How to Use Behavior Therapy to Get Control of Your Symptoms," for further information.)

Date	What You Practiced	Time Spent	Helped By
———	———————————	———————	—————————
———	———————————	———————	—————————
———	———————————	———————	—————————
———	———————————	———————	—————————
———	———————————	———————	—————————
———	———————————	———————	—————————
———	———————————	———————	—————————
———	———————————	———————	—————————
———	———————————	———————	—————————
———	———————————	———————	—————————

INDEX

methylphenidate (Ritalin), 188
Meyer, Victor, 33, 35
Minichiello, William G., xii, 3, 111, 195
mistakes, checking for, 17, 68, 232
  setting long-term goals for, 93
modeling, 126
monoamine oxidase inhibitors. *See* MAOIs
monosymptomatic hypochondriasis, 176–78. *See also* hypochondriasis
mood, sensitivity to, 213
mood, monitoring, 158
morality
  obsessions about, 65, 229
  overconscientiousness and inflexibility about, 26
motivation, 41, 42
MRI (magnetic resonance imaging) scans, 11
muscle relaxation, 114, 162–63

Nardil. *See* phenelzine
nausea, 185
neuroleptics, 188
neurosis, obsessional. *See* OCD (obsessive-compulsive disorder)
neurotransmitters, 11, 182, 184, 185, 189
noises, bothersome, 66, 230
Nopramin. *See* despiramine
normal behavior, 87, 125, 128
numbers, superstitions about, 20, 24–25, 66, 71, 230, 235
  long-term results of behavior therapy on, 149
  medication for, 149
  setting practice goals for, 105–6
  tailoring behavior therapy to, 135–6
Nunn, R. G., 158

obscenities
  fear of saving or writing, 62, 226
  shouting, 169, 170, 172. *See also* Tourette Disorder
obsessional neurosis. *See* OCD (obsessive-compulsive disorder)
obsessions
  aggressive, 62–63, 226–27

bowel, 156, 174–76
  medication for, 176
about child molestation, 22, 64, 228
  long-term results of behavior therapy on, 150–51
  medication for, 150
contamination, 2, 4–5, 13–15, 24, 115
  in case studies, 45, 56–57, 111–12, 120–21, 141–42, 193–94
  exposure and response prevention for, 34
  helpers for, 56–57, 111–12, 144
  long-term results of behavior therapy on, 141–42, 143–44
  medication and, 193–94
  overvalued beliefs and, 38–39
  prognosis for, 41
  setting long-term goals for, 90–92
  setting practice goals for, 101–3, 107
  tailoring behavior therapy to, 125–28
  Yale Brown Obsessive-Compulsive Scale Symptom Checklist and, 63–64, 67, 227–28, 231
defined, 7
about exactness, 65, 229
hoarding/saving, 21–22, 64, 228
  and obsessive-compulsive personality disorder, 26
  prognosis for, 43
involving incest, 64, 228
letting pass through mind, 117, 130, 138
about morality, 65, 229
need to know cause of, 196
rate of change with behavior therapy, 53–54
religious, 65, 229
about remembering insignificant information, 23, 49, 65, 229
severe depression and, 39–40
sexual, 2–3, 9, 22–23, 24, 49, 64, 228
  and exposure with audio and videotapes, 119–20
  setting long-term goals for, 95